8/8/09

D0819785

MOBILITY FIRST

Also by Sam Staley

The Road More Traveled: Why the Congestion Crisis Matters More Than You Think, and What We Can Do About It (with Ted Balaker)
Smarter Growth: Market-Based Land-Use Strategies for the 21st Century (with Randall G. Holcombe)
Planning Rules and Urban Economic Performance: The Case of Hong Kong
Drug Policy and the Decline of American Cities

Also by Adrian Moore

Curb Rights: A Framework for Free Enterprise in Public Transit (with Binyam Reja and Daniel Klein)

MOBILITY FIRST

A New Vision for Transportation in a Globally Competitive Twenty-First Century

Sam Staley and Adrian Moore

ROWMAN & LITTLEFIELD PUBLISHERS, INC.
Lanham • Boulder • New York • Toronto • Plymouth, UK

ROWMAN & LITTLEFIELD PUBLISHERS, INC.

Published in the United States of America
by Rowman & Littlefield Publishers, Inc.
A wholly owned subsidiary of The Rowman & Littlefield Publishing Group, Inc.
4501 Forbes Boulevard, Suite 200, Lanham, Maryland 20706
www.rowmanlittlefield.com

Estover Road
Plymouth PL6 7PY
United Kingdom

British Library Cataloguing in Publication Information Available

Library of Congress Cataloging-in-Publication Data:

Staley, Sam, 1961–
  Mobility first : a new vision for transportation in a globally competitive twenty-first
century / Sam Staley and Adrian Moore.
     p. cm.
  Includes bibliographical references and index.
  ISBN-13: 978-0-7425-5879-3 (cloth : alk. paper)
  ISBN-10: 0-7425-5879-7 (cloth : alk. paper)
  ISBN-13: 978-0-7425-5880-9 (pbk. : alk. paper)
  ISBN-10: 0-7425-5880-0 (pbk. : alk. paper)
  eISBN-13: 978-0-7425-6586-2
  eISBN-10: 0-7425-6586-8
  1. Transportation—Planning. 2. Transportation and state. 3. Urban transportation. 4.
Roads. 5. Transportation—United States--Planning. 6. Transportation and state—
United States. 7. Urban transportation—United States. 8. Roads—United States. I.
Moore, Adrian T. (Adrian Thomas), 1962– II. Title.
  HE151.S725 2009
  388—dc22
                                                                                    2008027364
Printed in the United States of America

To Bob Galvin, without whose leadership this book
would not have been written nor been as bold

Contents

Part IV   Making It Work

Foreword

Robert W. Galvin

TRAFFIC CONGESTION IS A TERRIBLE THREAT to our economy. The analogy is cardiovascular. If our bodies' arteries (arterials) clog, we have two choices: We can die, or we can surgically rebuild them a new way. Our cities are on course to die as their arteries clog with congestion. If we continue on this path, properties will devalue, people and jobs will leave the cities, and cultural institutions will decay. As cities die, their economic productivity disappears, crippling our national economy.

I have spent more than half of my life identifying and actively solving allegedly unsolvable fundamental issues from the privileged platform of Chief Executive Officer of Motorola Inc. (I was with Motorola for fifty years, thirty as CEO, mixed with service on major Federal commissions then and in retirement). I conceived and funded the Galvin Project, of which this book is a product, to help lay the groundwork necessary to eliminate road congestion. I was motivated by the following primary convictions:

First, the major cities of the United States and most of the developed world will *die* by 2050 from clogged arteries—commercial and private vehicular traffic gridlock—unless we do something now. Goods and people are already seriously compromised. Every ordinary citizen sees it. An inevitable civic fatality is apparent.

Second, this threat to city life is bound to the substantial depreciation of its commercial and personal property values due to their early-on inaccessibility.

Third, citywide property depreciation is avoidable just as human cardiac and orthopedic surgery can sustain the vitality of our bodies. The essential new procedures and solutions will be:

- *Prosthesis*: prefabricated, ready to install flyovers and queue jumpers of existing and prospective time-delaying intersections, and improvements to existing roads.
- *Major new arteries*: many underground tunnels with convenient parking terminals will network our metropolitan and suburban areas. Where fitable, a series of single pylon supports will elevate lanes adjacent to or in the median of existing roads or tracks. Many of the new arteries will employ electronic tolling with variable rates to control flow.

Fourth, an enlightened private sector—institutions and individuals—will take timely ownership of the problem and its prospects. Their self-interest will be to honorably protect the useful value of their property, and they would deservedly profit from an affordable, uncongested, toll road business. Businesses will appealingly open the entire city and region to timely, cost effective deliveries, unstressful job accessibility and unrestricted family activities from shopping, to school, to soccer, to social ties.

Herein, a substantial new industry will be founded. Little or no public funds will be required in countries like the U.S., Australia, the New Zealand, the U.K. and others to rebuild their transportation network to eliminate congestion. There will be international competition to invest in this emerging business sector creating many jobs that naturally must be learned and filled locally while this new strategy generates generic wealth countrywide.

Fifth, any city that ignores the threat will become an economic and personal-existence wasteland by mid-century. Any previously developed country that thinks it will be immune from this threat will blight itself and do a disservice to other countries it should support and serve. We must want most cities and all countries to responsibly succeed.

Accepting these convictions is one thing. Achieving the changes necessary to see them addressed is another. Human culture regarding change is well known. Our experience shows: Every change is resisted; major change at its origin is opposed; almost all changes "for the good" are adopted. Thus, there is light at the end of the tunnel.

The convictions supporting this project are sound and "for the good." The scores and scores of professional thinkers who have assembled, advised, stimulated and synthesized their ideas and judgments periodically over the last three years through the Galvin Project to End Congestion at Reason Foundation are almost of one mind. These primary changes must be in process shortly and must be accomplished by mid-century.

Of course, as our nation grapples with the immense task of financing our transportation infrastructure, many will wonder about the affordability of such an ambitious program. I have two responses.

First, a city cannot afford not to eliminate congestion. If it fails, the loss of productivity and aggregate of the depreciated value of all its properties will be multiples of the investment required to eliminate congestion. That investment will not only preserve property value but nourish the probability of its appreciation.

Second, although new flyovers and tunnels are more expensive than putting in place conventional surface arteries, the initial technology and means of provisioning will affordably launch the private sector founders of this new business. And just like founders of other sectors before them, they will accelerate improvements in technology, processes, costs, business models, etc., well beyond current imagination.

After all, haven't the "beyond our original imagination" benefits from past convictions to offer Air Travel, Cell Phones, Computers, Medical Solutions, etc.—almost every new service—dazzled us? Haven't they grown to a level of need that most of us cannot do without? And most of us can afford them. Congestion free ground travel may best them all!

Acknowledgments

ALL AUTHORS OWE AN INCREDIBLE DEBT to the people that provide input, comments, and feedback on their ideas and manuscript. We are no exception. Unfortunately, space (and memory!) does not permit us to thank the hundreds of students, professionals, and colleagues that have in some way influenced our thinking about cities and transportation spanning more than twenty years, all of which helped culminate in this book. Nevertheless, a few people had a direct impact on the book and our thinking, and we would like to acknowledge them. We, of course, remain solely responsible for any errors that might have made it through the drafts.

First and foremost we would both like to acknowledge and thank Bob Galvin. Bob is an amazing guy who thinks that problems simply need to be solved and that ignoring the people who say it can't be done is rule number one. His intellectual and financial support created the Galvin Project to End Congestion with Reason Foundation and all of the research and policy work that were crucial to making this book happen. Personally and professionally, we owe him a great deal more as well. Bob had the insight as an interested layman to foresee many of the things in this book and the kindness and wisdom to let us discover most of it on our own. His brand of strategic thinking is unique in our professional experience, and his continual prodding and perseverance left us intellectually stronger and fortified as a result. Bob's practical perspective and managerial drive frequently had us slapping our foreheads as he pushed us to the next level. Thanks, Bob.

This manuscript, of course, had many reviewers through its journey from draft to final copy. We are eternally grateful to Amanda Hydro, Len Gilroy,

Mike Flynn, and Shirley Ybarra for reviewing the entire manuscript and offering copious notes, corrections, and improvements. Bob Poole, Ken Small, Wendell Cox, and David Hartgen waded through several of the heavier chapters, keeping us from straying too far afield, making needed corrections, and reining us in at strategic places.

We would also like to thank Chris Anzalone and Ashlee Mills, our editors at Rowman and Littlefield. Chris saw the value of the project from the beginning and we appreciate his support throughout the process. Unfortunately, the book will not be published under his watch. He left the manuscript in the able hands of Ashlee Mills who helped shepherd the project into print and distribution.

Sam would like to acknowledge his intellectual debt to John Blair and the insights into urban economies and transportation he has gleaned over the years from Alain Bertaud, Alan Pisarski, Peter Samuel, and Ken Orski. Sam also thanks Sarah Bertke, who patiently explained basic engineering concepts over coffee at Starbucks. While the specific details of these discussions didn't make it into the book, the basic ideas are evident in the framework that became the core of chapter 5. Finally, and by no means least, Sam extends a heartfelt thanks to his wife Susan and the patience of their children Claire and Evan who had to endure, once again, their Dad sequestered away writing another "boring" policy book.

Adrian would like to acknowledge Dan Klein who first convinced him that transportation was an interesting and valuable area of study. Ken Small taught him about a third of what he knows about transportation, and Bob Poole taught him another third. The last (and most questionable third) came from his own discovery process that Ken and Bob still help him out with. Finally, Adrian thanks his wife Teri and daughters Iliana and Sequoia for tolerating his frequent travel and isolating himself in his office working on this project.

I

THE CONGESTION CONUNDRUM

1

It's the Cars, Stupid!

"ISN'T THE PROBLEM THAT OUR TRANSPORTATION SYSTEM is too efficient? Isn't the problem that too many people are driving their cars, and we need to get them out of their cars and onto mass transit?"[1]

The question from the television news anchor was rhetorical, but it revealed far more than she intended during the interview with Sam. Sam smiled. "I'm an economist. I believe efficiency is a good thing. We benefit when we can travel from point A to point B faster. So, if cars get us to where we want to go faster, that's not a problem."

The reporter's question was intended to provoke a more emotional response befitting a medium that depends on conflict and sound bites to convey information audio visually. But, her query was a good illustration of the upside-down nature of the debate over transportation in the United States, indeed the world. Even China is investing billions of dollars in subway systems that may well be obsolete within decades given recent trends in income and wealth.

Discussions about transportation are bogged down in a kind of "newspeak." "Transportation choice" means creating alternatives few people use. "Mobility" becomes code for neglecting transportation investments to the point commutes and everyday trips become longer and more laborious. "Mass transit" becomes an oxymoron as its contribution to the transportation system becomes smaller and smaller. George Orwell would not be happy. *1984* was written as a warning to the free world, not a prophecy.

While we're not talking about an Orwellian authoritarian government using language to stamp out freedom and individuality—the ways in which language is used to promote specific agendas shouldn't be ignored. And while the direct consequences are not as dramatic, the long-term effects of poorly designed and implemented transportation policy could dramatically undermine our nation's economic competitiveness. We are on the cusp of a new era in transportation policy. This era will require a wholesale rethinking of the kind of transportation network we need to be competitive in a global economy. Unfortunately, we have yet to begin a serious discussion about how our transportation system needs to be reformulated and redesigned to maintain our competitive edge. We are also in danger of seeing all the economic and social advantages from having the most mobile nation in the world disappear.

Just 40 years ago, investments in the national transportation network generated substantial economic benefits. Travel times fell, cities and people were connected, freight moved efficiently, and travel costs declined. Today, hundreds of cities are mired in traffic congestion. Travel costs are increasing and the quality of urban life is becoming more compromised for tens of millions of residents, businesses, and workers in cities faced with "severe" traffic congestion. At current trends, hundreds of millions of people and businesses will be suffering under severe traffic congestion by 2030, threatening the economic viability of large swaths of urban America, from Los Angeles to Chicago, Minneapolis to Miami, Dallas to Boston. Congestion weakens urban economies over the long run, undermining them to the point that they eventually erode and die with disastrous consequences to our national economy.

Transportation decision making in the United States has gone dramatically astray. Save for a few bold places, most notably in Texas and Georgia, no urban areas seem to be taking the threat of cities choking to economic death on congestion seriously despite the availability of practical solutions. No one—*no one*—is thinking about the dramatic redesign of our transportation networks necessary to ensure that mobility continues to be a cornerstone of the U.S. economy's competitive advantage in a global marketplace. A big reason these issues aren't getting the attention they deserve is the fact that the core economic argument for why mobility matters in our economy—and why congestion strangles it—has been lost in a political tug-of-war. Special interests vie for their share of the funding pie; whether it's a "Bridge to Nowhere" in Alaska, free federal money for a local project so local transportation funds can be diverted to pay for pension obligations, or spending only 50 percent of local transportation funds on the road system that carries 90 percent of local travel, too much time, energy, and money are spent on transportation projects that don't well serve an increasingly mobile and flexible society.

We're also not willing to think big enough. As the Australians and Chinese are digging deep underneath their cities to provide quick access to airports, downtowns and other destinations, Americans are wringing their hands over the poorly managed financial debacle of Boston's "Big Dig." As the French have unblocked decades of resistance to the desperately needed completion of its major ring road—once again using innovative tunnel design to save the cultural legacy of Versailles—U.S. policymakers insist on thinking "horizontally," staying inside the box by using conventional highway widenings to address bottlenecks. Even the Chinese have recognized the value of private capital to finance major new projects, particularly tunnels, bridges, and elevated roadways, while Congress dawdles and resists common sense options for using private industry to expand and upgrade our current highway capacity. Transportation needs to be thought of in a three-dimensional world—going up and down—not the two- dimensional approach of laying lane after lane of asphalt side-by-side, allowing infrastructure to unnecessarily gobble up neighborhoods and land. In the U.S. we simply don't take advantage of tunnels—3-D infrastructure—as a way to create the new road networks needed in major metro areas, particularly in those such as Los Angeles and Chicago that have very high traffic densities.

Meanwhile, rapidly rising traffic congestion is making mobility—the ability to travel where you want when you want, to connect to the places in a metro area you might want to go—a harder and harder goal to achieve in most major U.S. cities. This rising congestion makes it take longer to go the same distance, forcing workers and families into geographically smaller worlds, threatening the productivity, drive, and creativity that keep America's entrepreneurial economy a world leader. Unfortunately, too few policy makers are focused on the problems caused by declining mobility, and many others are reluctant to promote strategies with a track record of improving it.

Perhaps this is part of the reason our elected officials are reluctant to recognize the benefits of thinking big—using 3-D infrastructure and large scale projects such as tunnels in new ways to add capacity without disrupting our neighborhoods and local economies. Indeed, as we will point out in later chapters, traffic densities are high enough in many cities to warrant multibillion dollar investments in new capacity, including major new tunnels, perhaps even networks of underground roads, in cities such as Los Angeles, Atlanta, and Chicago, based on the simple economic concept of "willingness to pay." Thinking big in the twenty-first century means thinking vertically—up and down—not just horizontally.

Yet, a generation of government decisions has focused primarily on reducing mobility in urban America. Planners and activists have attempted to implement failed policies to reduce travel demand or channel travelers into alternatives to the automobile such as fixed route public transit, dramatically increasing travel times for travelers and lengthening average commutes. They have convinced many of us that expanding capacity, let alone a multilevel road network that might include tunnels or elevated facilities, is simply too costly. As a result, public policy has consciously underinvested in new road capacity and enabled dramatic increases in traffic congestion in all major urban areas in the United States.

Rising congestion is not a uniquely American phenomenon, despite the innovative efforts of places such as Shanghai, Sydney, and Paris. Cities across the world have failed to come to grips with the fundamental ways in which travel has evolved and expectations about mobility have increased. London may be the harbinger of these failed policies on the international level. Rather than addressing directly the desire for greater mobility and taking the necessary steps to transform their transportation system accordingly, London policymakers are turning back the clock. They are adopting policies with the expressed goal of reducing mobility, restricting access to places within the metropolitan area, and rigging the urban landscape to limit individual choice in housing and among neighborhoods. The city seems to have embraced the mantra "Congestion is Good." Paradoxically, the Global City that has received the most positive press for innovative transportation solutions, may in fact be undermining its own economic viability.

On the other side of the world, Chinese cities are struggling with the problems of rapidly rising wealth, increasing expectations about mobility, and massive migration from rural areas. These forces have produced some of the world's biggest and densest cities. Unfortunately, with the notable exception of Shanghai, too many Chinese cities are relying on Western models of transportation planning and management, most of which have failed to recognize the value of mobility in economic productivity. As the Chinese people give up their motorized bicycles, we have serious doubts that they will embrace fixed route mass transit rather than the automobiles more of them can afford each year. People certainly have not in contemporary North America, Europe, or Australia.

Restoring the efficiency and effectiveness of urban transportation will take a sea change in the way urban transportation is thought of and designed, and how decisions about it are made and solutions are implemented. One of the key ingredients for building a congestion-free transportation network is embracing the virtues of the personal, speedy, flexible and customized travel embodied in automobiles, trucks, buses and other forms of "rubber tire" transportation.

This means major institutional changes are coming down the turnpike, so to speak. First, the conditions that have long made roads a fuel-tax funded public good are fast eroding. Private sector involvement is burgeoning. France has privatized the management of its limited access highway system. The world's tallest bridge in southern France (the Millau Viaduct) was built using a public-private partnership (and U.S. technology). Australia relied on the private sector to infuse billions of new dollars into its urban transportation system, financing tunnels and highways to speed up traffic in its major cities. Even London is using the public-private partnership arrangement to completely retrofit the Underground (subway) and the region's extensive system of buses. A number of new highways in the United States have been built with private capital investment. Standard and Poor's estimates that in 2006 alone $100 to 150 billion was raised by private firms to invest in infrastructure, and the United States could capture a large share of those funds by opening markets up to investment in road projects.

At the same time, the fuel tax is an increasingly unsustainable means of funding transportation projects. We are driving more, increasing demand for infrastructure, but paying less fuel tax per mile as our vehicles get more fuel efficient. A shift to road pricing of some kind is inevitable—and desirable. Technological changes are rapidly making direct pricing more feasible, especially tolling specific roads. In the past decade about one-third of new freeway miles built in the United States were toll roads. Direct charges for using roads will lead to more efficient use of roads, reduce congestion and provide a revenue stream that allows private capital investment to increase our total infrastructure investment.

Direct pricing will also create the economic transparency necessary to make feasible many large-scale projects previously considered nonviable. Indeed, we are seeing this very effect in Atlanta where a largely underground north-south route paralleling the downtown is now on the drawing board as a result of new thinking about the traveling public's willingness to pay for new capacity through cutting-edge tolling technology. As the link between revenue and services becomes more apparent, the ability to use private capital and expertise to design, build, and operate these facilities increases exponentially.

Finally, urban transit needs to undergo a transformation. Instead of competing with roads for resources, transit and roads need to be planned and managed in a way where investments in infrastructure benefit both modes of travel.

In the end, policy is driven as much by ideas as by technical expertise and practical opportunity. Major institutional changes in the transportation system will grow out of basic changes in decision making, economics and engineering. And that's an important reason why we're writing this book.

A congested future for urban America (or *any* metropolis) is not inevitable. The pessimistic, nay saying attitude that underlies the myth "we can't build our way out of congestion" can be reversed. Throughout the nation and world, cities are adding new capacity by building elevated highways, burrowing under built-up areas with tunnels, and using "boothless" electronic tolling (open road tolling) to pay for new facilities and manage them more efficiently and effectively. These efforts show promising new ways to ward off America's free fall into congestion and, ultimately, lagging economic productivity.

Economically robust cities of the future can design and achieve a fast, efficient, and flexible transportation system. Attaining this goal will require grounding transportation decision making in the following fundamental concepts that anchor this book:

1. *Building three-dimensional road and transportation system capacity—3-D Infrastructure—to match rising travel demand* for customized personalized travel preferences. We can eliminate chronic traffic congestion and increase travel speeds by adopting cutting edge engineering solutions and embracing innovative road design, including underground and elevated roads and other facilities to provide multi-layered access to key destinations through tunnels, flyovers, queue jumpers (or duckers), and elevated expressways;
2. *Recognizing the many hidden costs of congestion* that go far beyond typical measures of lost time and wasted fuel that threaten to choke to death our urban economies, and embrace the commensurate benefits of solving congestion;
3. *Focusing long-term transportation policy on a "mobility first" strategy* that emphasizes connectivity with shorter travel times, lower overall travel costs for individuals and businesses, and expeditiously connecting people and businesses within metropolitan areas;
4. *Recognizing and supporting the role of market forces and the private sector* in meeting the traffic management and transportation infrastructure challenges of the modern city;
5. *Managing traffic effectively on existing roads* to further minimize traffic congestion and eliminate sources of temporary or unanticipated congestion such as bottlenecks arising from traffic accidents or bad weather; and
6. *Encouraging innovation in highway design and materials* by providing an environment in which the private sector can invest and flourish through competitive, market-based incentives and accountability.

Adopting these principles will be central to achieving a policy goal of eliminating congestion as a disease choking the life out our urban economies, improving accessibility to the goods and services we want, and putting urban America on a path of sustainable growth and development. Moreover, these goals can't be achieved unless we recognize the overriding salience of the first point—the need for 3-D transportation infrastructure.

The chapters that follow build on this vision for urban transportation, first outlining the need for a new vision, then outlining the conceptual and tangible steps needed to refocus transportation decision making in a way that supports the economic growth and sustainability of urban economies, and finally identifying the concrete steps we need to reform transportation systems and the types of investments needed to get America moving again.

Note

1. Interview with Sam Staley by Colleen Marshall, anchor, WCMH TV (NBC), Columbus, Ohio, 17 January 2007 for "Downtown Street Car Proposal Gathers Support, Critics," broadcast 19 February 2007, http://www.nbc4i.com/midwest/cmh/news .apx.-content-articles-CMH-2007-02-19-0014.html, accessed 17 October 2007.

2

Congestion's Relentless Pursuit

THE FIRST TIME SAM VISITED LOS ANGELES, he rented a car fresh off the plane from the Midwest. As the rental car agent filled out the paperwork, he looked up and asked: "Would you like insurance?"

Insurance? Why would he need insurance?

Sam had read how these insurance policies were really unnecessary. Besides, he had logged hundreds of thousands of miles as a driver. He had driven in Boston, New York, Washington, D.C., and other points in the Northeast and Midwest. He hadn't driven in Los Angeles before, but surely he could handle the traffic here. No snow. Dry pavement. Lots of sun. These were ideal driving conditions. Los Angeles couldn't be that much worse than navigating the paved-over cow paths of central Boston or inching through the congested grid of Manhattan. The rental car agent was just doing his job—trying to squeeze a few more bucks out of the rental contract. Sam looked at the agent and politely said "no."

Twenty minutes later, our author was back in the rental car agency asking for insurance. Now, it was the agent's turn to smile. "What made you change your mind?"

"The 405."

Anyone who lives in Los Angeles or visits regularly understands Sam's experience and what motivated him to get the insurance.

Los Angeles is a deceptively benign place to drive. Despite its reputation for being "car friendly," it's a hostile environment for even the most experienced drivers. It was the pragmatic reality of driving there (and a conservative tendency to avoid unnecessary risks) that pushed Sam back to the rental car office. This story is much more than a story of how a rental car agency earned a few more dollars. It's a warning for what dozens of cities will be like in the next twenty-five years unless we begin to address traffic congestion now.

Southern California is the most congested urban area in the United States. Its version of gridlock is legendary. Residents typically tack an additional 30 to 60 minutes onto their trips just across town simply because they have no way of predicting how long the trip will take. A fifteen mile trip from ocean-side Santa Monica to downtown Los Angeles should take twenty minutes, but business executives and soccer moms expect and plan for an hour or longer— each way. On some days, you simply can't get there from here.

It's hard to imagine that these conditions would be tolerated in one of the wealthiest countries and cities in the world, but they are. This isn't Mumbai, Beijing, Mexico City, or Llosa. Those cities are grappling with massive urban migration as rural peasants seek better economic opportunities in the cities and rising incomes drive up automobile ownership and driving.[1] Those cities exist in nations whose wealth is well below that of the United States, Europe, or Australia. We expect more from our wealth, our economy, and our political leaders.

Congestion, however, isn't just about travel delay. It's also about personal safety and public health. About one quarter of all traffic accidents may be the result of "rubbernecking"—drivers taking their eyes off the road to see what's happened elsewhere.[2] When crashes pile up, the problems faced by first responders are compounded. And the risks amplify as well. Research on emergency response times are finding that fatality rates can be reduced dramatically by cutting response times in half.[3] Fixing five of the nation's worst bottlenecks in Chicago, Houston, Los Angeles, and Phoenix could prevent 33,545 crashes, avoid 16,471 injuries, and prevent 133 deaths according to one estimate.[4] One study by a researcher at the International Stress Management Association found that British commuters experienced stress levels comparable to fighter pilots.[5] Indeed, many people are choosing to leave urban areas such as San Francisco, Los Angeles, and Atlanta simply to avoid the stress of commuting and congestion.[6] Thus, congestion does more than threaten our economy. It threatens our quality of life, our sense of place, and our sense of security. It also can threaten our very existence.

That's why insurance is necessary even for the most experienced drivers.

That's why our author went back to the rental car agency.

Notably, Sam had driven his rented four-door sedan out onto Century Boulevard and onto the 405. Century Boulevard wasn't the problem—Los Angeles's local road network is remarkably efficient and capable of smoothly handling large volumes of traffic through its neighborhoods. The 405, on the other hand, is a major north-south highway that runs just a few miles inland from the Pacific Ocean. In Southern California, the 405 skirts many of the nation's wealthiest beach communities—Newport Beach, Manhattan Beach, Marina Del Ray, Santa Monica, and others. It connects the San Fernando Valley (northern Los Angeles) to Orange County. It's a vital corridor. It's also perennially ranked as one of the nation's most congested roads. Even though Sam was traveling well past dinner time, he quickly learned why Los Angeles is the congestion capital of America—bumper-to-bumper traffic spanning more than a dozen lanes. And, he would find out, traffic didn't seem to let up much until well after midnight.

Bumper-to-bumper traffic doesn't have to be dangerous. Sam's sense of security and confidence was eroded by the stop-and-go nature of the traffic, the weaving between lanes as other drivers attempted to achieve reasonable travel speed, and the uncertainty about how the other drivers sharing the same road space would react. Speed kills, but so does bad behavior and poor decision making. Congestion provokes dangerous driving and unexpected behavior.

Up to half of the nation's congestion isn't "chronic" in the sense that traffic is slowed down to a crawl every day simply because there are too many cars on too few roads. Rather, more than half of all congestion is caused by "incidents"—unpredictable events such as car accidents or the weather that create temporary bottlenecks. Incident-related congestion is the most unsettling because it can't be anticipated or planned for. That unpredictability, and the added risks it entails, made rental car insurance seem like a bargain.

So, Sam's story is telling. Most people think of congestion's effects from its most visible and tangible impact—slowing down traffic and adding time to our commute. The media and researchers reinforce this. Travel delay is the primary barometer of congestion's toll. Each year, the Texas Transportation Institute (TTI) at Texas A&M University publishes the most widely cited reports on congestion's debilitating effects. The lead authors of the report carve out days of their schedules just to field media calls since their work is cited nationwide and in the most widely read newspapers.

In 2005, the Institute estimated that congestion costs Americans $73 billion.[7] This figure includes wasted gas and time, but it focuses primarily on passenger cars and sidesteps the impact on freight and commercial truck traffic. The report also significantly underestimates congestion's costs because it only covers 85 urban areas (although it includes all urban areas with a million people or more). When the impacts on lost productivity, unreliability, cargo delay, and safety are considered, the U.S. Department of Transportation's chief economist thinks congestion's toll is closer to $168 billion each year.[8]

That's a staggering number. It's also just a harbinger of what's to come.

BOX 2.1
Measuring Congestion

The most common way to measure traffic congestion is using a "travel time index," or TTI. The TTI measures how much longer it takes to get from point A to point B during peak periods compared to nonpeak. An index number of 1.0 represents free flow speeds in most urban areas.[1] An index greater than one represents congested travel—speeds slower than free flow. The Texas Transportation Institute uses 60 mph to benchmark free flow speeds on highways and 35 mph for arterials (local roads). So, for example, a TTI of 1.5 means travel during peak periods takes 50 percent longer than during free flow, implying average speeds have fallen to 45 mph on highways and 26 mph on arterials.

A 2006 Reason Foundation report by David Hartgen and Gregory Fields, at the University of North Carolina, Charlotte, estimated TTI's in 2030 for 403 urbanized areas.[2] Their estimates were based on current planned expenditures on transportation systems and past trends in congestion. The travel time indices in 2003 ranged from 1.04 (a barely perceptible amount of congestion) to 1.75.[3] Twenty-eight urban areas had estimated travel time indices in excess of 1.30 (severe congestion at "level of service," or LOS, of F).

All urban areas were expected to experience higher congestion in 2030 according to Hartgen and Fields' estimates, with TTI's ranging from 1.07 to 1.94. Minneapolis-St. Paul and Reno, Nevada, were expected to experience the fastest rates of increase in congestion over this period at 31 percent and 32 percent respectively. The results are pretty sobering for those interested in reducing congestion and improving mobility in urban areas. By 2030,

- Twelve urbanized areas will have congestion rise to levels equal to Los Angeles in 2003: Chicago, Washington, DC, San Francisco-Oakland, Atlanta, Miami, Denver, Seattle, Las Vegas, Minneapolis-St. Paul, Baltimore, and Portland (Oregon).
- Sixteen urbanized areas will have congestion levels increase to be equal to Chicago in 2003: New York, Sacramento, Dallas-Fort Worth, San Diego, San Jose, Phoenix, Riverside-San Bernardino, Charlotte, Bridgeport-Stamford, Boston, Houston, Philadelphia, Tucson, Salt Lake City, and Orlando.
- Twelve more urbanized areas will have achieved congestion levels equal to Denver in 2003: Austin, Tampa-St. Petersburg, Detroit, Cincinnati, Oxnard-Ventura, San Antonio, Louisville, Colorado Springs, St. Louis, Indianapolis, Sarasota, and Memphis.

In short, most urban areas can expect congestion to increase dramatically over the next 27 years. Congestion will become so severe by 2030 that 58 urban areas will have regional congestion levels high enough to qualify as "severe" (up from 28 in 2003).

Notes

1. Strictly speaking, this is not true. The Travel Time Index compares travel speeds during peak periods to travel speeds during off peak periods. Thus, if (as in Los Angeles) nonpeak periods already are slower than free flow, the TTI will not be a good barometer of congestion; it measures relative congestion. For most cities, however, nonpeak periods still represent times of the day where travel is at posted speed limits (or higher). For our purposes, that represents free flow travel speeds.

2. David Hartgen and Gregory Fields, *Building Roads to Reduce Traffic Congestion in US Cities: How Much and at What Cost?* Policy Study No. 236 (Los Angeles: Reason Foundation, 2006), http://www.reason.org/ps346.pdf.

3. Note that Hartgen and Fields' analysis is based on 2003 travel time indices generated by the Texas Transportation Institute using a methodology that was changed for the 2007 report (2005 estimates of congestion). We believe the basic trends are valid even though the specific point estimates for urban regions and years have changed.

By virtually every standard, our transportation system is becoming harder and harder to use. Congestion has risen well above being merely a nuisance. In 1982, Los Angeles was the only urbanized area in the nation where the average rush hour driver spent 40 hours in severe congestion each year—an entire work week stuck in traffic.[9] Thirteen years later, nine other urbanized areas met this threshold. But this was just the beginning. By 2005, 29 urban areas experienced congestion averaging 40 hours or more of delay per traveler. Six others faced delay of 38 or 39 hours of delay per traveler each year. Congestion in Los Angeles has become so severe that today's rush hour traveler spends 72 hours a year stuck in traffic—almost two work weeks!

In the past, we might have been able to dismiss Los Angeles as the exception—no other metropolitan area even approached its level of congestion. Unfortunately, Los Angeles seems to have a set a goal for other urban areas to aspire to. Now, every major metropolitan area in the U.S. is faced with rising traffic congestion, and many already face severe congestion regionwide.

We're not doing much about it, either. Most transportation agencies are quite content with letting it get worse, or, at best, simply slowing its rate of growth. A Reason Foundation study examined the long-range transportation plans in more than 50 metropolitan areas, finding that based on current plans, the number of urban areas facing severe congestion on a regional level would increase dramatically by 2030 (see box 2.1 and table 2.1). Cities such as Atlanta, Chicago, New York, Miami, and Washington, D.C. would face regional congestion as severe or more severe than current day Los Angeles. It wasn't just the big cities that were faced with congestion's relentless pursuit. Las Vegas, Portland (OR), and Seattle are going to face southern California-style

Table 2.1.　Urban Areas Facing "Severe" Congestion in 2030*

1982 (1)	2005 (32)	2030 (52)
Los Angeles, CA	Los Angeles, CA	Los Angeles, CA
	Chicago, IL	Chicago, IL
	Atlanta, GA	Atlanta, GA
	San Francisco-Oakland, CA	San Francisco-Oakland, CA
	Washington, D.C.	Washington, D.C.
	Miami, FL	Miami, FL
	Dallas-Ft. Worth, TX	Dallas-Ft. Worth, TX
	New York, NY-Newark, NJ	New York, NY-Newark, NJ
	Las Vegas, NV	Las Vegas, NV
	Minneapolis-St. Paul, MN##	Minneapolis-St. Paul, MN
	Portland, OR#	Portland, OR
	Seattle, WA	Seattle, WA
	Houston, TX	Houston, TX
	Boston, MA##	Boston, MA
	Phoenix, AZ	Phoenix, AZ
	San Diego, CA	San Diego, CA
	Riverside-San Bernardino, CA	Riverside-San Bernardino, CA
	Detroit, MI#	Detroit, MI
	Denver, CO	Denver, CO
	Sacramento, CA	Sacramento, CA
	Baltimore, MD	Baltimore. MD
	Orlando, FL	Orlando, FL
	San Jose, CA	San Jose, CA
	Austin, TX	Austin, TX
	Philadelphia, PA#	Philadelphia, PA
	Tampa-St. Petersburg, FL#	Tampa-St. Petersburg, FL
	Indianapolis, IN##	Indianapolis, IN
	Charlotte, NC##	Charlotte, NC
	Louisville, KY##	Louisville, KY
	Tucson, AZ##	Tucson, AZ
	Nashville-Davidson, TN##	Birmingham, AL
		Fresno, CA
		Oxnard-Ventura, CA
		Colorado Springs, CO
		Bridgeport-Stamford, CT
		Jacksonville, FL
		Sarasota, FL
		Palm Bay-Melbourne, FL
		Cape Coral, FL
		Honolulu, HI
		St. Louis, MO
		Kansas City, MO
		Omaha, NE
		Albuquerque, NM
		Raleigh, NC
		Durham, NC

Cincinnati, OH
Columbus, OH
Providence, RI
Charleston, SC
San Antonio, TX
El Paso, TX
Salt Lake City, UT
Virginia Beach, VA
Milwaukee, WI
Nashville-Davidson, TN

Notes: *Severe congestion defined as TTI >= 1.3 or 40 hours of congestion per traveler per year; # urbanized areas with a TTI= 1.28 or 1.29; ## urbanized areas with congestion equal to 40 hours of annual travel delay per traveler or more, but a TTI < 1.3.
Source: Transportation Indices for 1982 and 2005 from David Shrank and Tim Lomax, *2007 Urban Mobility Report*, Texas A&M University, Texas Transportation Institute, May; Forecasts for 2030 calculated in David T. Hartgen and M. Gregory Fields, *Building Roads to Reduce Congestion in America's Cities: How Much and at What Cost?* Policy Study No. 346 (Los Angeles: Reason Foundation, 2006).

congestion by 2030 based on current trends and planned transportation investments. Overall, of the 85 cities tracked by the TTI, almost two-thirds are on track to face "severe" system-wide congestion within 25 years.

In short, in every metro area it's taking us longer to get where we want to be. Inevitably, we have less time for things that matter to us—watching our kids' soccer games, making sure we are as productive as possible at work (or in the home office), or simply sampling life around us.

Congestion, the Mobility Killer

If you think you can escape congestion's impact, think again. Most Americans live and work in cities because that's where the jobs are. Seventy-three million Americans—more than the combined population of Canada and Australia—live in urban areas with congestion equivalent to the Denver urban area.[10] That means, under current policies, more and more of us will be grappling with congestion unless we do something about it now. The number of people living in severely congested cities will multiply by five times over the next 25 years. By 2030, 154.1 million people will live in 40 urban areas with congestion levels equal to Denver's today. That's more than the population of Japan, almost twice as many people than currently live in Germany, and almost as much as the combined populations of the United Kingdom, France, and Canada. Put yet another way, 42 percent of the U.S. population will live in urban areas where congestion is as bad or worse than Denver.

What does this mean for everyday travel? Traffic delays will double over the next 25 years in 16 of the 20 most congested areas even though they already face severe congestion.[11] The exceptions are the most congested cities in the nation: Los Angeles, Chicago, Washington, and San Francisco; their congestion is already so severe that doubling it is statistically difficult. They will still remain at the top of the list even though their *rate* of increase isn't as dramatic as smaller cities such as Las Vegas, Sacramento, or Portland, Oregon.

These numbers, unfortunately, are pretty abstract. How does congestion slow your everyday life? Let's trace out a few local examples. Free flow travel on highways, following the standard used by the Texas Transportation Institute, is pegged at 60 mph. Traveling 14 miles along the Santa Monica freeway (I-10) from the coast to downtown Los Angeles would take 14 minutes at free flow speeds, excluding time on local roads and parking the car.

A standard measure of travel delay is the travel time index. If the index equals one, congestion is zero: our 14 mile trip on the I-10 takes 14 minutes. Congestion, however, reduces travel speeds, increasing the amount of time on the freeway over the same segment of road. The estimated travel time index for the Los Angeles urbanized area, for example, is 1.50. Thus, regionwide the travel time during peak hours is 50 percent higher than during off peak. If this number were applied to the I-10, our trip now takes 21 minutes, seven minutes longer than during free flow, excluding the additional time it takes to get in the car and drive to the I-10, exit the freeway and drive to your destinations.

Many real world travelers on the I-10, however, would still feel "lucky" if they could go 14 miles on the I-10 in just 21 minutes.[12] Adrian made exactly this 14 mile commute for a year in the early 1990s, from Westwood to downtown L.A. On good days it was a 30 minute trip, and way too often it took 45 minutes or more. He had to leave for work one hour early to avoid occasionally being late, and so most of the time had about 30 minutes to kill before work in the morning.

Unfortunately, even this simple exercise underestimates the true costs of delay. The I-10, like the 405, is a highly congested route, and the index applies to an entire region. We're also not factoring in the "reliability buffer"—the amount we adjust our travel time to include uncertainty or unexpected delays. So, average travel speeds are already slower, and the amount of time Angelinos factor in to make their trip, as Adrian's experience showed, is typically much longer than these numbers suggest.

Nevertheless, by 2030, under current plans, measured congestion will almost double travel times along this route. When a "reliability buffer" is added, the 14-mile trip would extend to more than a half hour on the I-10 alone.[13]

Los Angeles is not unique. When we apply the same analysis to the top 20 most congested U.S. cities, the impacts can be seen more broadly. In most cases, travel times in 2030 will be almost two times longer than off peak and free flow even without a reliability buffer. While large cities dominate the top 20, some smaller cities—most notably Minneapolis-St. Paul and Portland, Oregon—will have achieved the dubious notoriety of having congestion levels as severe or more severe than New York City-Northern New Jersey, Dallas, and San Diego.

These lengthy travel times during peak hours translate directly into lower average travel speeds. Table 2.2 provides a few "back of the envelope" estimates of the average travel speeds along freeway routes in what will likely be the nation's 20 most congested urban areas in 2030. Congestion causes travel speeds to plummet along each section of interstate highway. Angelenos will experience travel highway speeds of just 23 mph once the reliability buffer is factored in. Chicago and Miami travelers fare the worst: with highway travel speeds falling below 20 mph. Minneapolis-St. Paul, Baltimore and San Diego fare the "best" with highway travel speeds averaging 36 mph, or about the same speed as free flow arterial (local) roads. Indeed, in every urban area except these three, traffic congestion will slow average speeds on these freeways to levels below local arterials. Thus, allowing congestion to increase will result in dramatically lower levels of mobility for large swaths of the American urban population.

Unfortunately, lower travel speeds tell only part of the story. In truth, congestion has a much more debilitating impact on our mobility. The exercise above was simply to make a point—congestion slows us down. Congestion also disrupts just about everything in our day. The speeds in Table 2.2 are *average* speeds based on everyday traffic flow. Some days it will take a lot longer to drive that stretch. Drivers have to plan for much longer trips or else risk missing their business meeting, their children's soccer game, making a doctor's appointment, or picking up their children at daycare. It's not just the speed. It's the reliability we depend on for planning our trips. Congestion makes our personal and professional days harder to plan, disrupting our family life and our businesses. We get back to this topic in much more depth in the next chapter.

Congestion and Sustainable Cities

What got us to this point?

Part of the answer is that we simply haven't paid attention to congestion as an important policy issue. We have focused on other concerns, like health care, poverty reduction, environmental protection, national economic growth, and international trade and foreign policy. While infrastructure has

Table 2.2. Estimated Speeds along Selected Freeways for the Top 20 Most Congested Urban Areas in the United States

| Urbanized Area | Sample Freeway | Estimated Avg. Freeway Speed (mph) | | | |
		2003	2030	2030 w/ reliability buffer	Difference from Free Flow Arterial
Los Angeles, CA	I-10, Santa Monica to Downtown LA	34.3	31.0	23.3	–11.0
Chicago, IL	I-190/90, O'Hare to downtown	29.7	24.8	18.7	–11.0
Washington, D.C.	I-66, Fairfax to Potomac River	37.1	29.9	22.5	–14.6
San Francisco, CA	SR 101, SF Airport to Bay Bridge	42.0	34.8	26.1	–15.9
Atlanta, GA	I-75, Galleria/285 to downtown	52.3	41.3	31.0	–21.3
Miami, FL	I-95, Ft. Lauderdale Airport to downtown	29.6	22.9	17.2	–12.4
Denver, CO	I-25, Northglenn to downtown Denver	50.0	38.8	29.2	–20.8
Seattle, WA	I-5, Lynnwood to downtown Seattle	40.6	31.3	23.6	–17.0
Las Vegas, NV	I-515, Henderson to downtown	40.3	31.4	23.6	–16.7
Minneapolis-St. Paul, MN	I-35, Bloomington to downtown Minneapolis-St. Paul	62.7	47.9	36.0	–26.7
Baltimore, MD	I-195/95, BWI Airport to downtown	61.3	48.1	36.1	–25.2
Portland, OR	I-5/405, Tualatin to downtown	51.1	40.1	30.1	–21.0
New York, NY	US 1/9/Holland Tunnel, Newark to Lower Manhattan	54.9	43.8	32.9	–22.0
Sacramento, CA	I-5, Laguna West to downtown	47.2	37.3	28.1	–19.10
Dallas, TX	US 75, Plano to downtown Dallas	34.3	27.0	20.3	–14.0
San Diego, CA	CA 94, Spring Valley to downtown	57.8	48.0	36.1	–21.7
San Jose, CA	US 101, Palo Alto to downtown San Jose	50.3	41.7	31.4	–18.9
Phoenix, AZ	AZ 202/I-10, Mesa to downtown	46.4	38.3	28.8	–17.6
Riverside-San Bernardino, CA	CA 91/I-215, Riverside to San Bernardino	49.1	41.0	30.9	–18.2

Source: Author's calculations based on David Hartgen and Gregory Fields, *Building Roads to Reduce Traffic Congestion in America's Cities* (Los Angeles: Reason Foundation, 2006), appendix, http://www.reason.org/ps346.pdf.

periodically been a priority of federal and state governments, other issues have become more dominant, and transportation needs to compete with more programs for funding and attention. Besides, congestion wasn't that big of a problem when the Interstate Highway System was completed. So, we sat back and relaxed.

For example, few long-range transportation plans for major metropolitan areas take congestion reduction seriously. Most don't even come close to proposing policies that reduce it. It's just not a high priority. Most of the planning agencies have either been asleep at the wheel, or simply ignoring the potholes in the road no matter how bumpy they make the ride.

In Minneapolis-St. Paul, congestion was practically nonexistent in 1982. By 2001, residents were wasting 28 hours per year on average on congested roads according to the local regional plan.[14] Highway congestion is now expected to double, absent new road improvements, increasing to 40 hours of delay in 2030.[15] The regional planning agency's attempts to address congestion are halfhearted at best—even with recommended road improvements, congestion will increase to 37 hours by 2030.

Put another way, planned road improvements in the Minneapolis-St. Paul region won't reduce congestion; they will simply keep it from growing faster. Urban congestion will be "only" 32 percent higher in 2030 compared to current levels rather than the 42 percent higher congestion drivers will face without the improvements. At this pace, drivers there will navigate the nation's tenth most congested road system in 2030.[16]

Hundreds of other metro areas are looking at a similar future, spending vast sums over 25 years while congestion gets worse. Adrian met with the Mayor of Albuquerque recently for a brief discussion of local transportation issues. The mayor pointed out that the city was just completing a new regional rail transit link to Santa Fe and the city experiences very little congestion. So, he asked, "What's the problem?" Adrian pointed out that Albuquerque's long-range transportation plan called for spending hundreds of millions of dollars over the coming two decades. Yet, at the end of plan, Albuquerque's congestion is projected to be as bad as Phoenix today. "Do you think," he asked the mayor, "the people of Albuquerque would be excited to know that the official plan for the city is to have Phoenix's congestion?" Probably not, the mayor replied.

Fortunately, some are recognizing that reduced mobility and rising congestion cannot be tolerated. The U.S. Department of Transportation launched a six-point urban congestion reduction agenda in the spring 2006.[17] Citing this plan in his farewell remarks, former department Secretary Norman Mineta soberly observed,

> We can and we must address the congestion that is so pervasive in today's America before it seriously undermines our economic competitiveness and quality of

life. Nationwide, the economic price tag of congestion is already a whopping $200 billion a year, not to mention the largely unmeasured social costs when parents leave for work at dawn, only to get home just as their children are about ready to go to bed.[18]

Current transportation secretary Mary Peters is also committed to moving forward on this agenda, and President George W. Bush gave congestion relief a prominent place in his proposed FY 2008 budget request.[19]

But as we write this, George W. Bush's second term is almost up. His successor will have to ramp up a transportation agenda very rapidly. The five-year transportation reauthorization process began in 2008 and will reach a climatic pitch in 2009. The federal government plays a much bigger role than it used to, and any new administration will not be immune to the political pressures of using the reauthorization process to prop up special interests, including those hostile to needed improvements in the transportation network.

The Interstate Highway System and the full funding of a national road network during the middle and latter half of the twentieth century positioned the federal government as the major player in financing new road infrastructure at the national, state, and local levels. This role was reinforced when the national freight and passenger rail companies failed financially in the 1970s and were replaced by government-run enterprises (CONRAIL on the freight side, which was privatized in 1987, and AMTRAK on the passenger side, which still operates with steep public subsidies). The federal government is also a primary supporter of local and regional mass transit systems.[20] The federal government, however, was content to play a supporting role in infrastructure during most of this period. Not so now.

Policy makers will build on the initiatives established by the U.S. Department of Transportation and a few pioneering states in the early part of this decade. The anticongestion initiatives championed by secretaries Mineta and Peters represent the first coherent federal policy on traffic management and congestion in more than fifty years. But federal resolve will not be enough.

Congestion is primarily a local phenomenon with local solutions, and unfortunately state and regional governments are not nearly as focused on congestion as the Feds are. That's why state experiments will be crucial to tackling the problems of congestion and reduced mobility. Texas, Georgia, and more recently Florida have become the bellwethers for reform on the local level. After a statewide initiative driven by the governor's office, Texas adopted an Urban Mobility Program focused on actual reductions in congestion in each of its major urban areas.[21] Georgia's Transportation Board has also adopted recommendations from the governor's Congestion Mitigation Task Force to reduce overall congestion.[22] Florida is moving forward with innovative user-financed expansions of its road network. As these initiatives play out, state policy makers and transportation planners will reap windfalls from these early adopters by learning what works and what doesn't.

Another element in solving congestion is figuring out how to combat a misguided yet growing sentiment among some planners, urbanists, and others that congestion is beneficial. Higher densities and congestion, they believe, will encourage investment in street-level retail and boost transit ridership (see box 2.2). There are many problems with this approach, as we discuss in chapter 10. Nevertheless, roads, highways, and automobiles have developed opponents, and these opponents have used the regulatory process to stifle new projects.[23] This is an inevitable consequence of legislative approaches to funding transportation. Funding streams create focused political supporters while road users are ordinary people with busy lives and not organized into an interest group. With the exception of the trucking industry, automobile users are a fractured group with disparate interests, resisting the singular drive necessary to coalesce into a unified lobbying group as effective as mass transit or extreme environmental groups.

BOX 2.2
Is Congestion Good for Us?

A conventional wisdom has emerged within some urban planning circles claiming traffic congestion is desirable. The argument rests on two assumptions. First, most neighborhoods suffer from too little density. Higher densities put more goods and services within walking distance of residents. High levels of foot traffic also create the consumer densities necessary to support retail shopping, grocery stores, and other neighborhood services such as laundries and restaurants.

Higher density, mixed-use neighborhoods do not necessarily imply higher traffic congestion, but that is most often the case. Planners assume that higher densities will reduce automobile travel because most people will use transit or walk. But not enough people shift to walking and transit to offset the congestion caused by more cars and more people living in an area as density increases.

To see this, suppose a suburban community of 7,000 people generates 2,000 automobile trips of equal distance (so we can hold vehicle miles traveled constant). The city's population doubles to 14,000, but its boundaries stay the same, so density doubles. This would double the number of commuter trips to 4,000. If the city is well served by mass transit—everyone lives within a quarter mile of a bus, van, or rail transit stop—research suggests automobile trips might fall by as much as 30 percent, or 600 trips. Using the most optimistic estimate, growth would still generate 1,400 additional automobile trips even though vehicle miles traveled per person falls. If road capacity doesn't increase, or fails to keep pace with the increase in travel demand, congestion increases. Moreover, if the local transit agency adds routes and busses to meet rising demand, congestion will get even worse as additional vehicles compete for scarce roadway. Thus, compact and higher density development becomes congestion-inducing development.

The view by some planners that congestion is a healthy sign of economic activity confuses correlation with causation and is inconsistent with recent quantitative studies on the impacts of congestion on the economy and labor market (see chapter 3). While congestion may be an external indicator of a healthy economy, it reflects a mismatch between the infrastructure necessary to support mobility and the rising demand for transportation services. Mobility and lower transportation costs improve productivity, not congestion and higher transportation costs. While communities may be able to endure high levels of congestion in the short run, the long run consequences are economically debilitating.

The economic vitality of a few highly congested areas may, in fact, reflect their unique characteristics, not a general rule. Manhattan, for example, serves as the financial services hub of a national economy and the symbolic center of a global city. It is also marked by high levels of traffic congestion. Manhattan survives in large part because of its unique place in the economic and social hierarchy of the national economy, not because it has fostered congestion to maintain a sense of vitality. We discuss the special case of Manhattan and New York City in chapter 4.

The third element figuring into efforts to increase mobility is the long-term character of transportation investments and benefits. A study by the Federal Highway Administration (FHWA) examined road projects over a 30 year period and found, on average, a new highway took 13.1 years to plan and build.[24] The effects of good (or bad) transportation policy are hard to see during an election cycle, presenting yet another challenge to addressing the emerging congestion crisis in a practical way. The prospect of a future governor, congressman, legislator, or mayor cutting the ribbon on a new highway ten or 15 years from now isn't very appealing to an elected official who votes for it today; many of her constituents will not recognize the benefits of, or for that matter, even use the new road facilities. Some who will use the new road are not yet old enough to drive, let alone vote!

This is the central political dilemma of investments in transportation infrastructure. Roads have "economic lives" longer than the time it takes to build them or the election cycles of the elected officials who support them. Roads, bridges, and other transportation infrastructure can expect to have useful life spans of 50 or 100 years. Complicating the problem even further, road networks historically have been built with excess capacity. Congestion on the interstate (or intercity traffic) remained negligible for decades until the growing local economy filled that road space with local travelers and commuters. As a city grew, the story continues, policymakers failed to ensure their road network kept pace. Travel times increased. Travel speeds fell. Congestion worsened. In some cities, congestion reached crisis levels.[25]

Unfortunately, we are now paying the price for our unfocused and fragmented approach to transportation policy. While many factors contribute to the growth and decline of cities, congestion is one of the few that falls directly within the realm of public policy. Sociologists and economists, for example, know that crime increases and decreases to a large extent based on trends in the average age of the general population, regardless of specific policy decisions. Any time the population experiences a "bubble" of teenagers, crime goes up. Similarly, we can do little directly through public policy to counter (or nurture) broad globalization trends that influence the ability of our domestic firms to compete. We can try to create a climate more conducive to entrepreneurship, innovation, and economic adaptation, but there is little we can do directly to influence globalization.

Congestion's different. Federal, state, and local decisions can have such a direct impact on congestion that we can use (and have used) very blunt and inefficient strategies to quell it. During the late twentieth century, U.S. policy makers reduced congestion through an investment in a national network of limited access highways and significant upgrades to local road networks in part through the Interstate Highway System.[26] We simply put down enough asphalt and linked far-flung places like San Francisco and Baltimore. Although congestion relief was not a central justification for this strategy, the effect was to dramatically reduce congestion in most major urban areas. It was blunt, and expensive, but it worked. Mayors across the nation were concerned about high population densities and snarled traffic in downtowns at the beginning of the twentieth century. By 1982, only the Los Angeles metropolitan area faced severe congestion on a regional scale.

Notably, the Interstate Highway System was largely complete and federal new highway construction effectively stopped by the early 1980s. Vehicle miles traveled on all Interstate highways nearly doubled and the system expanded by just four percent.[27] Urban areas fared somewhat better, but demand far outstripped new capacity. Between 1980 and 2004, travel demand on U.S. *urban* Interstate highways increased by 182 percent (measured by vehicle miles traveled) while federal urban Interstate highway lane-miles increased by just 64 percent.[28] Travel demand on the non-federal urban highways increased by 141 percent while lane miles increased by just 32 percent.[29]

To make matters worse, the FHWA data likely overestimates the number of miles actually added to the transportation network. Urban highway data are based on census designations of an "urbanized area." Urbanized areas change, often bringing formerly rural areas into their boundaries as they become more urban (achieving suburban and urban population densities). Thus, some of the "new miles" may be a statistical artifact of bringing previously existing highways into the revised boundaries of newly expanded urban area.[30] In other words, the lane-miles "added" may have been reclassified roads, not new ones. The road network may not have been expanded to meet rising travel demand. Gross measures of lane-miles added don't necessarily capture whether the lane-miles are in the right place or whether new investments have been made to expand the network to meet rising demand. This is a crucial issue we return to in chapter 5.

Transportation in a Changing World

It's tempting to blame rising congestion on politics. Or to say that we can solve the problem by simply laying more asphalt. Of course, the world is more complicated than that, and dismissing the congestion problem in these ways trivializes the nature of the task before us. Rising congestion is only partly a function of politics. More fundamentally, rising congestion is also a function of how we design and manage our transportation network.

Complicating our task is the changing nature of the economy and the competitive position of our cities. The contemporary urban area is more dynamic, and travel patterns more complex, than in the nineteenth and twentieth centuries when the current "DNA" of the transportation system was established. As urban areas have become more geographically balanced, the suburb-to-downtown commute has become a twentieth century transportation anachronism. Of the 89.5 million commuting trips made in the typical urban area in 2000, just 18.5 percent involved a "traditional" suburb to central city commute.[31] The dominant commuting pattern is now suburb-to-suburb, making up 46 percent of all commute trips.[32] Suburban employment, shopping, and residential centers compete effectively with downtowns and central business districts. Also, "pure" commuting trips make up only about 18 percent of all trips during weekdays, and its share is declining.[33] The rest of trips are commutes combined with travel to other locations on the way to or from work, or just trips on personal business. Thus, while important, making transportation investments solely or even largely based on traditional commuting trends may well lead to more inefficiency and congestion.

Americans historically have had the luxury of moving to less congested parts of a city in order to minimize congestion's economic and social damage. Unfortunately, the scope for making these adjustments is much more limited now. Particularly in growing cities where technology and innovation are common, labor markets are fluid and long-term employment with one firm is becoming less important.[34] The typical baby boomer has held more than ten jobs by the time he turns 40, and 72 percent of these jobs ended within five years.[35] While time spent with one employer edged up from 3.8 years to four years between 1996 and 2006 for all workers, it fell for the age groups in the prime work range of 35 to 64 years.[36] Not surprisingly, one-fifth of today's workers have held 15 or more jobs by the time they turn 40.[37] People are changing jobs more often and using the increasing flexibility of a service-based economy to tailor their travel to individual lifestyles and needs.

Contract, temporary, and "contingent" labor is becoming more common as technology allows employees to adopt more flexible and customized work schedules. In decades past, when employment was stable, buying a new home to be closer to the work place made sense. In the current work environment, employment is dynamic as workers switch jobs more quickly and more often while home choices tend to be driven by lifestyle. Buying a new home or moving to a new apartment every five years is not practical or desirable for most families, particularly when raising children. The current transportation system is a recipe for traffic congestion. It was designed to accommodate traditional commutes—leaving a suburban home and traveling to a central city work location. Due to the decentralization of employment, growth of trip chaining, and increased flexibility in the work place, today's patterns are much more complex.

These patterns suggest that the traditional "hub-and-spoke" transportation network that is the foundation of the current urban highway (or transit) system is no longer viable. Instead, policymakers need to consider redesigning the regional transportation network to resemble a "spider web." Rather than funnel traffic through a select few major corridors (spokes leading to a downtown hub), a web-like network allows travelers to make dynamic, spontaneous adjustments to maximize travel speeds and minimize travel times. Employment and residential centers are connected by transportation links that are relatively equal in weight and role to reflect more balanced (yet dynamic) traffic patterns and allow for more effective systemwide flow management.

In Atlanta, for example, local roads are not built to handle enough capacity to serve as a meaningful alternative to the major highways running north and south through downtown or the beltway. A spiderweb design, a concept developed more fully in chapter 5, builds capacity into the links between major routes so that if an interstate is backed up or congested, travelers can easily detour onto local roads. The mesh of the local road system allows travelers with diverging final destinations to choose different routes, preventing one road from becoming too overloaded. The dynamic nature of travel patterns suggests that these links need to be robust and able to adapt to changing traffic conditions based on the economic and demographic evolution of the metropolitan area.

Transportation for the Twenty-First Century

Expanding physical road capacity will be an essential ingredient to any menu of policy options intent on controlling and reducing congestion's burden. While important efficiencies can be gained by managing the existing capacity more efficiently, most major urban areas will need to expand their existing network to match rising travel demand. This expanded capacity can be achieved efficiently through a variety of new applications of engineering technology, including elevated highways and tunnels.

These physical capacity improvements will be different in kind from those used in the past. Past approaches have used a proverbial sledge hammer to pound a carpenter's nail, in effect laying copious amounts of asphalt without building in the flexibility necessary to adapt to long-term trends and the dynamic impacts of travel behavior. This approach reduces congestion, but it is not an efficient approach and is now inconsistent with the needs of the modern urban economy.

Modern urban travel patterns suggest transportation policy makers will need to rethink the kind of capacity that must be developed to meet the contemporary needs of cities and urban regions. The fluid and dynamic nature of commuting and travel behavior in contemporary urban areas has exposed a "missing link" in the regional transportation network. A high volume urban arterial can serve as an intermediate link between slow local roads and high volume expressways with limited access. New design concepts allow for using engineering innovations such as "flyovers" and queue jumpers to permit local traffic to avoid traffic lights completely and maintain free flow speeds. Adding this intermediate road tier could increase travel speeds as much as 40 percent over current approaches and double the capacity of intersections.

Fortunately, an era of tight public sector budgets and the ongoing quest to lower taxes may be leading some highway agencies to become more willing to try different things. The recent leases of toll roads in Illinois and Indiana and the ongoing highway expansion programs in Texas, Virginia, and Florida are proving that private capital markets are willing and able to step in to fund and manage major infrastructure projects when the demand from travelers and motorists is there. Where the private sector has scaled back, the primary resistance was political, not economic or financial. In many urban areas, traffic densities have increased enough to economically justify higher-cost solutions like tunneling, trenching, and elevated roadways. New advances in composite technologies are allowing new infrastructure to be developed off-site and transported to locations at lower cost.

Improvements in engineering have greatly expanded the potential throughput capacity of these facilities (while maintaining relatively high travel speeds for users), improving their economic viability. The A86 tunnel in Paris, for example, is a double-deck facility, holding twice as many lanes as a conventional tunnel of the same diameter, thereby dramatically reducing the cost per lane. In Australia, tunnels include underground interchanges, raising the prospects of entire regional transportation networks being developed underground. Advances in engineering now allow four lanes or more to be elevated over existing roads and streets with a small footprint, such as the cast-offsite approach developed for Tampa's new elevated express toll lanes (opened in August 2006). Engineers at the Illinois Institute of Technology are developing an innovative cable suspension design for elevating roads in urban areas with little room for expanding physical infrastructure.

Electronic Tolling Systems (ETS) have greatly increased the capacity to fund new facilities by eliminating tollbooths and allowing for variable rate tolling. Variable rate tolling, in particular, provides a new way to segment the market for travel, offering services tailored to the travel needs of individual drivers. More specifically, free flow travel can be provided to those travelers willing to pay for that level of service. In addition, ETS allows higher prices to be charged for peak periods where demand is strongest, and lower prices during off-peak periods to encourage use. ETS technologies also reduce the time and convenience costs to motorists (and truckers), increase travel speeds, and provide more opportunities to fill niche markets through new facilities for specialized routes (such as High Occupancy Toll lanes, truck-only toll roads, and express toll lanes). By creating a dedicated, facility-based revenue stream, smaller capacity improvements such as queue jumpers and flyovers can, in some cases, be self-financing. This reduces political obstacles to funding new facilities and increases the attractiveness of these investments to private sector capital.

More substantively, ETS provides a mechanism for incrementally reconfiguring the regional transportation network in a way that is more consistent with twenty-first century travel and commute patterns. Traffic densities become a primary, market-driven criterion for determining where new facilities should be developed and at what intensity by linking potential revenues to actual use. These facilities can be created incrementally by implementing a network of High Occupancy Toll lanes (HOT lanes). Each HOT lane would guarantee free flow travel speeds by using prices to regulate the volume of traffic. These lanes would be linked together to create a regional network of free flow travel lanes, reducing uncertainty and providing a congestion-free alternative for those willing to pay for it.

Perhaps, however, we are getting ahead of ourselves. We still haven't fleshed out the consequences of "doing nothing," nor whether the trends we are seeing are in fact universal enough to reconfigure our transportation network along the lines we propose. We'll turn to these two issues in the next three chapters.

Notes

1. One of the most forceful and cogent arguments for this relationship has been made by Joel Schwartz at the American Enterprise Institute in Washington, D.C. See, for example, Joel Schwartz, "The Social Benefits and Costs of the Automobile," in *21st Century Highways*, ed. Wendell Cox, Alan Pisarski, and Ronald D. Utt (Washington, D.C.: The Heritage Foundation, 2005), pp. 37–67.

2. Ted Balaker and Sam Staley, *The Road More Traveled: Why the Congestion Crisis Matters More Than You Think, and What We Can Do About It* (Lanham, MD: Rowman & Littlefield, 2006), p. 38.

3. The current standard provides for an eight-minute window. Recent research on emergency medical services response times suggest that cutting the window down to four minutes could dramatically improve outcomes. See Peter Pons, Jason S. Haukoos, Whitney Bludworth et al., "Paramedic Response Time: Does It Affect Patient Survival?" *Academic Emergency Medicine*, Vol. 12, No. 7 (2005), pp. 594–600; Jill Pell, Jane Sirel, Andrew K. Marsden et al., "Effect of Reducing Ambulance Response Times on Deaths from Out of Hospital Cardiac Arrest: Cohort Study," *British Medical Journal*, Vol. 322, No. 7299 (2001), pp. 1385–1388; Elizabeth Ty Wilde, "Do Response Times Matter? The Impact of EMS Response Times on Health Outcomes," 17 November 2007, unpublished paper.

4. Ted Balaker, *Why Mobility Matters, Policy Study No. 43* (Los Angeles: Reason Foundation, 2006), table 1, p. 9.

5. Ibid., p. 12.

6. See the extensive discussions in Balaker, *Why Mobility Matters*.

7. David Shrank and Tim Lomax, *2005 Urban Mobility Report*, Texas Transportation Institute, Texas A&M University.

8. Jack Wells, Chief Economist, U.S. Department of Transportation, "The Role of Transportation in the U.S. Economy," presentation to the National Surface Transportation Policy and Revenue Study Commission, June 26, 2006. These numbers are based on the 2003 estimates and not revised based on the new methodology contained in the 2005 Urban Mobility Report published (in 2007) by the Texas Transportation Institute for 2005 calendar year.

9. David Shrank and Tim Lomax, *2007 Urban Mobility Report*, Texas Transportation Institute, Texas A&M University, table 1, pp. 32–33.

10. A Travel Time Index of 1.33 or higher, according to the Texas Transportation Institute. Population data is for urbanized areas and calculated from the complete TTI dataset. The urbanized areas include: Atlanta, Chicago, Dallas-Ft-Worth, Denver-Aurora, Houston, Los Angeles-Long Beach-Santa Ana, Miami, New York-Newark, Riverside-San Bernardino (Southern California), San Diego, San Francisco-Oakland, San Jose. Urbanized areas not included but close to the Denver threshold include Phoenix, Seattle, Orlando, Baltimore, Sacramento, Las Vegas.

11. Roughly, any region where peak-hour traffic delay is 30 percent slower than off-peak, or a TTI of 1.3 or more, is considered "severe" and roads perform at an LOS of F.

12. Importantly, this calculation probably underestimates travel times along this freeway because the I-10 is a particularly heavily traveled roadway even by L.A. standards and the TTI is a regional index, not a local one.

13. A "reliability buffer" is the difference between the amount of time it takes, on average, to get to a destination and the amount of time someone should *plan* to make the trip. In regions (or along routes) with stop-and-go traffic, travel times can be very unreliable, so we build in a time buffer to ensure we get to our destination on time. The Texas Transportation Institute calls this the "Buffer Index." In Chicago, for example, average traffic conditions suggest that travel takes about 50 percent longer during peak times than off-peak times—a half hour trip would take 45 minutes. Once the Buffer Index is calculated, travelers should plan for a trip twice as long as off-peak times (one hour rather than a half hour). See Shrank and Lomax, *2007 Urban Mobilty Report*, pp. 12–13.

14. These estimates come from the regional planning agency, not the Texas Transportation Institute. The Institute estimated that Minnesotans spend 43 hours stuck in traffic each year.

15. Met Council, 2030 Regional Transportation Plan.

16. Based on estimates from David Hartgen and Gregory Fields, "Building Roads to Reduce Traffic Congestion in America's Cities: How Much and at What Cost?", Policy Study No. 346 (Los Angeles, CA: Reason Foundation, August 2006), http://www.reason.org/ps346.pdf

17. U.S. Department of Transportation, *National Strategy to Reduce Congestion in America's Transportation Network*, May 2006.

18. Norman Y. Mineta, "Facing the Truth about Transportation in the 21 Century," farewell remarks delivered at the U.S. Chamber of Commerce, Washington, D.C., July 6, 2006, http://www.dot.gov/affairs/mineteasp070606pm.htm.

19. John D. McKinnon, "Bush Plays Traffic Cop in Budget Request; President Suggests 'Congestion' Tolls To Ease Rush Hour," *Wall Street Journal*, 5 February 2007, p. A6.

20. Federal Transit Administration, National Transit Database, 2005 National Transit Profile, http://www.ntdprogram.com/ntdprogram/pubs/national_profile/2005 NationalProfile.pdf, accessed 2 February 2007.

21. See the discussion on Texas in Balaker and Staley, *The Road More Traveled*, pp. 125–138.

22. Georgia's approach has been to increase the weight congestion is given in the formula to determine priorities for transportation projects. Congestion now counts for 70 percent of the weight in determining priorities for specific projects. Prior to this new policy, congestion received a weight of just 10 percent.

23. These groups make up the "Congestion Coalition" and are the focus of chapter 6 in Balaker and Staley, *The Road More Traveled*. See also Ted Balaker and Sam Staley, "How Traffic Jams Are Made in City Hall," *Reason* (April 2007), http://www.reason.com/news/show/119192.html, accessed 14 April 2008, and Robert Atkinson, "An Exchange on Building U.S. Road Capacity: The Politics of Gridlock," in *Moving People, Goods, and Information in the 21st Century: The Cutting-Edge Infrastructures of Networked Cities*, ed. Richard E. Hanley (New York: Routledge, 2004), 117–133.

24. *Evaluating the Performance of Environmental Streamlining: Development of a NEPA Baseline for Measuring Continuous Performance*, 5.1 Conclusions. http://www.environment.fhwa.dot.gov/strmlng/baseline/index.asp.

25. The correlation coefficient, a standard measure of how strongly two variables are related to each other statistically, between population growth and TTI's travel time index between 1983 and 2003, is 0.0827. Congestion "lags" population growth. Congestion should increase more quickly as the road network's excess capacity is used up, and after people have started to move in. Not surprisingly, the relationship between population growth and congestion is even stronger when congestion in urban areas between 1993 and 2003 is compared to population growth during the previous decade (1983 to 1993).

26. In then Vice President Richard Nixon's speech to the nation's governors in Lake George, New York, five reasons were given for a billion dollar investment in what would become the Interstate Highway System. The second reason listed by Nixon was "the annual wastage of billions of hours in detours, traffic jams, and so on, measurable by any traffic engineer and amounting to billions of dollars in productive time," http://www.fhwa.dot.gov/infrastructure/rw96m.htm, accessed 14 April 2008.

27. U.S. Department of Transportation, Federal Highway Administration, "An Initial Assessement of Freight Bottlenecks on Highways," October 2005.

28. U.S. Federal Highway Administration, Office of Highway Statistics.

29. Ibid.

30. The authors thank Wendell Cox for bringing this point to their attention.

31. Alan E. Pisarski, *Commuting in America III*, NCHRP Report 550/TCRP Report 110 (Washington, D.C.: Transportation Research Board, 2006), p. 47.

32. Ibid.

33. See the discussion in Pisarski, *Commuting in America III*, pp. 5–7. While about 70 percent of the travelers during peak periods are commuters, the share of "pure" residence-to-work trips is declining.

34. These changes in labor force dynamics have received substantial attention in the academic and policy literature. See "Labour Market Trends and Globalization's Impact on Them," International Labour Organization, Bureau for Workers' Activities, n.d., http://www.itcilo.it/english/actrav/telearn/global/ilo/seura/mains.htm#Flexible %20forms%20of%20work%20in%20developed%20countries.

35. U.S. Department of Labor, Bureau of Labor Statistics, "Number of Jobs Held, Labor Market Activity, and Earning Growth Among the Youngest Baby Boomers; Results from a Longitudinal Survey," Washington, D.C., 25 August 2006, http://www.bls .gov/news.release/pdf/nlsoy.pdf.

36. U.S. Deparment of Labor, Bureau of Labor Statistics, data from Current Population Survey and available at http://www.bls.gov/news.release/tenure.t01.htm. The complete release can be read at http://www.bls.gov/news.release/tenure.nr0.htm.

37. U.S. Department of Labor, Bureau of Labor Statistics, data from the National Longitudinal Survey of Youth, 1979 and available at http://www.bls.gov/nls/y79r21 jobsbyedu.pdf.

·

II
MOBILITY AND GLOBAL COMPETITIVENESS

3

The Need for Speed

C ONGESTION IS GROWING UNCHECKED in metropolitan areas across the nation. So what?

At any given point in time, the delay we experience in rush hour doesn't seem to really influence the economic health of cities. After all, Mexico City is one of the most congested cities in the world, but it ranks among the fastest growing. Silicon Valley was a hub of national economic growth during the 1990s as its traffic congestion became legendary in the United States. The regional economies of New York, Chicago, and Los Angeles hum along despite regional congestion that is perennially ranked "severe."[1]

But congestion's costs are largely hidden. They include the economic, cultural, entertainment and other activities that don't happen because congestion makes them too difficult to get to. At a minimum, congestion reduces the vitality of cities below what they could be. In truth, congestion left unchecked can kill cities as we currently know them, choking economies and making them less competitive and strangling many of the cultural activities that make cities unique.

This chapter lays out the case for why and how congestion could ultimately kill our cities. To argue otherwise—that congestion is good for our cities—requires making the rather large intellectual leap that businesses become more profitable, and families improve their quality of life by taking longer to get to their destinations. This is not just implausible. It's wrong. To show why, this chapter explores more fully the economics of traffic congestion. It explains why congestion weakens urban economies over the long run, undermining them to the point they eventually die. Indeed, increasing the *speed* of travel is critical to increasing the productivity of cities and producing the wealth necessary to sustain our neighborhoods and improve our quality of life. A speedy and efficient transportation system may be more important than ever in the context of today's globally competitive, information-based service economy.

The Economic Consequences of Congestion

Growing cities typically face rising congestion when local infrastructure fails to keep pace with growing travel demand. During the short run, perhaps even a decade or two, it might seem that rising congestion and economic growth go hand in hand as more jobs and cars are added to a largely stagnant road system. This perception is deceptive. Public policy shouldn't be based on casual observation, and there's much more to the congestion story than lots of cars and trucks running around on roads. Congestion exerts a distinctly negative impact on the economy, even if its effects are overshadowed by stronger forces that boost productivity more than the rising toll of lower mobility dampens it. Like the proverbial frog sitting unaware of the rising heat in a pot of water, drivers often find themselves boiling in congestion because no one adjusted the heat.

Urban economists explicitly refer to congestion as a "tax." Arthur O'Sullivan's leading textbook on urban and regional economics devotes an entire chapter to automobiles, travel, and the effects of congestion.[2] Congestion is considered an "external" cost—a cost imposed on others without their consent—and external costs cause inefficiencies. As drivers enter an already busy road, for example, the traffic slows. Since the benefits of travel are primarily measured in time, any additional time penalty from slower traffic is imposed on current travelers because their travel times are longer with more cars crowding into the same space. Existing travelers didn't "agree" to allow the new cars on the road. In most U.S. cities, access is unrestricted. Thus, the slower travel times are a cost imposed by a third party—the new drivers on the road. A city that solves the congestion problem, O'Sullivan notes, is able to grow faster than one that doesn't because it enhances the welfare of its citizens by maximizing travel times and minimizing transportation costs.

John P. Blair, an expert on cities and author of a leading book on urban development policy, understands that transportation systems and their ability to move people, goods, and services to their destinations quickly and efficiently are important to the economic health of cities. "Metropolitan regions have been compared to machines," he writes. "If the metaphor is useful, the transportation system can be considered the oil that lubricates the machine."[3]

A machine *is* a useful metaphor. Without a well-functioning, efficient, and safe transportation system, economies simply can't function. Their most productive forces become seized up because of a lack of economic lubrication. In the most extreme cases, they revert to their pre-industrial roots and effectively die.

The academic discipline of urban economics is built on the concept of transportation costs for good reason. Historically, access to transportation was a driving force in where cities were located.[4] The Phoenicians built a commercial empire based on trading routes through the Middle East and Mediterranean Sea before the Greeks used their military might to cement these (and other) ports into a true empire. The first cities in the U.S. (and Europe) were built on major bodies of water—oceans, lakes, or rivers—to reduce the costs of transporting goods and services to markets. More importantly for our purposes, the creation of new transportation links dramatically changed the economic fortunes of cities. The Erie Canal linked New York City with agricultural regions in upstate New York in 1825, cutting freight costs from 20 cents per ton mile to 1.5 cents.[5] Another canal linked the Big Apple to northern New England, helping foster an economic boom that pushed its population to 500,000 by 1850.[6]

The economic benefits were not just from water. In 1792, a private toll road expanded the economic reach of Philadelphia 62 miles to Lancaster and allowed new parts of the region to develop. The economic benefit from road construction was so significant nationally that by 1845 more than 1,500 turnpike companies had been incorporated and, at their peak, accounted for 27 percent of all business incorporations.[7] All told, eighteenth and nineteenth century turnpike investments in roads and transportation systems exceeded the levels of investment during the highway building boom of the late twentieth century.[8] The privately funded portion of the road network may well have rivaled today's federally funded Interstate Highway System.[9] This is a startling statistic because toll roads were money losers. They stayed in business because the owners—the region's merchants, farmers, landowners, and ordinary residents—benefited from the mobility and trade they made possible.[10] In short, the economic benefits of improved transportation justified the private and public investment.

More recently, the Interstate Highway System produced significant financial benefits for industries when it knitted urban regions into a national market for domestically produced goods and services at a level unknown since the nineteenth century investment in railroads. Economists Chad Shirley and Clifford Winston found that investments in highways significantly improved the profitability of businesses, although the benefits of these investments appear to have declined in recent years.[11] In the 1970s, highway investments generated rates of return of 15 percent or more by helping businesses lower transportation costs. These benefits included lower freight rates, decreased travel times, greater reliability within the transportation system, and allowing firms to reduce their inventory and adopt "just in time" manufacturing and supply strategies. "In our analysis," they conclude, "highway spending raises productivity by improving the cost, speed, and reliability of highway transportation which reduces inventories."[12]

So, mobility is important. The role transportation costs play in promoting national *and* regional economic growth was and continues to be significant. It's the way in which these costs factor into economic decision making that has changed, with significant implications for how we design and build our transportation network in the twenty-first century. But, here's where it gets complicated.

Transportation is not the only factor driving urban productivity. Lots of other elements are important, too. Firms in cities have access to a bigger and wider labor pool. They can draw on secretaries, computer programmers, computer networking specialists, writers, and copier repair technicians. Cities also have a large and vast array of companies available that provide customized services, such as print shops, translation services (handy in a global economy), temporary work agencies, personal security, catering, or specialized computer programming. Cities have more efficient and deeper capital markets with the experience and networks necessary to finance new ventures. In technology-driven economies, even the location of similar firms (or workers) together breeds new ideas that foster even more innovation. Indeed, recent research has found that urban areas tend to have higher rates of innovation and invention. A city with twice the employment density as another city within a metropolitan area will have a rate of invention 20 percent higher.[13] In short, cities have advantages, and these advantages make them productive.

Thus, urbanization is a key byproduct of economic growth and wealth creation. Cities bring people, technology, ideas, and equipment together, using proximity and concentration to foster innovation and productivity. That makes them attractive places for people to live and work, too. As economist Arthur O'Sullivan writes: "Production happens in cities, so that's where most of us live and work."[14] Combined, the factors that drive up productivity because firms, workers, and other people are close together are called "agglomeration economies."[15] They are so widespread and well recognized that they are a key part of all coursework in urban economics and economic geography. These increases in production *and* productivity (amount produced per worker) translate into higher incomes, creating markets for an infinite variety of goods and services. Cities can provide generic goods—commodities—as well as specialized and niche goods, drawing on their size, ease of movement, and the low costs of serving customers and suppliers. Urban societies, not surprisingly, tend to be wealthy ones.[16]

That's not the whole story. Agglomeration economies are powerful forces that promote city growth. But cities also have forces working against them, including pollution, noise, crime and congestion. Cities grow when the positive agglomeration forces are stronger and more powerful than the negative congestion forces. Some of the benefits of locating together have to do with the scale: cities provide a more hospitable environment for production capable of nurturing more diverse products, services, and firms. Finding the balance between positive and negative influences on urban performance has spurred an entire research program on the so-called (and unresolved) issue of "optimal" city size—the point at which the economic costs of urbanization equal their economic benefits.[17] Urban economist Alain Bertaud sums up the problem nicely: "If we consider that congestion is a tax on increasing returns to scale due to urbanization, there must be a point where the tax offsets all the gain. But before this point is reached metropolitan areas are still bound to grow."[18]

The key question here, however, is: What role does the speed of travel play in urban development? Theoretically, it should be important, as we've already discussed. Faster travel speeds drive transportation costs down. These lower costs affect the bottom line for firms—lower costs mean higher potential profits and lower prices for consumers. But, is there any direct evidence that travel speeds influence economic growth? The short answer is "yes."

Economists Rémy Prud'homme and Chang-Woo Lee found that higher travel speeds expanded the labor and employment pool in cities. For every ten percent increase in travel speeds, the labor market expanded by fifteen percent and productivity by three percent.[19] Unfortunately, their study focused on cities in France. An extension of this analysis to include larger cities in other countries (but not the U.S.) by Prud'homme, however, found similar results.[20] Researchers have also found that slower growth in core urban areas in the Netherlands can be attributed to the "negative congestion effects caused by traffic jams."[21]

Closer to home, planner Robert Cervero extended Prud'homme and Lee's work and found that every ten percent increase in commuting speed in the San Francisco Bay area increased worker output by one percent.[22] Average speed had a bigger impact on land use and employment clustering than factors such as employment density and racial composition of the work force. Importantly, Cervero found that as the labor market "shed" (the number of workers within a certain distance of their employers) expanded from 30 minutes to 60 minutes, labor productivity increased by 25 percent.

BOX 3.1
The Travel Shed

The concept of the "travel shed" or "commute shed" is useful in thinking about how congestion and travel times impact economic productivity and where firms and families choose to locate. The commute shed is the geographic area within which commuters will live. Think of it as an "opportunity circle."[1] The bigger the circle, the more employment and residential opportunities someone has. The smaller the circle, the fewer opportunities available. The size of the circle is determined by time, not physical distance. So, the longer it takes to travel somewhere, the smaller the opportunity circle will be.

According to the Law of Constant Travel Time, the commute shed would include all those areas (and jobs) that could be reached within thirty minutes. In some urban areas, this may include almost the entire work force. As congestion reduces mobility, however, it takes longer to get to those jobs. The commute shed shrinks. Rather than traveling fifteen miles to a job, commuters may only be willing to travel twelve miles, or ten miles. Workers stay closer to home in distance, but not time. For the individual worker, the job possibilities shrink; his "world" becomes smaller and less connected to the rest of the urban area.

Note

1. For a more complete discussion of this concept, see Ted Balaker, *Why Mobility Matters*, Policy Study No. 43 (Los Angeles: Reason Foundation 2006), http://www.reason.org/pb43_whymobilitymatters.pdf, accessed 30 April 2008.

Congestion also influences different industries in different ways.[23] Manufacturing companies, for example, should find that congestion impacts their productivity by lengthening the time it takes to ship final products to their respective markets, often in other nations or regions. Congestion can disrupt "supply chains"—the economic linking of suppliers of different inputs or parts at different stages of the production process—forcing firms to stock larger amounts of inventory to compensate for the uncertainties of deliveries. These types of disruptions are different from those faced by retailers and wholesalers shipping goods from warehouses and distribution centers intended for direct sales to consumers at the neighborhood level. In a "just in time" economy, congestion's negative impacts loom large.

Similarly, technology and service based industries are more labor intensive and will be far more interested in how congestion influences the ability of their employees to organize and participate in meetings, deliver intermediate products to vendors, or simply make it to work on time. Congestion influences our quality of life, making it harder to predict schedules for spouses, colleagues, and babysitters, complicating errands, and frustrating attempts to socialize with others. Notably, the disruptive impacts of congestion on personal life and individualized work schedules were a primary factor behind a threatened boycott of a technology conference in Bangalore, India, by the business community.[24] Infrastructure had not kept pace with the city's stunning economic growth in the information technology industry—Bangalore is India's version of Silicon Valley—extending commute times and imposing significant burdens on the technology companies located there.

Are these effects just speculation? No. Daniel Graham, a transportation economist at Imperial College in London, England, provides some compelling evidence on how congestion influences different sectors of the economy. Using data from thousands of neighborhoods in London, Graham examined congestion's impacts on productivity based on two factors: how far people traveled and how much time it took them to get to their destination.[25] Different industries seem to benefit from cities at different points in their industry's growth cycle. Manufacturing, information technology, and construction firms experienced the maximum point of productivity in cities sooner than catering and distribution.[26] Services such as finance, insurance, and banking benefited the most from locating in the city. Similarly, some industries were more influenced by congestion and reduced travel speeds than others. Graham speculates that if travel speeds increased by five percent, productivity for firms located in London would increase by one percent.[27] Interestingly, these estimates are within the same range as those discovered by Prud'homme.

What about the U.S.? University of North Carolina, Charlotte, transportation researchers David Hartgen and Gregory Fields examined congestion's effects on eight urban areas, ranging from Salt Lake City with an urbanized area population of just 1.5 million people to the San Francisco Bay area with an urbanized area population of 6.8 million people.[28] Their analysis looked at how travel times influenced the size of the labor market as well as access to key destinations within the region, specifically the downtown central business district, large shopping malls, major universities, major suburbs, and airports. Their analysis used 25 minutes as the standard for access since this travel time was the median commute time for workers in major U.S. urban areas.

Not surprisingly, they found that congestion reduced accessibility to these key areas because fewer people could access them in a reasonable amount of time. Perhaps more surprisingly, the magnitude of the effects is similar to those of Prud'homme and Graham. The central business districts, in particular, were most vulnerable since most growth was already going to the suburbs. Congestion simply reinforced these trends, making the downtown more isolated from the rest of the region. Over time, this result implies rising congestion will make downtowns less productive and, ultimately, less viable. In seven of the eight urbanized areas, Hartgen and Fields found the downtown would be helped by eliminating congestion because it expanded its ability to tap into growing suburban markets and decentralizing labor force. The same benefits were found for shopping malls and universities.

Of course, not all downtowns or economic regions were affected the same way. Congestion relief in Salt Lake City had small effects because travelers there experience relatively little congestion on a regional scale (although those driving north or south on I-15 during peak hour times might have a different perspective). The largest positive effects from improved accessibility were found in Charlotte and Denver.

But what of economic performance? Hartgen and Fields' analysis uncovers several salient points. First, access to jobs has a much bigger impact on economic performance than access to residents. So, the key was to ensure employers have access to as large of a labor pool as possible. Second, while the most accessible place in these areas was the downtown, regional economic performance appears to hinge on other destinations, most notably growing suburbs and universities.[29]

The effects were also large. If Dallas could maintain free-flow conditions on its highway network, its regional economy would generate $46 billion more dollars by improving access to its universities, $23 billion by improving access to its major suburbs, $18 billion through improved access to its shopping malls, $8 billion from improved access to its airport, and $6 billion through improved access to the downtown. Denver would reap economic benefits of similar magnitudes. Atlanta would benefit, but not by quite as much: $15 billion from improved access to its growing suburbs, $24 billion by improving access to its malls and universities, and about $10 billion by improving access to its airport and downtown.

Thus, congestion limits productivity by restricting access to a core input in the production process—people. As congestion increases, fewer people have access to jobs while businesses have access to fewer workers. Productivity is shortchanged, and we all suffer. In large metropolitan areas, congestion has the effect of "balkanizing" the local economy as businesses cluster close to their potential workers but can't access workers or services in other parts of the region.

Perhaps, then, we should not be surprised that while outsiders see Silicon Valley as a single entity, in truth it represents a series of industry clusters. Hardware clusters involving semiconductors and disk drives tend to locate in the southern parts of the Valley near San Jose and Santa Clara while software companies locate closer to San Francisco.[30] Location can make or break a start-up company. "You locate a company where the engineers are," Nir Zuk, founder of Palo Alto Networks told the *New York Times*. "You would never locate a networking company in Palo Alto."[31] Thus, Palo Alto Networks is based about 12 miles south of Palo Alto. While that may seem like a short distance for Midwesterners or southerners unaccustomed to long commutes, congestion in Silicon Valley can turn a 12-mile commute into an hour or longer. Traffic congestion shapes regional economies, and constrains them by tying location decisions to the commuting distance of potential workers—their labor supply.

Changing Travel, Changing Transport

The economy is changing, and the factors that boosted productivity for manufacturing companies in the twentieth century are not necessarily that ones that keep technology-based economies humming at top speed in the twenty-first century. In the past, investments in transportation improved economic competitiveness primarily by lowering the costs of moving goods and services to markets, whether domestic or international. Thus, reducing the cost of transporting wheat, wool, or corn from 20 cents per ton mile to 1.5 cents had a big impact on the bottom line of business, which also translated into cost savings for consumers. Today it is as much about a firm's access to labor.

In service-based economies where workers are highly mobile, workers decide where to live and work based on "amenities," or quality of life factors such as climate, affordable housing, quality of schools, and health care.[32] Mobility not only boosts access to labor, but directly impacts lifestyle choices, access to places and services we want to use, and how we arrange our work lives. Alan Pisarksi, author of *Commuting in America III*, believes that this amenity effect is just as important, if not more so, in a service-based economy where human capital (people) can move about unconstrained, and the most productive workers choose their work and home locations freely.[33] "The affluence of the emerging society," Pisarski says, "and the resulting immense value of time, will drive most decisions, including those related to transportation. Areas of the country will compete for workers on the basis of life-style, climate, and ease of living. Good transportation will be one of those competitive amenities."[34] This is already happening. An examination of 81 U.S. metropolitan areas found that highway congestion was a "disamenity" for workers and reduced net in-migration.[35]

Congestion figures more prominently in this "choice" equation than in the past. Traditionally, Americans adjusted their travel, particularly commuting, several ways to minimize the negative impact on their lives. First, they often simply moved. If they believed their new job was permanent or stable, they purchased a home that was closer to where they worked. "Dynamic market adjustments," note economists Peter Gordon and Harry Richardson, "the suburbanization of jobs for example, is the explanation [for historically stable commute times]—'rational relocation' by both firms and households is the solution, not the problem."[36]

These adjustments were possible because the traditional commute, unlike the current pattern, was highly structured and predictable. Workers left their home, drove directly to a centralized work place, and then parked their car for most, if not all, of the work day. Now, as work schedules become more flexible and the demands of families with multiple income earners become more complex, workers are likely to break up their work day for personal trips and "trip chain"—tag on multiple destinations during their commute such as dropping off (or picking up) their children at school or daycare, picking up dry cleaning, shopping for groceries, shuttling kids to soccer games, meeting clients for coffee, etc. One could easily see a graphic designer or consultant, for example, leaving home, dropping her kids off at school, meeting a potential client for coffee, setting up a temporary workstation at the coffee shop, and then meeting another client or vendor for lunch, before getting to her office.

In fact, this is exactly what's happening. By 2001, nonwork trips made up more than 83 percent of all trips. Forty-six percent of all trips were for family and personal reasons, ten percent for school or church, and 27 percent were for social and recreational purposes. Even in rush hours, nonwork trips accounted for more than 62 percent of all trips in the mornings and afternoons. More importantly, perhaps, nonwork trips grew at 30 percent between 1990 and 2001, almost one-third faster than traditional work trips. Moreover, these trips are more likely to be chained. Thus, travel has become more complex as our lifestyles and work habits have evolved with the flexible demands of a service-based economy. These changes have significant implications for travel and congestion especially chained trips in the morning rush hour that contribute substantially to congestion.[37]

The details of changing trip patterns do not fundamentally alter the logic of how we decide where to live or work. Rather, they change the calculus or formula applied to the choice. Since more households optimize their location based on two jobs rather than one, and long-term employment with one firm is less common, the complexity of this decision making process probably lends itself to longer commutes on average because fewer options are available to the household. In addition, increased trip chaining—linking several destinations or purposes in one trip—may lengthen the average trip or commute time.[38]

A second way households traditionally adjusted was by moving their work closer to where they lived. Moving the workplace can be accomplished by physically moving the jobs closer to where someone lives, or using technology to transfer work into the home through telecommuting or telework. Telecommuters already outnumber transit users in more than half of U.S. metropolitan areas with more than one million people (see table 3.1).[39] More importantly, telecommuting is now the fastest growing segment of the commuting market.[40]

However households adjust, the effects are the same. As congestion increases, households tend to narrow the scope of their travel to stay within the 30 or 45 minute commute shed. This result is remarkably stable and applies to large and

**Table 3.1. U.S. Metropolitan Areas Where
Telecommuters Outnumber Public Transit Riders**

- Austin, TX
- Charlotte, NC
- Columbus, OH
- Dallas, TX
- Denver, CO
- Detroit, MI
- Grand Rapids, MI
- Greensboro, NC
- Indianapolis, IN
- Jacksonville, FL
- Kansas City, MO
- Louisville, KY
- Memphis, TN
- Nashville-Davidson Co., TN
- Norfolk, VA
- Oklahoma City, OK
- Orlando, FL
- Phoenix, AZ
- Raleigh, NC
- Richmond, VA
- Rochester, NY
- Sacramento, CA
- Salt Lake City, UT
- San Diego, CA
- St. Louis, MO
- Tampa-St. Petersburg, FL
- W. Palm Beach, FL

Source: Ted Balaker, *The Quiet Success: Telecommuting's Impact on Transportation and Beyond*, Policy Study No. 338 (Los Angeles: Reason Foundation, November 2005), http://www.reason.org/ps338.pdf.

small areas. In smaller areas with little congestion, workers and residents have access to large swaths of the region. In more dense areas, such as New York, regional access to jobs and destinations is geographically more limited. Also, as we saw in our example of Silicon Valley, employers tend to look for workers within the same commute shed. Thus, congestion balkanizes an urban area as households and employers geographically narrow their economic and social playing field.

This balkanization is a threat to the service- and technology-based economy of the modern city. It cuts the connections that make the eclectic style of urban life valuable. It prevents people and business from tapping into the diversity that makes them great. New York City is not a great city because China Town, Little Italy, Greenwich Village, SoHo, and the dozens of other trendy or fashionable neighborhoods act as independent, isolated villages. They thrive because they are part of an integrated urban area, tapping into the labor, capital, and wealth of more than a million people in Manhattan, eight million people in the five boroughs of New York City, and twenty million people in the greater New York area. The neighborhoods would not thrive in isolation. It is the coming and going, the flow of people enjoying the unique features of a neighborhood, whether they live there or not, that keeps it vital. Every thriving neighborhood needs access to the larger city to remain vibrant and strong. The same is true for global cities such as London, Paris, and Beijing.

Modern cities, however, aren't as constrained economically or geographically as cities in the past. Historically, physical barriers to mobility were common and expensive to overcome. Rivers, hills, and mountains would cut off cities from their hinterlands, and these barriers would direct urbanization toward certain areas before bridges and tunneling techniques knitted regions together. As technology improved, and our wealth increased, these physical barriers were gradually overcome in city after city. Examples of how engineering solutions enabled large urban regions include: connecting the San Fernando Valley on the north side of the Santa Monica Mountains and Los Angeles on the south side in Southern California; downtown Seattle and the eastern reaches of the Seattle urban area; San Francisco and Oakland in northern California; and Cincinnati and Covington/Newport, Kentucky.

These regions were connected through the engineering marvels of the nineteenth and twentieth centuries—bridges and tunnels. Indeed, when transportation (and water) investments overcame the physical barrier of the Santa Monica Mountains, large swaths of land opened up that fed the growth of Los Angeles. The San Fernando Valley's population of 1.6 million, while a formal part of the city of Los Angeles, would now rank it as the nation's fifth largest city. While it has a thriving local economy, the Valley provides important economic benefits to the greater Los Angeles area, particularly in technology and entertainment industries.[41]

Congestion has the same effect as those physical barriers once had in previous centuries. By limiting mobility, it narrows access to other parts of the urban region, separating north from south, east from west, and downtown from the periphery. The economic benefits provided by the San Fernando Valley are jeopardized by rising congestion that balkanizes Southern California. Some have already noted the Valley's robust local economic growth and its role as an emerging independent economy. This growing sense of independence helped fuel a secession movement.[42]

Another compelling example can be taken from the Midwest's economic powerhouse: Chicago. About 250,000 people now live downtown.[43] Yet, nearly 500,000 people work downtown. Downtown's economic survival depends on its ability to bring workers to their jobs quickly and efficiently. If congestion makes access to the downtown impractical for those in the hinterlands, Chicago's city center loses its economic luster.

While congestion is already driving a social and economic wedge between the San Fernando Valley and the southern reaches of the city of Los Angeles (and downtown Chicago and its suburbs), it doesn't have to. The physical barrier of the Santa Monica Mountains was conquered with a dedication to solving key infrastructure problems by building an aqueduct that fed water to the undeveloped part of northern Los Angeles (and elsewhere in the region) and building roads through passes that created core transportation routes that connected to the city. Bridges, tunnels, and transit have been used to feed the economic vitality of Manhattan by bringing the boroughs of Staten Island, Brooklyn, Queens, the Bronx, and the cities of northern New Jersey within the commute shed of one of the world's most dynamic cities. Similar creativity and dedication will be needed to re-engineer our transportation networks to meet the competitive and dynamic needs of the twenty-first century economy and society. Different times call for different measures.

Progressive Strategies for Dynamic Times

This clarion call may sound well and good, but doesn't it run counter to other studies that seem to suggest that investments in transportation infrastructure are losing their economic luster? The rate of return for highway investments had fallen to just five percent by the 1980s and 1990s by some estimates.[44] Some have taken these data as evidence that highway investments are no longer needed, or that we only need to shore up worn-out roads and bridges or other facilities destroyed by natural disasters such as hurricanes or earthquakes.

Moreover, shouldn't we be worried about broader issues such as climate change and land use? Can we afford to keep investing in a road-based strategy? Both questions deserve forthright answers. Unfortunately, we are unable to thoroughly answer them in the depth many of our readers were prefer. Nevertheless, we believe the financing issue is central and devote chapter 11 to these questions. We have left the issues of climate and land use to admittedly brief appendices that we hope will provide an outline of how we approach these issues, even if they don't fully satisfy our critics.

The studies apparently showing the declining economic benefit of new roads, and other questions outside the main focus of this book, do not fundamentally question congestion's negative economic impacts. In fact, as we mentioned at the beginning of this chapter, most economists agree that congestion is a drag on city economies. Congestion has been growing more than twice as fast as the national economy. Over the next 20 years, the cost of congestion could amount to $890.5 billion, or 4.3 percent of the value of the entire national economy.[45]

Rather, studies suggesting a decline in the value of new road investment should be considered as a healthy dose of skepticism about solutions that may have worked in the past but might not work in today's economy. It is not that building more roads won't help. Rather, building roads the old fashioned way won't help. We need to use new approaches to building networks, build new types of roads that meet the needs of modern travel patterns and behavior, adopt new technologies, and improve network management to make the transportation network of the twenty-first century work. We need a more nuanced and layered approach to why and how congestion impacts cities and the economy. We also need a better sense of just how widespread these changes are. For that, we turn to America's city of cities: New York.

Notes

1. See also Samuel Staley, "A Congested Economy," *New York Times*, 15 November 2007, http://www.reason.org/commentaries/staley_20071125.shtml, accessed 23 January 2008.

2. Arthur O'Sullivan, *Urban Economics*, 6th edition (New York: McGraw-Hill, 2007), pp. 207–224.

3. John P. Blair, *Urban and Regional Economics* (Homewood, IL: Irwin, 1991), p. 454.

4. See the brief overview and description in O'Sullivan, *Urban Economics*, pp. 20–23; Ted Balaker and Sam Staley, *The Road More Traveled: Why the Congestion Crisis Matters More Than You Think, and What We Can Do About It* (Lanham, MD: Rowman

& Littlefield, 2006); Joel Kotkin, *The City: A Global History* (New York: Modern Library, 2005).

5. O'Sullivan, *Urban Economics*, p. 21.

6. Ibid.

7. Daniel Klein and John Majewski, "America's Toll Road Heritage: The Achievements of Private Initiative in the Nineteenth Century," in *Street Smart: Competition, Entrepreneurship, and the Future of Roads*, ed. Gabriel Roth (New Brunswick, NJ: Transaction Publishers, 2006), pp. 280–281.

8. Klein and Majewski, "America's Toll Road Heritage," p. 286.

9. Klein and Majewski estimate that private toll roads built and managed roads ranged between 30,000 and 52,000 centerline miles.

10. Klein and Majewski, "America's Toll Road Heritage".

11. Chad Shirley and Clifford Winston, "Firm Inventory Behavior and the Returns From Highway Infrastructure Investments," *Journal of Urban Economics*, Vol. 55 (2004), pp. 393-415. Notably, this and other studies do not take into account environmental regulation, economic impact statements, and other factors that have significantly increased the costs of building roads.

12. Shirley and Winston, "Firm Inventory Behavior," p. 412.

13. Gerald A. Carlino, Satyajit Chatterjee, and Robert M. Hunt, "Urban Density and the Rate of Invention," *Journal of Urban Economics*, 2006, doi:10.1016/j.jue.2006.08.003.

14. O'Sullivan, *Urban Economics*, p. 17.

15. Importantly, agglomeration economies are not the same as scale economies. Economies (and diseconomies) of scale result from expanding output within one facility or firm, spreading costs over a larger number of units produced. Agglomeration economies result from the concentration of firms in one area, usually (but not always) urban areas.

16. See, for example, Vernon Henderson, "How Urban Concentration Affects Economic Growth," Policy Research Working Paper, The World Bank, Development Research Group, April 2000. This is not universally true. In some nations, urbanization is promoted as a matter of policy to reduce reliance on the agricultural sector. This is particularly evident in many African countries. Nevertheless, even in these cases, an economy's wealth is primarily generated by cities.

17. For an extensive discussion of this concept, see J. Vernon Henderson, *Urban Development: Theory, Fact, and Illusion* (New York: Oxford University Press, 1988). See also, Henderson, "How Urban Concentration Affects Economic Growth."

18. Email correspondence with Samuel R. Staley, 17 August 2006.

19. Rémy Prud'homme and Change-Woo Lee, "Size, Sprawl, Speed and the Efficiency of Cities," *Urban Studies*, Vol. 36, No. 11 (October 1999), pp. 1849–1858.

20. Rémy Prud'homme, "Transportation and Economic Development," paper prepared for ECMT 199th Round Table, March 2000.

21. Lourens Broersma and Jouke van Dijk, "The Effect of Congestion and Agglomeration on Multifactor Productivity Growth in Dutch Regions," *Journal of Economic Geography*, Vol. 8, No. 2 (2007), pp. 181–209.

22. Robert Cervero, "Efficient Urbanization: Economic Performance and the Shape of the Metropolis," *Urban Studies*, Vol. 38, No. 10 (2001), pp. 1651–1671.

23. For an interesting examination of how agglomeration economies influence the productivity of firms in different industries, see David L. Rigby and Jurgen Essletzbichler, "Agglomeration Economies and Productivity Differences in US Cities," *Journal of Economic Geography*, Vol. 2 (2002), pp. 207–432.

24. This situation is discussed in more depth in Balaker and Staley, *The Road More Traveled,*, Chapter 7.

25. Graham used data from 10,780 wards in London. Daniel J. Graham, "Variable Returns to Agglomeration and the Effect of Road Traffic Congestion," *Journal of Urban Economics*, (2007), doi:10.1016/j.jue.2006.10.001.

26. Graham, "Variable Returns to Agglomeration," p. 11.

27. Graham, "Variable Returns to Agglomeration," p. 16.

28. The other urbanized areas (and populations) were Charlotte (1.7 million), Seattle (3.3 million), Denver (2.6 million), Atlanta (4.3 million), Detroit (4.9 million), and Dallas (4.8 million). David T. Hartgen and Gregory Fields, "Accessibility, Traffic Congestion, and Regional Economic Performance," (Los Angeles: Reason Foundation, in press).

29. Notably, airport access does not appear to have significant impacts on regional economic performance.

30. Steve Lohr, "Silicon Valley Shaped by Technology and Traffic," *New York Times*, 20 December 2007.

31. Quote in Lohr, "Silicon Valley Shaped by Technology and Traffic."

32. Jennifer Roback, "Wages, Rents, and the Quality of Life," *Journal of Political Economy*, Vol. 90 (1982), pp. 1257–1278. For a more contemporary and popular statement of this effect on cities, see Richard Florida, *The Rise of the Creative Class* (New York: Basic Books, 2002).

33. Alan Pisarski has made this observation at numerous times, including a presentation on mobility made to the annual American Dream Conference, sponsored by the American Dream Coalition in San Jose, California on 12 November 2007.

34. Pisarski, presentation to the American Dream Coalition, 12 November 2007.

35. Soojung Kim, "A New Approach to Measuring the Effects of Infrastructure on Regional Economic Performance: U.S. Metropolitan Areas," paper presented to the Western Regional Science Association, Santa Fe, New Mexico, February 2006. For earlier studies, see also Marlon Boarnet, "Highways and Economic Productivity: Interpreting Recent Evidence," *Journal of Planning Literature*, Vol. 11 (1997), pp. 476–486 and "Infrastructure Services and Productivity of Public Capital: The Case of Streets and Highways," *National Tax Journal*, vol. 50 (1997), pp. 39–57.

36. Gordon and Richardson, "The Geography of Transportation and Land Use," p. 44.

37. Bumsoo Lee, Peter Gordon, James E. Moore II, and Harry W. Richardson, "Residential Location Land Use and Transportation: The Neglected Role of Nonwork Travel," School of Policy, Planning and Development, University of Southern California, Los Angeles, California, 23 January 2006, unpublished paper.

38. Ibid.

39. Ted Balaker, *The Quiet Success: Telecommuting Impact on Transportation and Beyond*, Policy Study No. 338 (Los Angeles: Reason Foundation, October 2005), http://www.reason.org/ps338.pdf.

40. Balaker, *The Quiet Success*, p. 10.

41. Joel Kotkin, *Older Suburbs: Crabgrass Slums or New Urban Frontier?* Policy Study No. 285 (Los Angeles: Reason Foundation, September 2001), pp. 28–33, http://www.reason.org/ps285.pdf.

42. While it failed at the ballot box in 2002, a majority of those voting within the San Fernando Valley favored separating from the City of Los Angeles.

43. Downtown Chicago is bounded by Lincoln Park to the north, North Halstead, and Cermak.

44. Shirley and Winston, "Firm Inventory Behavior." For a review of the recent literature, see also Eric Thompson, *If You Build It Will They Come? An Examination of Public Highways Investments on Economic* Growth, Center for Applied Economics, School of Business, University of Kansas, May 2005, pp. 11–14.

45. Jack Wells, "The Role of Transportation in the U.S. Economy," presentation given to the National Surface Transportation Policy and Revenue Study Commission, 26 June 2006, http://www.surfacecommission.gov/The%20Role%20of%20Transportation%20in%20the%20U.S.%20Economy.ppt, accessed October 31, 2006.

4

The Apple of Automobility

![decorative line]

W ITH NEARLY EIGHT MILLION PEOPLE in the Big Apple itself, and 11 million more in nearby counties (including Long Island), New York ranks as the nation's largest city, the classic gateway to opportunity for foreigners and Americans alike. Climbing the steps from the Eighth Avenue subway stop at 42nd street, or walking out the doors of Penn Station can overwhelm visitors with the immensity of the life, vibrancy, and bustle of the city. Manhattan skyscrapers swallow up workers and spit them out, overwhelming pedestrians. The glitter and glitterati of Times Square now rivals the Vegas Strip, juxtaposing the streaming ticker of NASDAQ with the youthful irreverence of MTV's *Total Request Live* and the more mainstream ABC's *Good Morning America* broadcasts.

The implications for travel and mobility are not clear if one limits one's idea of New York to Wall Street or Times Square, or simply accepts the vibrant veneer of Manhattan's contemporary urban streetscape. A more nuanced and layered look at Manhattan, New York City, and the larger metropolitan region can tell us a lot about the powerful demographic and technological forces shaping our culture and the implications for transportation and travel. It turns out the Big Apple is a lot more like the rest of us than we think. Many of the insights we can glean from travel behavior in New York and its surrounding area provide surprising and confirming evidence about how our current sensibilities are undermining our nineteenth century conceptions of urban transport.

New York also faces severe transportation challenges. Commuters and other travelers in the New York City area—which includes northern New Jersey, lower New York State, Long Island, and southwestern Connecticut—spend more than 384 million hours stuck in traffic every year. This waste adds up to more than $7.4 billion each year according to the Texas Transportation Institute.[1] That ranks the region second only to Los Angeles in congestion costs despite New York boasting the nation's most extensive and most utilized system of public transit. "The city's transportation system is increasingly under stress," notes a report prepared for the recent citywide planning initiative. "Congestion is affecting nearly all modes of travel and putting a strain on critical infrastructure, such as bridges, and tunnels, streets, sidewalks and subways."[2] Ken Orski of the Urban Mobility Corporation puts the problem as directly as anyone: "New Jersey-New York-Connecticut is one huge bottleneck."[3]

It's also going to get worse. The city's planning office expects the Big Apple to add 900,000 people by 2030, yet public transportation officials have failed to upgrade the road network to keep up with population growth. Over the next 20 years city planners expect automobile traffic to grow by 10 percent and freight traffic to increase by 64 percent. But of the mayor's 16 major transportation recommendations in the city's long-range plan, not one would significantly increase the road system's capacity. Gridlock is inevitable without major shifts in transportation policy and strategy.

New York City and its region, then, is a good case study for this book. It's our largest city playing an iconic role in our national economy. At the center of the region is a downtown—Manhattan—that many believe is the heart of the region's competitiveness. This heart is connected by arteries extending out into the hinterlands, tracing a classic path of urban development. What can this city and its environs tell us about mobility in the twenty-first century? A lot. The issue is figuring out where to start because each layer of the region has its own story to tell. We'll split this story into two parts—one at the center of the metropolitan area and the other at the regional level. We'll begin our journey at the center.

Cities Are More Than the Downtown

Downtowns are funny places. For most of us, they represent the image of everything we think of that makes a city—skyscrapers, busy streets, buses, and roads choked with traffic. But, we don't live there. Most of us don't even work there. They are in many ways relics of a past era of urban development. New York, it turns out, isn't that much different from most other cities' downtowns although history and geography are conspiring to keep its place as the über-downtown of the Americas. Despite the real vibrancy of Manhattan, most

New Yorkers live outside the downtown (below 59th street in Manhattan) and 80 percent of the city's residents live in the other four boroughs. Sixty percent of the region's residents live outside New York City proper in surrounding states, counties and cities.

Traffic and transportation is thus a regional issue "writ large." The New York Metropolitan Transportation Commission covers 25 counties in three states: New York, New Jersey, and Connecticut. Twenty million people (seven percent of the U.S. population) are distributed across this region in the following way:

- New York City: 8.2 million
- Long Island: 2.8 million
- Mid-Hudson/Downstate New York: 2.0 million
- Northern New Jersey: 5.6 million
- Connecticut: 1.9 million

This is only the first slice out of the region. New York City is *also* a massive place by U.S. standards, both in terms of people and economic activity. The City consists of five boroughs, all of them big enough to be major cities in their own right:

- Manhattan: 1.6 million
- Bronx: 1.4 million
- Brooklyn (Kings Co.): 2.5 million
- Queens: 2.3 million
- Staten Island (Richmond Co.): 0.5 million

Notably, Queens and Brooklyn have larger populations than Manhattan and would independently rank as the third and fourth biggest cities in the U.S. behind Los Angeles and Chicago.

These boroughs, with their immense size and diversity, also pack more people onto each square mile than almost all other cities in the U.S. Manhattan averages population densities of 70,000 people per square mile, and some neighborhoods reach densities of 150,000 or more. Manhattan alone would rank as the densest large city in the United States.[4] But Manhattan is an outlier among outliers. No other city or borough comes close to these kinds of densities or, for that matter, the mixes of land uses. Manhattan is twice as dense as Brooklyn and the Bronx, three times as dense as Queens, and nearly ten times as dense as Staten Island. Manhattan's employment market share is also almost three times that of Brooklyn and four times that of Queens.

By contrast, the nation's third most populous city, Chicago, has a population density of 12,750 people per square mile. Among major cities, Chicago is the tenth densest.[5] Los Angeles, the nation's second largest city, has a population density of a mere 7,877 and ranks 28th densest among major cities. Phoenix seems to barely register on the density charts with 2,782 people per square mile (ranking 147th), about the density of a typical U.S. suburb. Of course, as we mentioned in earlier chapters, the cities that are growing look much more like Phoenix and Los Angeles than New York or Chicago.

New York City's boroughs are further subdivided into 59 separate planning districts that include hundreds of separate neighborhoods. Take Manhattan. This borough includes 37 neighborhoods recognized by the New York City planning department. At the southern tip of the island, neighborhoods are as diverse as the Financial District, Gramercy, SoHo, Chinatown, Little Italy, Greenwich Village, East Village, and Tudor City. The northern reaches of Manhattan include Harlem and Washington Heights. With a population of 1.5 million people, the borough of Manhattan by itself would rank as the nation's fifth largest city (smaller than Houston but a shade bigger than Philadelphia, Phoenix, San Antonio, or Dallas) and the nation's 35th largest metropolitan area. New York is a big, diverse place, any way the statistical pie is sliced.

Not surprisingly, transportation options are more diverse as well, in keeping with the massive mobility needs of the region as well as the historic densities and concentrations of economic activity. Thirty percent of the Big Apple's residents use the nation's largest system of buses, trains, and taxis to get to work, shop, watch movies, play baseball, or attend to other personal business every day. The city's transit system carries 8.6 million passengers each day, more than the next five largest U.S. systems combined.[6] Chicago and Los Angeles have the next highest ridership, hovering around 1.5 million riders per day. Chicago's system, by contrast, serves just 3.6 percent of all travel in the urbanized area and meets the needs of about 11 percent of commuters.[7] "You cannot talk about improving circulation within the Tri-State," notes Ken Orski, "without talking about improving transit service."[8]

So, here we have it: New York City is the largest, densest, most transit-oriented city in the U.S. It also faces some of the nation's most severe mobility challenges and problems.

New Yorkers Like Mobility

New York is indeed travel challenged, not only on a regional level but also within the Big Apple. Commutes in Queens, Staten Island, Bronx, and Brooklyn rank as the nation's longest, averaging 60 minutes or more each day.[9]

About half of New York's commuters expect to spend at least 40 minutes getting from point A to point B, regardless of the type of trip.[10] Regionally, the *average* one way commute is 34 minutes, the longest of any U.S. metropolitan area. So, the average commuter in Northern New Jersey, the Mid-Hudson, southwest Connecticut, or Long Island is spending more than an hour on the road or in a train getting to work.[11] Compounding insult to injury, New York is the king of the extreme commute: 18 percent of New Yorkers commute for an hour or longer each way![12]

In one sense, it's not surprising that the only city in the U.S. where mass transit legitimately earns its name is New York. The longer the commute, the more likely people get on a bus or train.[13] Almost half (45 percent) of those working in the region's "central cities"— Newark, Edison, Union, and Wayne in New Jersey, White Plains and New York City in New York—use transit, almost twice the share of the next largest urban area (Chicago).[14] Three-quarters of those going to the downtown (lower Manhattan) use transit to get to work.[15] In short, transit is essential to regional mobility.

But, mobility in New York is not all about transit. In fact, it turns out, mobility in New York is not even primarily about transit. The New York urban area, as we will see, is an automobile-oriented metropolis—with an important twist. This doesn't imply that transit is unimportant. Quite the contrary. Transit plays a vital role in the city's mobility, particularly in places with exceptionally high densities. Fewer than five percent of Manhattan's residents use cars for making trips, which means its population relies almost exclusively on buses, taxis, trains, or walking to get around.

Nevertheless, while important, transit is not dominant. In fact, it's losing ground for the same reasons downtowns and central cities have been losing ground across the nation. Fully 70 percent of all trips within the Big Apple proper include some form of flexible mobility through walking, personal cars, or taxi. Thus, while transit may be an essential component of the transportation system, New York City is not transit "oriented" or "dependent" in the way critics of American suburbs label so-called urban sprawl "automobile oriented" or "autodependent."

This observation may be a bit hard to swallow for most, so let's take a closer look at Manhattan, arguably the "hardest case" for our automobility thesis.

Manhattan is unique for its size, density, and travel patterns. Just a few bridges and tunnels provide access to the megacity's downtown from the other boroughs (Brooklyn, Bronx, Queens, Staten Island) or neighboring cities and states (New Jersey, the Lower Hudson, Connecticut, or Long Island). In some categories, fixed-route transit—subway or bus—is truly dominant, and travelers are transit dependent. Three-quarters of all commuters, for example, use buses or trains to get to "downtown" New York—Manhattan destinations below 59th street.[16]

But that's for *commuting* trips into Manhattan. Just 16 percent of all trips in New York are commuting trips. Eighty percent of New Yorkers don't live in Manhattan, and most do not work in Manhattan, and most trips are not for commuting purposes. Those living outside Manhattan tend to avoid travel by fixed route transit. They travel by car or walk. In other words, they prefer flexible and adaptable ways of traveling that allow them to customize their trips. Even for the niche travel market of commuters, car trips (not transit trips) make up 52 percent of commutes into the Bronx, 45 percent in Brooklyn, almost 60 percent in Queens, and 71 percent in Staten Island.

Secondary business centers in the outer boroughs, like downtowns in most cities and urban areas, are exceptions to the general rule. While just one-third of commutes into downtown Brooklyn and the Bronx Hub are by automobile, the share jumps to 41 percent in Flushing, 45 percent in Long Island City, and 48 percent in Jamaica—all in Queens.[17] Interestingly, and perhaps more telling, 70 percent of workers commuting into the JFK airport employment hub come by car.[18] Of the 1,700 workers living within a half mile of the airport, 1,400 use cars to get to work![19]

Once again, these are commuting trips, and they represent an ever smaller share of the overall market. For noncommute trips, New Yorkers prefer flexible, self-directed travel choices to fixed routes systems that depend on set schedules. In Manhattan and the Bronx, the two boroughs with the highest transit use, walking is the primary way residents conduct everyday personal shopping. The car and walking split mode shares (30 to 40 percent) for shopping in Brooklyn and Queens. On Staten Island, cars rule. Short, fixed-route, schedule-driven transit trails walking and car-based automobility everywhere, even Manhattan (where walking trumps transit).

In the end, travel behavior in New York is not that much different from travel in the rest of the nation. While the legacy of very high densities and the dominance of the Manhattan office market provide an unusually hospitable climate for traditional fixed-route forms of transit, commuting is the only travel category where automobility seems to be at a disadvantage (and even here the barrier may be the high cost of parking, not lack of mobility). In short, New York City, despite the advantages of hyperurbanity, is not immune to the same travel preferences and trends experienced elsewhere.

So, the core city of the New York urbanized area reflects many of the choices we've discussed in earlier chapters. But the full flavor of these choices and the trends they have sparked in travel aren't apparent by looking simply at New York City. The City is one part of a much bigger urban area. The full context becomes clear when we look at the entire region.

BOX 4.1
Building Road Capacity in the Big Apple[1]

Few U.S. cities provide a bigger challenge to adding physical road capacity than New York City, and Manhattan in particular. Many, including elected officials and transportation planners, simply presume that capacity cannot be increased, relying exclusively on transit and law enforcement approaches to manage traffic and "tame" bad driver behavior. But, this isn't quite true. Several opportunities exist to add physical road space in Manhattan, even if (like transit expansion in the rest of America) it isn't a complete solution to the problem.

Much of Manhattan's congestion stems from vehicles passing through the island on their way to destinations outside or on the outskirts of the borough. These travelers would love to bypass most or all of Manhattan, but the roadway network isn't built to allow it. Instead motorists are crammed together, turning crosstown travelers into local travelers. Many become what New Yorkers call "box blockers," drivers closing intersections when the traffic backs up and preventing cross traffic from moving through.

This isn't the only alternative. In cities across the world, drivers can choose to drive up and over intersections on humps called queue jumpers, or they can duck under intersections through short tunnels. Queue jumpers and tunnels make sense in dense urban areas and neighborhoods, as well as areas constrained by environmentally sensitive lands, because they operate within existing rights-of-way. They can also be configured for many different types of roads, from two-lanes on a one-way street (sending one lane over the intersection) to streets with six or more lanes.

In New York, the Murray Hill Tunnel serves this function, allowing express traffic to bypass local traffic. The tunnel, which carries two lanes of car traffic from East 33rd Street to East 41st Street, is effective for avoiding the congestion on Park Avenue. Cities like Paris, Sydney, Melbourne, Tokyo, and even Tampa, Florida, have upgraded beyond queue jumpers to provide longer under- and aboveground motorways. While much of a metropolitan area is packed with subway and train tunnels and other utilities, elevated facilities need only airspace, and wide swaths of subterranean space remain uncluttered.

On the western edge of Manhattan, for example, no serious underground obstructions from the Battery to the George Washington Bridge would prevent building these express intersection bypasses. Various east-west streets are also free of subway tunnels. One analyst points out that a north-south truck-only tunnel could be built in Westside that would take many lane-cloggers off surface streets.[2]

Notes

1. This section is adapted from Ted Balaker and Sam Staley, "Thinking Over the Box," *New York Times*, 15 July 2007, http://reason.org/commentaries/balaker_20070715 .shtml.

2. Peter Samuel, editor, TollroadsNews.com, email correspondence with Sam Staley and Ted Balaker, 12 July, 2007.

Regional Transportation Blues

In some ways, the New York region's transportation story is the flip side of the transit story we just discussed. Transit dominates commutes into Manhattan because the road capacity simply doesn't exist to carry the number of cars that would accommodate the volume. This isn't the case for the region, which is much more broadly connected through highways. Access to Manhattan is severely limited because all commuter and commercial traffic is routed over a few major roads onto the island, and the city's five boroughs lack a fine mesh of arterials connecting them to provides alternatives. That constraint doesn't exist for the metropolitan area. Yet the road network still performs miserably.

But perhaps this is the least surprising fact about New York's regional road system. After all, the New York regional population is the largest, and the transportation system is among the oldest. It also hasn't been retrofitted significantly (under the assumption that New York City, and Manhattan, will remain the center of the region's economic, political, and cultural universe). An indication that this world is changing can be found in the numbers. The Texas Transportation Institute estimates that the annual hours of delay per traveler has ballooned from just twelve in 1982 to 46 in 2005.[20] And it's getting worse.

With so much popular and political attention focused on the City, it's easy to forget that more than half the region's population lives outside its five boroughs. The Big Apple, it turns out, isn't quite as dominant as a commuting hub as many people might think. A recent analysis of commuting patterns by the North Jersey Transportation Planning Authority, for example, found that just ten percent of northern Jersey residents commuted into the City. More than half worked in their home county and another 24 percent worked in another county in northern New Jersey.[21]

Hudson County, for example, starts on the west bank of Hudson River across from Manhattan, and Staten Island sits to its south. About 600,000 people live in the county. Its population has been relatively stable, but Hudson County lost about 9,000 residents, or 2,000 workers, between 1990 and 2000.[22] The number of people working in the county, however, *fell* by about 20,000 during the same period.[23] Where did these workers go? While some moved out of the county, most started commuting to jobs in other counties in the urban area. About 6,000 began commuting from Hudson County into Manhattan. More than 10,000 people began commuting to jobs in other New Jersey counties, including Bergen, Essex, Middlesex, Morris, and Union. Thousands more started commuting to more than a dozen other counties in

New Jersey, New York State, Connecticut, and even Long Island. Commuting, on the whole, become more dispersed, not more centralized.

New Jersey is not unique within the region. Further north, employment in Westchester County, New York, fell by about 15,000.[24] Meanwhile, Connecticut's South Western Regional Planning Agency found that 6,000 of Westchester's residents now worked in Greenwich while another 6,400 worked in Stamford.[25]

As in other places, these shifting travel patterns create a significant challenge for the region's transportation planners. People are driving to more locations and their trips are more dynamic than in the past. Even though the New York area remains one of the most concentrated and densely populated areas of the nation, the quest for mobility and improving transportation technologies has allowed more and more people to adapt their lifestyles to account for more customized travel and lifestyle choices. In most cases, the geographic result has been a less dense, more decentralized urban landscape.

These decentralized and dynamic travel patterns don't lend themselves to the fixed-route transit system that has served Manhattan commuters so well in the past. In fact, transit's share of work trips in the region fell by 6.3 percent between 1990 and 2000.[26] We explore more fully the implications of these demographic changes for public transit in chapter 10.

It doesn't help that New Jersey, New York State, and Connecticut have shortchanged investments in their road systems. David Hartgen, a transportation planner and engineer at the University of North Carolina, Charlotte, has been evaluating and ranking road investments by state departments of transportation for nearly 20 years. Guess what? New Jersey ranked last among U.S. states in overall cost-effectiveness of its highway investment in 2005.[27] New York State didn't fare much better—48th. Neighboring Connecticut performed marginally better in the tri-state area, ranking 39th. High costs, rising congestion, and a general unwillingness to invest in adequate road capacity drove the tri-state's rankings to the bottom of the barrel.

The New York-Northern New Jersey metropolitan area will need at least 2,446 new lane-miles of road to eliminate severe congestion by 2030.[28] The Bridgeport-Stamford, Connecticut metropolitan area to the northeast of New York City would need to add at least 554 lane-miles of new road capacity. These capacity additions would effectively eliminate severe congestion in the New York metropolitan area.[29] Overall, these investments add up to about $40 billion while saving nearly 1.3 billion hours of traffic delay each year.

As we mentioned in the previous chapter, the "fix" for New York is not simply to lay more asphalt. The roads will have to be the right type built in the right place. The tri-state's Manhattan-centric approach to its transportation system is outdated and inefficient, causing bottlenecks and needless congestion. Planners need to build roads that facilitate travel around and within the City, and connect smaller but growing employment centers in New Jersey, New York (below I-84), Long Island, and Connecticut. In short, the region needs strategic investments in *new* road capacity to keep traffic flowing and congestion in check.

BOX 4.2
How New York Can Reduce Regional
Congestion Through Road Capacity Expansion

Transportation planners and elected officials in the New York area are not hog-tied when it comes to highway investments that can make a real impact on improving traffic flow and reducing congestion. Planners could, for example, recommend

- Adding new limited access highways that link the northern counties of New Jersey to Westchester County and Fairfield County, including new bridges across the Hudson, both north and south of the Tappan Zee Bridge.
- Expanding local and arterial roads in New Jersey to recognize the more decentralized and fragmented nature of employment growth.
- Building east-west routes linking Westchester (New York) and Fairfield (Connecticut) counties, by expanding existing roads or building new ones.
- Linking Long Island to Connecticut via bridges (or tunnels) across Long Island Sound.

Other opportunities exist as well, but they require political leadership and fortitude. Underutilized rail right-of-way, for example, could be dedicated to roads for freight, truck, or passenger car traffic, significantly expanding road capacity cost effectively. One idea would convert the Staten Island Railway into a dedicated busway and premium toll road for passenger cars to improve access to the Verrazano Narrows Bridge and ferries at St. George.[1]

Another ambitious project idea is to link 494 lane miles of existing interstate and HOV lanes into an integrated busway and toll road priced to provide free flow access to Long Island, northern New Jersey, Westchester, and southwestern Connecticut. Building elevated highways (or tunnels) in existing highway right-of-way can also work in more densely populated areas of the region.

While the New York region's traffic woes are daunting, they are also solvable. Planners, elected officials, transportation policymakers, and citizens, however, will need to apply the latest technologies within a pragmatic framework consistent with modern travel patterns if they want to remove the region's dubious reputation as "the nation's chokepoint."

Note

1. Peter Samuel, editor, TollroadsNews.com, email correspondence with Sam Staley, July 2007.

Conclusion

So, what can New York tell us about mobility, travel behavior, and the challenges of modern transportation planning? First and foremost, even cities that rank among the most dense and diverse are not immune to the broader economic and demographic shifts that result in greater automobile use. Employment and lifestyles are becoming more decentralized, fragmented and dynamic. Travel consumers want transportation options that maximize their ability to customize trips to fit their changing needs and priorities. Thus, fewer and fewer people are working close by and travel destinations are becoming more fluid. We need a transportation system and network that reflects the complexities of modern day travel, where commutes are less important that the myriad of other choices we face on a daily basis.

If improving mobility is a key goal of policy makers, developing a transportation network that accommodates flexible and dynamic travel patterns will be critical. Addressing current urban traffic problems is *not* just about laying more asphalt or pavement. It's about putting the right capacity, in the right place, at the right time. This is where our transportation system fails, and we need a new way of thinking about the needs of a modern transportation network before we can make serious inroads into reducing congestion, let alone banishing it from our lives and economy. But, what does that network look like? How does it compare to the current system? How do we build it, or retrofit the existing one? These questions are the focus of the next several chapters.

Notes

1. David Shrank and Tim Lomax, *2007 Urban Mobility Report* (Texas Transportation Institute, Texas A&M University), Table 2, p. 34.

2. "New York City Mobility Needs Assessment: 2007–2030," Technical report prepared for PlaNYC effort, p. 23.

3. C. Kenneth Orski, editor, *Innovation Briefs*, email correspondence with Sam Staley, July 16. 2007.

4. Based on 2000 census data reported in the Statistical Abstract of the United States, http://www.census.gov/compendia/statab/tables/07s0031.xls, accessed 27 July 2007.

5. Cities with populations of 100,000 or more. The U.S. has 254 cities meeting this population threshold. Nine have populations greater than 1 million: New York City, Los Angeles, Chicago, Houston, Philadelphia, Phoenix, San Diego, San Antonio, and Dallas. Estimated from *Statistical Abstract of the United States*, Table 31, "Incorporated Places with 100,000 or More Inhabitants in 2005: 1970 to 2005."

6. PlaNYC, Transportation Technical Report, p. 6, Figure 2.1.

7. Transit market share for travel in the urbanized area is Census Data calculated by Wendell Cox and can be found at http://www.publicpurpose.com. City of Chicago Journey to Work data are reported at http://www.publicpurpose.com/ut-jtw-chicagocity.htm and were accessed 27 July 2007. Commuting data are taken from U.S. Bureau of the Census, Journey to Work data for 2000, metropolitan area profiles, and accessed on 27 July 2007, http://www.fhwa.dot.gov/ctpp/jtw/chi_mtw.htm.

8. C. Kenneth Orski, principal, Urban Mobility Corporation and editor, *Innovation Briefs*, email correspondence with Sam Staley, 16 July 2007.

9. PlaNYC, Transportation Technical Report, p. 78.

10. PlaNYC, Transportation Technical Report, p. 9, Figure 3.2.

11. Alan E. Pisarski, *Commuting in America III* (Washington, D.C.: Transportation Research Board), p. 106, table 3-41.

12. Pisarski, *Commuting in America III*, p. 107, Table 3-42.

13. Pisarski, *Commuting in America III*.

14. Pisarski, *Commuting in America III*, p. 94, Table 3-34.

15. Ibid. Chicago is a close second, with 61 percent of workers going to downtown Chicago using transit. About half the commuters working in downtown Boston and San Francisco use transit.

16. PlaNYC, Transportation Technical Report.

17. PlaNYC, Transportation Technical Report, p. 14, Table 3-1.

18. PlaNYC, Transportation Technical Report, p. 21.

19. Ibid.

20. Ibid., Table 4, p. 38.

21. *Journey-to-Work Data: Census 2000 County-to-County Worker Flow Data for the NJTPA Region,* North Jersey Transportation Planning Authority, November 2003, p. 2, available at http://www.njtpa.org/DataMap/Perf/JTW/default.aspx, last accessed 28 April 2008.

22. According to the 2006 estimates calculated by the U.S. Census Bureau.

23. Census estimates show the population of the county declined to 601,146 from 608,975. between 2000 and 2006 after the county grew by 10 percent between 1990 and 2000.

24. U.S. Census Bureau estimates.

25. U.S. Census, 2000 Journey-to-Work data analyzed by the South Western (Conn.) Regional Planning Agency (SWRPA), http://www.swrpa.org and http://www.swrpa.org/pdf_files/JTW_SWR/JTW_SWR_WC_Walll_Map11-2003.pdf, accessed 28 April 2008.

26. Wendell Cox, "Urban Transport Fact Book: Journey-to-Work Data by Metropolitan Area: 2000 and 1990," http://www.publicpurpose.com/ut-jtw2000metro.htm, accessed 31 July 12007.

27. David Hartgen and Ravi Karanam, *16th Annual Report on the Performance of State Highway Systems*, Policy Study No. 360 (Los Angeles: Reason Foundation, 2007), http://www.reason.org/ps360.pdf.

28. David Hartgen and M. Gregory Fields, *Building Roads to Reduce Traffic Congestion in America's Cities: How Much and at What Cost?* Policy Study No. 346 (Los Angeles: Reason Foundation, 2006), http://www.reason.org/ps346.pdf. See also the state specific data at Reason Foundation's web site, http://www.reason.org/ps346/state_by_state_congestion.pdf.

29. Hartgen used the standard of a Level of Service of 1.18 or higher as "severe congestion."

5

A New Approach to Congestion and Road Networks

O KAY, HERE'S THE STORY SO FAR: Congestion is increasing unchecked in almost all major U.S. metropolitan areas. Most policy makers and planners are resigned to letting it get worse. Rising congestion is strangling our urban economies and making our cities less and less competitive on the local and global levels. Complicating matters is the fact our urban transportation network was designed and built in a different economic era. The network no longer functions effectively in a dynamic, globally competitive service-based economy.

How do we get out of this mess?

The simplistic answer to our transportation infrastructure woes is to write it off as a money problem: We haven't spent enough. If we've underfunded roads, bridges, airports and other critical infrastructure, just turn up the faucet and pump more money into these and other improvements. So, if travel demand has doubled, we need to double our road capacity. Besides, we know how to build bridges and roads, right?[1]

Unfortunately, this approach is not going to cut it. Not in the twenty-first century at least. Our infrastructure problems run much deeper than simply building more roads and bridges and repairing old ones. In many cases, the obstacles are practical: We simply don't have the space in many cities to add more lanes to freeways that are already six and eight lanes wide. In most cases, however, the obstacle is much broader. We simply aren't thinking about how new capacity needs to be added and designed. We don't think about our investments in infrastructure in a strategic (or economic) way. The key to addressing our mobility challenges (and ultimately eliminating congestion) rests on building the right kind of roads, creating new types of networks, putting them in the right places at the right times, using the best technologies to provide innovative new routes and designs, and managing our transportation system at peak efficiency. (Transit also has a role, but we reserve this discussion to chapter 10 because its success requires a more extensive discussion than we can provide here.) Adding road capacity *will* be the critical element of this twenty-first century network, but we will have to do a lot more than lay asphalt. We have the tools—tunnels, elevated highways, variable rate tolling, optimizing traffic signals. We just need to be smarter about how they are used and more comprehensive in the way we think of how the network will function.

How? Like most big changes in thinking, we have to start at the beginning. How we travel. In the real world. Our previous chapters discussed at length how the world of travel and mobility today is fundamentally different from yesterday. Now, in this chapter, we begin the hard process of thinking about what this means for building a peak-performance twenty-first century transportation network. We need to move from a two-dimensional world view to a three-dimensional one. To do this, we need to understand the design behind our current 2-D transportation network.

A Brief Political History of U.S. Highway Design

The overarching goal of the U.S. program creating the Interstate Highway System was strategic: Link America's major urban areas through a national road network designed to move traffic efficiently and quickly from one region to the next. This network boosted economic productivity because it dramatically reduced transportation costs by increasing the speed at which goods could be shipped across the country. In addition, the road network could link up easily and frequently to other existing and proposed roads that served local markets and functions. Thus, goods could be distributed more efficiently by avoiding the bottlenecks of a centralized collection area for people and freight.

The Interstate Highway System also built on an existing network of national highways. The national highway network provided a mechanism for the federal government to fund upgrades to roads that served regional functions, such as linking cities and towns within a region or providing better connectivity for commercial freight traffic. While these highways linked towns and cities, they did not significantly enhance regional connectivity by providing limited access, high speed expressways between states and major metropolitan areas. Many of the highways, in fact, were two-lane roads upgraded with shoulders and turn lanes. Some became four-lane roads. In short, it was a 2-D way to look at the road system.

Since the Interstate Highway System was designed as a national network of inter-regional expressways, its primary design features focused on linking major employment centers (typically downtowns or central business districts). Thus, within economic regions, the highways tended to converge on a central place, or hub. Not surprisingly, the outlines of the interstate system resemble a "hub and spoke," where the highways are the spokes that converge on the downtown core as a "hub." An excellent illustration of this design is Atlanta (Figure 5.1) where Interstates 85, 75, and 20 converge on the city center. A beltway, I-285, circles the core of the metropolitan area. Without the beltway, all through and local traffic converges on the center of the city. The beltway, originally designed to route through traffic away from the central city, now accommodates local cross-county traffic as well.

The basic "hub and spoke" regional transportation system is most obvious in regions without major natural barriers or obstacles. The Phoenix downtown is the focal point of Interstates 10 and 17 without a beltway (although *state* routes 101 and 102 create a beltway around Phoenix and Tempe). Denver grapples with the convergence of Interstates 70, 76, and 25. The specific configuration of the expressway network, however, changes by location, reflecting physical and natural barriers. Rivers, for example, inhibit building arterials, collectors, and other local roads. Bridges (and tunnels), on the other hand, carry high-volume traffic on limited access highways across these barriers. Most still converge on the central city, even without beltways.

This hub and spoke design of the Interstate system is consistent with the central goal of the Interstate Highway System to connect America's major metropolitan areas. It is a very efficient design if these centers are clearly identifiable and economic activity is concentrated in one central place. (Notably, we also begin to see more features that are vertical rather than horizontal— elevated expressways and tunnels—to cross over arterials and even neighborhoods to reach central destinations. Roads, like early rail transit lines [e.g., the EL in downtown Chicago], are beginning to have 3-D elements even though they are not a central principle of network design.)

The hub and spoke system, however, served another important purpose, unanticipated perhaps by the network designers, with significant implications for how we design the twenty-first century transportation system. At the same time regional planners and policy makers were trying to link up the nation's major urban centers, our metropolitan areas were decentralizing.[2] Jobs and population were steadily moving out of the central city and new employment and residential centers where being created.[3] The hub and spoke transportation system turned out to be an excellent way to channel large volumes of traffic for conventional suburb-to-central city commutes. Suburban residents would use their local roads to access the newly created Interstates and drive to their jobs in the central cities on the high capacity highways. As suburban

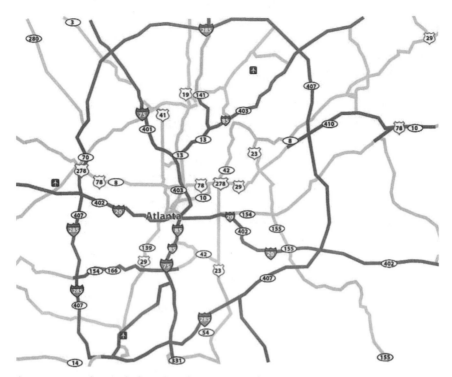

Figure 5.1.   Atlanta's hub and spoke transportation system

growth drove traffic densities up, and central cities became more congested, beltways and ring roads on the Interstate system were used to connect the suburban population and employment centers within the region rather than simply to divert through traffic away from the downtown. Thus, the hub and spoke system evolved into a wagon wheel. Now, while still used as a connector, most traffic on urban interstate highways is local passenger car traffic. In Chicago, 95 percent of traffic on interstate highways is local and regionally internal traffic, not through traffic.[4] Eighty-eight percent of the traffic on San Diego's freeways is local and 86 percent of the traffic in Phoenix is local.[5] For most large cities, about 85 percent of traffic on the limited access highway network is local, not interstate or interregional traffic.

Unfortunately, this original highway design, the transportation network's DNA, has not evolved to meet the needs of the modern city. The highly structured, centralized design of the urban transportation network doesn't fit the needs of a dynamic, decentralized, service-based urban economy in the twenty-first century.

It's not hard to see why. The current hub and spoke transportation system is based on simplistic travel behavior: home-office-home. Today, work and home schedule flexibility adds much more complexity to travel in urban areas as we discussed in detail in chapters 3 and 4. The adaptability of the automobile, combined with the dynamics of the modern work environment, gives us the flexibility to trip chain. Moreover, these economic and lifestyle changes make the nature of the chain itself dynamic. A contemporary transportation network needs to accommodate this diversity and dynamism which are inevitable consequences of the modern economy. Because our current transportation network is *not* designed to accommodate these dynamics, it causes congestion.

Regardless of the applicability of the hub and spoke system to modern travel needs, the process of creating and financing the Interstate Highway System established an approach to transportation investment that is no longer reasonable or viable in current times. One element of this approach is that we can enhance mobility (and productivity) by linking urban centers through a vast network of high volume limited access highways. Another element is that incremental capacity expansion based on the local road network will give us a road map to an efficient transportation network.

Most development within urban areas followed existing road networks as homes and businesses expanded into the periphery. As densities increased from agricultural to residential, and neighborhood commercial centers developed at key intersections, roadways quickly filled beyond capacity. Politicians responded by adding and widening roads, but these improvements typically lagged actual increases in travel demand.

The "old" way of relying on the legislative decision-making process politicized transportation investments *and* service delivery. Unlike in the private sector, revenues in transportation were not tied directly to consumer preferences. Where roads go, both on the network and within the region, is a political decision, not a market-based one, since government controls the process and decision making. Rural roads, for example, are typically designed and initially built at excess capacity—farm tractors and trucks rarely need the full capacity of a two-lane paved road. Suburban development tends to overtake the road capacity before the legislative process can come up with sufficient new investment to respond to rising congestion. Thus, short of a periodic crisis such as a bridge collapse, the deliberative process inherent in representative democracy tends to perpetuate a lag in investment. Combined with the long-term character of road investments, which also attracts a higher level of legislative scrutiny, significant delays in infrastructure investment are the rule rather than the exception. Clearly, reforming how we finance roads will be a fundamental building block for how we go about implementing a congestion-free transportation network in the twenty-first century, and we discuss this in detail in chapter 11.

The U.S. commitment to the Interstate Highway System should be considered the exception rather than the rule. The highway system's metropolitan congestion reduction benefits were not central to its political support.[6] Rather, the program was an interurban connector that knitted vast metropolitan regions together. It successfully met this goal. Rates of return on highway investments paid substantial economic dividends. The first series of investments in the 1950s and 1960s improved mobility by creating an entirely new system for transporting goods and services. Local drivers and commuters were another primary (although unintended) beneficiary because the new wave of limited access highways greatly improved circulation within the metropolitan area, keeping severe congestion in check.

Urban expressways serve a wider range of purposes in the twenty-first century than they did in the twentieth century. Transportation and mobility are critically important to the global competitiveness of regional and national economies, but the way in which mobility influences competitiveness is much different, as we saw in chapter 3. In addition to reducing transportation costs associated with moving goods and services between regions, efficiency is gained now by improving the mobility and access to human resources and improving quality of life within regions. In an economy where most new wealth is created in high-end services, "back office" administrative functions, telecommunications, and technology-based industries, access to a high quality labor force is critical. Now, the most productive and talented portion of the labor force—entrepreneurs, software engineers, designers and service-based workers—is also among the most mobile.

What happens when this mobility breaks down? Economic stagnation. Lower productivity. Lower efficiency. Lower standards of living. Workers can't get to jobs; employers can't find workers. The urban economy balkanizes as the region fragments into isolated neighborhoods and small towns, unable to pool resources at a high enough level to take advantage of specialized skills. The agglomeration economies that are so important to boosting urban productivity fall. The economic benefits of cities—the concentration of people, workers, and firms—shrinks as the best and brightest can't be brought together to come up with the best solutions possible.

Charting a Course for a Congestion-Free Metropolis

Economic balkanization, and the resulting losses in economic competitiveness, can be avoided by aggressively refocusing national and regional transportation strategies. Rather than seeing the end of a national infrastructure effort, we're just beginning to grapple with the trillion dollar task of how to reconfigure, rebuild, and redesign our highway system in the face of the clash between rising congestion and the competitive pressures of a global economy. Our road network needs to be more balanced to accommodate these wider ranges of choices about travel times and purposes rooted in a desire for customized travel flexibility.

An important part of the solution will be managing flows more efficiently. Most urban areas face the problem of too little capacity during peak travel times (i.e., "rush hour") and too much capacity during off-peak times. Managing existing travel demand more effectively can help reduce the peaks and valleys that characterize our current transportation system. Effective management can only be achieved by more efficient "user signaling" strategies such as variable rate tolling that conveys information to drivers about the congestion costs of using roads at heavily used times. As toll rates go up with the level of congestion, drivers with the flexibility in their schedule have the incentive to use the roads at different times. These technologies, along with other techniques such as traffic signal optimization, ramp metering, and more effective incident management ensure that existing capacity is used most efficiently, essentially "creating" new capacity during peak times by removing less valuable trips (from the drivers' perspective) from high demand periods of road use.

An equally important but more daunting part of the solution will be reconfiguring the metropolitan transportation network to meet modern travel needs. Applying new techniques and strategies is a bigger job than most people realize. It calls for a full-scale reconfiguration of our regional highway system, both in terms of basic design and the approach we take to managing it. It will also call for creating new types of roads and adding capacity in creative ways—what we term moving from 2-D to 3-D infrastructure investments.

Fortunately, we have more effective tools to work with than ever before. Rather than using grand highway plans to determine where and what kind of road should be built, we can ask travelers. More importantly, they can tell us. They can tell us the same way we tell our local retailers how many tomatoes to stock in the fresh produce shelves, how many shirts should be on the racks, how many Xboxes or PS3's to inventory. We have to price our roads.

Prices coordinate the supply of the things we want with our willingness to pay. If we want fresh tomatoes, the grocer will determine how many she can provide based on the price we are willing to pay; if we are willing to pay enough, she will make sure tomatoes are there for our picking 365 days a year, even 24 hours a day, in and out of season.

For transportation, electronic tolling provides the technology necessary for a fast, efficient, and effective way to gauge traveler (consumer) interest in new facilities of all kinds, and the ability of private companies (transportation

agencies and private leasing companies) to provide them. By tying a consumer-driven revenue stream to a particular project, tolling provides a practical way to raise the money to expand our nation's transportation infrastructure without raising taxes.[7] It's a pretty direct relationship. If the toll road use
goes up, the company earns more revenue. In order to keep drivers coming
back, they have to maintain reliable free-flow conditions. Higher toll revenue
is also an important signal that *expanding* capacity is warranted (and one reason why lease agreements with private companies typically include triggers for
new investment at certain performance thresholds). So, toll road operators
have strong incentives to reinvest in new road capacity because the demand is
high enough to support it financially.

Pie in the sky? Not for people traveling on roads like the Indiana Toll Road,
the A86 tunnels outside of Paris, the congestion-free 91 Express Lanes in
Southern California, or State Highway 183 north of Austin, Texas, or the
dozens of other electronically tolled facilities in the U.S. and around the
world. These are all facilities that were built because tolling provided a way to
measure consumer demand—willingness to pay—and apply that to the cost
of building these facilities. In fact, in the past decade about one-third of new
limited-access highway lane-miles built in the United States were tolled.[8]
Tolling let these roads pass a market test, and they were built. New innovations
in highway design have expanded our ability to increase traffic flows and increase traffic densities to the point where even tunnels and elevated highways
can be economically viable and in some cases self-financing. The A86 tunnels
underneath Versailles, France are completely self-funded through the private
sector.

The idea that consumers should pay for road services they want is relatively
new in U.S. transportation policy circles even though economists have been
recommending this approach for at least 100 years.[9] This concept works in almost every other part of the economy. Now we have the tools and the technology to make it work in transportation, especially limited-access highways.
We need to begin treating roads like other economic products and services.
This will be the key to attracting the billions of dollars from the private sector
necessary to reconfigure and rebuild our regional transportation system and
make the ideas in this and subsequent chapters a reality.

The new primarily private financing that tolling will inevitably draw into
the transportation system is only one benefit. Another perhaps even more important advantage of tolling is the ability to prioritize projects based on willingness to pay. Investors can literally use consumer demand and willingness to
pay to determine when, how, and where new capacity should be added. This
is a capability the system simply didn't have before electronic tolling and dy-

namic pricing became practical. In the end, the result will be a more dynamic, consumer centric network more consistent with the need.

What will a system like this look like and how will it function?

A 3-D Spiderweb

Southern California is a remarkable place. Despite suffering from the worst congestion in the United States, the region moves a surprising number of cars, trucks, and buses on its roads efficiently—on *secondary* roads. The freeways are a clogged mess. The local roads, particularly in Orange and Riverside Counties, flow reasonably well, even in rush hour. How can this be? On local roads, drivers can "exit" frequently and often, weaving their way from one road to the next, skipping intersections and even highways that are anything but flowing freely. In short, connectivity allows individual drivers to adjust their trips and routes to keep traffic moving. This principle is fundamental to understanding how regional transportation networks need to be redesigned in modern urban economies.

A cutting edge, modern transportation system will need to be more like the flexible mesh of a spider web than the rigid hub and spoke. Consider this. In addition to catching prey, a web is tailored for quick movement by the spider. Rather than following one strand from the center (a spoke) to the end of the web (the rim or edge), or following the rim to another strand (another spoke), the spider can move deftly across strands, using the mesh of the network to support it. No matter how big or small, the spider can get to its prey using its network of strands to go sideways, straight, or even over the web.

In a weblike transportation system, the road network is balanced and inter-connected (see figure 5.2). This provides options for travelers. Since destinations are dispersed and varied, travelers with different purposes can choose from a series of options. Rather than one area such as a downtown serving as a core or urban center, the network links multiple centers of residential, commercial, mixed use, and (to a lesser extent) industrial clusters. Thus, the purpose of a "beltway" is not to funnel traffic onto a major highway leading to a downtown. Rather, the beltway is one link in an interconnected network of similar high volume traffic links that bind together geographically dispersed towns, villages, and emerging cities. Because traditional downtowns remain one of the city's job clusters, and serve important functions—often as regional government, cultural, and entertainment centers—the network cannot ignore them. Yet, the downtown's role is more balanced to reflect its economic significance in a region with multiple large employment centers and dispersed low-density residential living preferences. The network is not just about

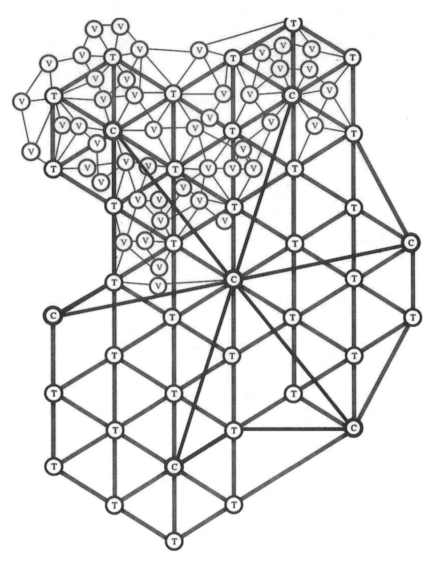

Figure 5.2.   The spiderweb approach to transportation networks

linking downtown L.A. It's also about linking Wilshire Boulevard, West Los Angeles, the San Fernando Valley, Burbank, Palmdale, Ontario, Santa Ana, and Manhattan Beach.

Creating a web like this in cities suggests building up, rather than tearing down, the regional network of major arterials and limited-access highways.

We need to think 3-D. Many of the links in the system will have to be added below or above, either by boring regional tunnels, elevating expressways, or hopping over and under clogged intersections (see chapters 6 and 7). These may be the only practical solutions in built up urban areas where we need many new links to implement the mesh described in figure 5.2. In our most dense and heavily traveled cities, a *network* of tunnels may well fill most of these gaps, connecting parts of the transportation network and parts of the city that are not well connected by the existing surface transportation network.

How might this look in the real world? Fortunately, we don't have to start from scratch. We don't even have to start in the United States. We can look at cities in the industrializing world that are grappling with rising car ownership and traffic congestion in the automobile age. Cities like Chengdu, a metropolis of almost 10 million people (nearly the size of Chicago) in the heart of the Sichuan Province of mainland China, and Shanghai, one of the fastest growing cities in the world and a major Asian trading hub.

Most Americans probably never heard of Chengdu before the tragic earthquake (that killed tens of thousands of people in May 2008) despite its size and its role as a logistical center for one of the world's largest and fastest growing economies. Asian food enthusiasts would have recognized the spicy taste of Sichuan food. Our children might have recognized Sichuan because it is the home of the famous panda bear, a staple of any collection of stuffed animals. For those fortunate enough, like the authors, to have traveled to Sichuan (before the earthquake), they may have also had the chance to visit Du Jiang Dam, a 2,300-year old hydraulic works that stands as testimony to China's prowess as innovators and engineering skill. More directly, this example is a useful reminder of China's growing economic power, its commitment to building a first class road system to move freight and people, and an inspiration for the rebuilding of this devastated region. While the earthquake is an economic and social setback, our experience with the citizens and public officials of the city and the province leave us convinced Sichuan's economy will be back on track quickly and its lessons will be all the more important for analysts in the U.S.

Chengdu has a geographic "hub," similar to many North American and European cities, but growth is radiating outward. As the principal city serving the interior of China, Chengdu is a freight, logistics, and rail center. As the city has grown, and the wealth of its citizens has increased, Chengdu's traffic challenges have magnified. Higher incomes have triggered dramatic growth in automobile ownership. While private automobiles numbered just 600,000 in the spring of 2007, this statistic is misleading. Over one-third of Chengdu's citizens get to work or shop using bikes. Not manual bikes—electric bikes that can reach speeds of 35 mph. As incomes have increased, residents have been opting for the automobile. While local transportation officials are doing their best to keep people on public transit, including building a subway line, the long-term prospect for keeping increasingly wealthy citizens out of cars is dim.

More importantly, the growth of people *and* jobs is putting pressure on local officials to reduce congestion. Chengdu has a relatively small old core, with much of the city growing and building out in the last two decades of rapid urbanization. High tech office parks are springing up in suburban areas, and freight traffic is becoming more important as the "last mile" consists more and more of getting goods onto the shelves in neighborhood stores. In addition, manufacturers are making deliveries within the city to multiple clients, requiring a more complex transport system suitable to using trucks and cars. The geographic distance between firms has increased as well as the number of trips.

The solution? The first phase was to get the existing system to work more efficiently. The city invested a lot in traffic signal coordination. These efforts paid off, improving through-put by 15 percent according to local transportation officials. The city has also invested in freight corridors. Since 60 percent of the freight volume is trans-shipment—moving goods onto other points in the interior—city and provincial officials have worked on developing direct supply routes that avoid putting undue burden on the local network. Most importantly, Chengdu grew up with an existing web of surface streets, and now they have added capacity, and this capacity has been added in a way that resembles the mesh of a spiderweb rather than a wagon wheel.

The city has three official "ring roads" that encircle the entire city and the city is in the process of building a fourth. Each ring road is connected by a series of smaller large volume roads, some connecting movement into older neighborhoods, others connecting outlying neighborhoods and points, including the high tech business parks. In addition to these ring roads, the city has designed five "trunk" roads for carrying high volumes of traffic to improve circulation within the city, ensure freight moves quickly out of the city, and ensure traffic (and freight) not needed inside the city is not directed into those areas. In short, the road network is a mesh of multiple road types that *connect* places and roads, but serve different functions, and are linked together as part of one system. The approach has the benefit of allowing incremental capacity additions to meet new demands and needs as the city grows.

Minneapolis-St. Paul provides an illustration of how this prototype road system might be configured in the U.S. (figure 5.4). The metropolitan area is also relatively young, developing mostly in the era of automobility. It has two central cities (polycentric core) with numerous limited-access highways providing ample routes around the central cities as well as into them. Interstate

CHENGDU CITY

Figure 5.3.   Spiderweb road network surrounding Chengdu, Sichuan, PRC

Figure 5.4.   Major road network in Minneapolis-St. Paul

highways 694 and 494 provide the outlines of an outer beltway, and I-394 provides direct (and linking) access to the downtowns. Other major roads enhance this road system by providing easy access to other parts of the metropolitan area without forcing travelers into the downtown core. Route 169, for example, links the northwest and southwest quadrants of Minneapolis with a grade-separated limited-access highway. Route 100 provides a similar function for the southwest quadrant of the city but for a shorter distance that links Route 5 with I-394.

Both Minneapolis-St. Paul and Chengdu represent a 2-D approach to the spider web. Is there a city trying to accomplish this in 3-D? While not specifically embracing the comprehensive approach we have described, Shanghai comes close.

Shanghai is now a world megacity of more than 20 million people. It's an old and dense city that grew rapidly when motorized vehicles were still rare. As one of China's "open trade" cities during the colonial era, it grew to become one of Asia's premiere trading centers and a leading multinational financial hub by the 1930s. The Communist revolution put the brakes on growth throughout most of the late Twentieth century, but reforms in the 1990s opened the doors wide for rapid growth once again.

Not surprisingly, Shanghai's road network reflects its colonial, pre-automobile legacy and consists mostly of narrow and winding streets. Ironically, many people don't think of transportation in Shanghai today in this way. They think of the much-touted Maglev train, a 30-kilometer long high-speed train running from Pudong airport to the suburbs that connects to the city's extensive subway system. Indeed, as the first commercial Maglev line in the world, the train is impressive, and a worthy symbol of China's re-emergence as a global economic powerhouse pushing the boundaries of productivity and innovation. But in many ways the maglev train is the least amazing element of Shanghai's recent transportation infrastructure investments.

Faced with severe and rising traffic congestion and goods-movement problems in an old city divided by the Huangpu river, a branch of Yangtze river delta, Shanghai had to think creatively about how to solve its mobility and logistics challenges. With nearly 230 kilometers of subway carrying over 3 million passengers per day and growing, the city still faces rising congestion. So city officials committed to an expressway network designed to put every resident within 15 minutes of a branch and to enable any traveler to reach any part of the city in 60 minutes or less.

The city is also thinking of the network in three dimensions, recognizing that much of the road system will have to be tunnels to provide connectivity across the entire city. Shanghai now has three major road tunnels that pass under the river and plans at least six more in the next few years. These tunnels will create an underground network, a second layer of road infrastructure below the surface of the city that also links to the surface expressway system. This network will allow rapidly growing vehicle traffic to move people and goods throughout the city quickly.

Returning to the web analogy, a spiderweb is held together by a finely integrated mesh of silk links. The silk links are of varying densities and thicknesses. In a spiral spiderweb, the peripheral silk links are thicker, but thinner links hold the major sections of the network together.[10]

The spiderweb exemplifies two important network attributes. First, a well-integrated network of links allows ease of movement over a (relatively) large space. Second, a series of smaller segments can hold together a large geographic space by using a network design. No spoke or segment of the transportation system dominates at any given point in time. The silk links in a spiderweb carry similar burdens to maintain the structural integrity of a web. Much like how a grid pattern moves traffic very quickly, smoothly, and efficiently on the local level, a series of network concentric rings or links of higher volume arterials and limited access highways can greatly improve circulation within an urban area on a regional level.

The wagon wheel, hub-and-spoke system is much more cumbersome, fixed, and static in comparison to a web-based network. The limited access highway that is the backbone of the current interurban highway system is designed for long-distance travel—thick roadway trunk lines linking downtowns and major urban centers. Highways, for example, typically have exits a mile or more apart, and many states prohibit exit and entrance ramps within one mile of each other. These highways are designed to funnel traffic over long distances.[11]

In contrast, neighborhood roads have frequent intersections, stops, and yields, and are designed for very low speeds (for safety and aesthetic reasons). The grid system in many twentieth century cities maximizes traffic flow by providing maximum visibility along the road and minimizing obstructions. From this level, road capacity is expanded by lane widenings or additions. Local roads can become very wide—six and seven lanes across in areas attempting to channel very large volumes of local traffic.

Yet, these roads are still designed based on basic principles of local traffic. Large intersections with stoplights that release traffic at specific, timed intervals are the dominant traffic management strategy. South Los Angeles and the northern part of neighboring Orange County provide good examples. This vast suburban area, composed of a number of cities inland from Long Beach, was built out with a great network of four to six lane boulevards. Many boulevards, like Beach, Brookhurst, and Harbor, run north-south, while many more, like Lincoln, Katella and Chapman, run east-west.

In practice and by design, these boulevards serve as an alternative to the freeway network for medium length trips within a city or between neighboring cities. But they are not managed and operated to serve this function. Instead they are treated much like neighborhood streets, with frequent stoplights, rarely more than a mile apart, and often much less, and not synchronized. They could do so much more to serve mid-length trips if they were run differently. We believe that this feature of a web-based transportation system is so important we have dedicated chapter 8 to a full length discussion of how these roads function, how they can be built, and where they need to be in the network.

New Networks for Modern Needs

How can the road network accommodate modern day travel behavior and maintain mobility?

First and foremost, the physical capacity must exist to handle a core level of traffic flow. No matter how well managed an existing facility may be, sufficient road capacity needs to exist to handle the volume of traffic. Capacity also needs to be added as land uses evolve and greater demand is placed on the existing infrastructure. In built-up parts of cities, we will need to go 3-D. Tunnels and tunnel networks will be crucial to providing this new capacity, creating a second (or third?) layer of the road network and expanding it into a more complete web. As cities grow, new surface road networks should be built with the 3-D web in mind.

But network design is also a critically important function. On the neighborhood level, a local road system established on a grid pattern is likely to keep traffic moving relatively quickly. At some point, the city grows to the point it needs to accommodate regional trips and destinations. Higher level roads are needed to provide efficient access and avoid clogging up local roads. Then, as the city evolves into an urban region, high-speed roadways will be necessary to keep traffic flowing.

This is where older cities such as London, England, face significant challenges—the circuitous nature of their road network makes navigation difficult for all except those intimately knowledgeable about the city. While this encourages public transport, it degrades mobility and creates congestion that the best attempts at traffic signal optimization and demand management can't overcome.

This is where the examples of Chinese cities such as Chengdu and Shanghai are so useful. They have added capacity as travel demand has increased, building tunnel networks and ring roads that connect farflung parts of the city. While these cities still face daunting challenges with congestion, they are establishing a basic framework for a road network that will be much easier to modify and adapt to the rising travel needs and demands of their citizens.

Technology is also quickly evolving in ways that allow transportation infrastructure to be built and managed more efficiently. These innovations are providing unprecedented opportunities for the public and private sectors to remake the transportation system to conform to contemporary demands and needs. Advances in composite materials are allowing road facilities to be fabricated off site and assembled on site, cutting construction times dramatically. One design currently under development at the Illinois Institute of Technology could double an intersection through-put, cut construction time by one third, and shrink costs dramatically. Thanks to rapid advances in electronic tolling system (ETS) technologies, revenues can be closely aligned with the costs of adding specific types of new capacity. This was an important step toward making Chengdu's fourth ring road a reality, as well as building new self-supporting roads in Southern California, Minneapolis-St. Paul, Denver, Austin, Dallas and elsewhere.

We have tried to show how the twenty-first century regional transportation network will function and operate much differently from the current one. Connecting people and businesses will be much more important because these connections are essential to business innovation and a service-based economy. The key will be to maximize access to a labor force over a geographic area while accommodating and catering to the diversity of tastes and lifestyles that workers and their families desire. In most U.S. and wealthy metropolitan areas, this implies a web-based transportation network that maximizes automobility. As a practical matter, the approach to transportation must focus on redesigning and rebuilding the road network by both adding new physical capacity and managing that capacity efficiently based on what consumers (users) want from their transportation system.

The practical ways we accomplish this are the subject of the next four chapters, but it probably makes sense to first ask a basic question: Does building physical road capacity work? The answer is yes, and we'll use the historical case of the nation's most congested city to show why.

L.A. Confidential

Los Angeles: gridlock capital, USA.

What could anyone learn from Los Angeles about building road capacity and its impact on mobility? A lot, it turns out. Although conventional wisdom holds L.A. up as the example of what happens when a city builds too much, the reality is the opposite: L.A. didn't build enough roads, and it's suffering the consequences now. Moreover, despite its current reputation, the city is a useful *historical* case study for illustrating the *importance* of building roads.

We've spent a lot of time in this chapter discussing the need to redesign our urban transportation systems to recognize the singular importance of auto-mobility to a productive society. Los Angeles has a lot to teach us about this, both in terms of its current failures to encourage mobility and its past success in embracing automobility. This story, then, provides important context for the practical ideas for physically reconfiguring our transportation network later in the chapter.

More than three-quarters of American households already owned at least one car by 1930, but Los Angeles was one of the first cities to grow to prominence and mature within the automobile age. Most cities in the Northeast and Midwest were built during the rail and water era, where personal mobility was either by foot (the majority), streetcar, or by riverboat. Densities were necessarily high in order to provide reasonable access to jobs, stores, and friends.

The automobile changed all that by providing unparalleled access to new jobs, shopping, and communities. It didn't take an hour to travel four miles anymore. Instead, a four-mile trip could be taken in ten minutes or less. Los Angeles was the first city to grow in this era without an infrastructure of cow paths and trolleys that provided the infrastructure DNA for traditional cities that so fundamentally shaped their early development.

More to the point, Los Angeles faced huge traffic problems early in its development. In the 1930s, Los Angeles's local planners and engineers were grappling with downtown congestion as public transit (primarily rail) lost ridership rapidly. City planners and local officials believed the solution was not in expanding the existing transit system, but in creating a network of boulevards and parkways that recognized the dominance of the car. The transition from a streetcar network to automobile-oriented boulevards was "abrupt" in the words of planner Peter Hall.[12] But, by the 1950s, the city (with the assistance of a state highway program), transformed itself into "a city of freeways."

Thus, Los Angeles was the first city to accept and internalize the decentralized, customized technology of the automobile. The transportation investment that made the most sense was the highway. The one that made the least sense was the streetcar.

The incongruity between the twentieth century auto mobility and the nineteenth-century urban pattern is hard to underestimate. In 1919 automobile registrations doubled in number from the previous year as the number of automobiles increased to 100,000 in 1920 (from 55,000 in 1915).[13] By

1930, 800,000 cars were plying the rough streets of the city. Downtown was gridlocked. The city council considered a ban on downtown parking as a way to discourage automobile traffic. The council eventually established a 45-minute limit and a ban on parking during peak hours (4:00 p.m. to 6:15 p.m.).[14]

The controversy unleashed a new wave of thinking about how to accommodate traffic that would profoundly change the direction of transportation policy in Los Angeles and the rest of the nation. Rather than fight progress, they accepted it.

In the early decades of the twentieth century, Los Angeles was already about one-third as dense as New York and 40 percent as dense as Chicago and Cleveland. This is not surprising since by 1930, 94 percent of homes in Los Angeles were detached structures and the multistory tenement house was not the architectural feature it became in older, northeastern cities. About half of the homes in Chicago, New York, and Boston were single family. By 1940, more than 60 percent of downtown Los Angeles's workers commuted by car.

The first wave of transportation improvements was in widening streets. The investment made a difference, significantly cutting congestion and improving traffic flow. It also left an important legacy: Los Angeles still has one of the most efficient and well developed systems of arterials in the nation.

What, then, accounts for the near gridlock experienced by modern day Los Angeles?

While the city invested early in a system of boulevards, parkways, and highways, the investment didn't continue. On the contrary, the last major freeway in Los Angeles, the Century Freeway, was slated for completion in the early 1980s but wasn't completed until the early 1990s because of litigation. Meanwhile, the city of Los Angeles grew by another million people and the larger urban region ballooned to 12.4 million. Now, Los Angeles has among the fewest miles of roadway per capita than any other urban area over one million in population.[15]

In the first half of the twentieth century, Los Angeles "managed" congestion using three strategies:

- Local governments built roads to accommodate rising demand;
- Demographic decentralization lowered the densities of traffic and people; and
- Residential "sorting" allowed families and households to keep commuting times manageable since the fragmented and decentralized nature of the metropolitan area allowed people and jobs to move closer together (creating suburban employment centers).

As a result, despite sprawling development and a seemingly relentless pursuit of lower density lifestyles, travel times remained constant. Commute times in Los Angeles remained steady at 24 minutes between 1967 and 1997.[16]

Lessons Learned?

Is Los Angeles a special case? No. At least not according to the best available data.

The Texas Transportation Institute collects information on the demand for travel in urban areas, measured by vehicle miles traveled (VMT). They also collect information on the size of the road network (although not necessarily its efficiency). These measures include the number of lane miles that are on freeways (highways that limit access typically using on-off ramps) and local roads (arterials and "collectors" that circulate traffic within the neighborhood or provide access to highways). Thus, the size of the road network can be tracked over time and compared to the change in the demand for highway facilities.

What happens when urban areas don't keep pace with rising travel demand? Congestion skyrockets. None of the 85 urban areas tracked consistently by the Texas Transportation Institute were able to expand their road network at the same pace as travel demand. But, for those that added major road capacity, the growth of congestion slowed significantly.[17]

The other cities let travel demand run away without significantly adding capacity. The third tier of 38 urban areas where travel demand grew 30 to 45 percent faster than travel demand saw congestion double on average in the 1980s, moderate somewhat in the 1990s, and then double again by 2005.

The fourth group of 15 urban areas let travel demand outstrip road capacity by more than 45 percent. Atlanta, Chicago, Columbus, Dallas-Fort Worth, Minneapolis-St. Paul, Las Vegas, and Washington D.C. are among the high growth urban cities in this category. The congestion has *quadrupled* since 1982, consistently doubling every decade.

In the words of the researchers at the Texas Transportation Institute:

> *Additional roadways reduce the rate of increase in congestion.* It appears that the growth in facilities has to be at a rate slightly greater than travel growth in order to maintain constant travel times, if additional roads are the only solution used to address mobility concerns. (Emphasis in original.)[18]

In short, adding capacity does improve mobility and keep congestion in check. Most urban areas are now faced with two substantial transportation network challenges: a road and highway system that is poorly matched to the travel needs of residents and businesses (hub and spoke versus spiderweb) and a lack of a road capacity because travel demand has outstripped road building. Meeting these challenges will require a substantial investment to ensure the new road capacity is in the right place efficiently and cost effectively, and new technologies are adopted to manage existing traffic more efficiently while accommodating rising travel demand. In most cases, regions will need to address their mobility needs by addressing all three challenges at once. Nevertheless, it can be done. And that's what the next chapters are about.

Notes

1. Some planners and analysts believe that adding new capacity would be counterproductive since new roads seem to fill up so quickly and become congested. This "induced" or "latent" demand negates the effects of improving traffic flow by encouraging new drivers onto the road, degrading performance. We believe the logic behind this thinking is fundamentally flawed. Rather than going into this discussion in detail, we refer readers to the eminently readable overview of this issue and others by UCLA urban planning professor Brian D. Taylor, "Rethinking Traffic Congestion," *Access*, No. 21 (Fall 2002), pp. 8–16.

2. For excellent reviews of this process, see Robert Bruegmann, *Sprawl: A Compact History* (Chicago: University of Chicago Press, 2005) and Joel Kotkin, *The City: A Global History* (New York: Modern Library, 2005), chapters 15–17.

3. This process is well recognized now, but an accessible, pioneering contribution to this phenomenon is Joel Garreau, *Edge City: Life on the Frontier*.

4. Transportation Research Board, National Cooperative Highway Research Project, Report 365, Chapter 5, Table 10.

5. Ibid.

6. *A 10 Year National Highway Program: Report to the President*, The President's Advisory Committee on a National Highway Program (Clay Committee), January 1955.

7. Some critics of tolling incorrectly argue that tolls are taxes. Tolls are user fees. Taxes, based on standard public finance principles, are applied generally to a population regardless of whether they use the service or not. We discuss this in much more detail in chapter 8 when we discuss how we finance the ideas we recommend in this and subsequent chapters.

8. Benjamin Perez and Stephen Lockwood, *Current Toll Road Activity in the U.S.: A Survey and Analysis*, Office of Transportation Studies, Federal Highway Administration, August 2006, p. 2.

9. For an excellent overview of the history of road pricing with a focus on the economics profession, see Robin Lindsey, "Do Economists Reach a Conclusion on Road Pricing? The Intellectual History of an Idea," *Econ Journal Watch*, Vol. 3, No. 2 (May 2006), pp. 292–379. Adam Smith includes one of the first known treatments of tolling in *The Wealth of Nations* (1776), but Lindsey believes Arthur Pigou is credited with beginning the modern English language discussion. The first extended treatment and

development of road pricing as a way to manage road space more efficiently was pioneered by William Vickrey in 1948.

10. Notably, some webs have silk links formed in concentric circles where all links are similar in thickness. (These links also serve as an efficient transportation network for the spider when it descends on its prey.)

11. This design begins to break down near downtowns or central business districts when exits are spaced closer together. Traffic is diverted to local roads, and the freeway is modified to take on the function of a high volume urban arterial serving local destinations.

12. Sir Peter Hall, *Cities in Civilization* (New York: Pantheon Books, 1998), pp. 819–831.

13. Hall, *Cities in Civilization*, pp. 813, 814.

14. Hall, *Cities in Civilization*, p. 814.

15. Although it is tied with San Francisco-Oakland and San Diego.

16. Peter Gordon and Harry W. Richardson, "The Geography of Transportation and Land Use," in *Smarter Growth: Market-Based Strategies for Land-Use Planning in the 21st Century*, eds. Randall G. Holcombe and Samuel R. Staley, pp. 27–58 (Westport, CT: Greenwood Press, 2001), p. 45.

17. David Shrank and Tim Lomax, *2007 Urban Mobility Report*, Texas A&M University, pp. 22–23, 44. Five urban areas—Anchorage, Dayton, New Orleans, Pittsburgh, and St. Louis—were able add road capacity within 15 percent of traffic growth. In fact, congestion declined in absolute levels after 2000. Of course, these were also urban areas that experienced low population and job growth. A more interesting group is probably the 27 areas in the next tier. These urban areas were unable to match the growth in travel demand with expanded road capacity. Nevertheless, the mismatch was somewhat manageable. Road capacity expansion was within 15 and 30 percent of the growth in travel demand. Congestion doubled between 1982 and 2000, and the rate of increase moderated, at least in the early part of this decade. This group includes urban areas such as Honolulu, Houston, Tampa-St. Petersburg, Boulder, Cleveland, Nashville-Davidson, and Philadelphia.

18. Shrank and Lomax, *2007 Urban Mobility Report*, p. 23. Shrank and Lomax also note that only five urban areas came close to matching road capacity expansion with travel demand, suggesting that alternative strategies will also be necessary to mitigate congestion. Our view is that the barriers to expanding road capacity are primarily political, largely a result of ideological opposition to roads, a pervasive hostility toward cars within the transportation planning community, and a lack of creative thinking about road network design and management.

III

GETTING FROM HERE TO THERE

6

Boring Urban Roads

WE ENDED THE LAST CHAPTER with the imperative of keeping the supply of transportation infrastructure on pace with travel demand. We can't lose sight of the far more important point we made: we need to think about infrastructure in 3-D. But how do we create an a 3-D transportation system? Ideas are great, but the nuts and bolts are what counts. We take on this task—identifying the nuts and bolts of transforming our 2-D transportation network into a multidimensional one—in the next four chapters. This chapter starts us off with what many will think is the most ambitious of our proposals: Going underground to add that third dimension.

An efficient metropolitan transportation system will have a sufficiently robust road network that allows most of the metro area to be reached in 30 minutes. We talked about that critical feature in chapter 3. Residents should be able to do their errands, make appointments, and conduct personal business and other family tasks like grocery shopping or attending home soccer games in even less time. Achieving that standard requires new roads and establishing new routes to knit together a regional transportation network that recognizes the cross-city and noncommuter travel behavior that dominates the modern metropolis. In congested urban areas, this will require major investments in a new underground layer.

Unfortunately, adding new capacity in urban areas is almost always thought of horizontally—roadways are expanded outward, covering more space, and forcing traffic to shift over larger and larger expanses of asphalt and concrete. This approach has been highly disruptive for cities: Urban freeways often bisect or destroy entire neighborhoods and are often the ugliest public structures we build.[1] Not surprisingly, substantial political opposition has emerged to these projects as local residents attempt to protect their homes, businesses, and neighborhoods.

Capacity expansions do not have to be horizontal, eating up gobs of open space or acquiring expensive rights-of-way. Using tunnels is a common practice in Europe and Asia, but less common in the United States, where an abundance of flat, open land has let transportation engineers and planners take the easy path to capacity expansion—linear, outward expansion. That's changing. Modern engineering techniques such as advances in tunneling technologies and tunnel lining materials, and new designs for cheaper, low-clearance, auto-only tunnels allow us to move beyond simplistic horizontal views of capacity building. Shanghai is showing how to think of roadway tunnels under the city as a network on a new layer, connecting into the surface network to create a transportation web linking the city and improving mobility.

Few places however serve up iconic imagery more than Versailles, France and how tunnels can address important urban problems. The palace built by the Sun King, Louis XIV, attracts more than ten million visitors each year. The palace served as the de facto capital of France under Louis XIV, Louis XV, and Louis XVI. Its monarchist opulence helped lay the cultural foundation that triggered a revolution for equality, liberty, and brotherhood. In fact, during the French Revolution, the city was even renamed "The Cradle of Liberty," and it served as the first seat of the revolutionary government in the summer of 1789.

Now, however, Versailles is more than a symbol of former monarchist glory. It's a wealthy suburban city, less than eleven miles from the center of Paris, with a deep history, that now houses almost 90,000 people. It is in a growing suburban area of about 1.3 million people. The city is also the center for the *académie de Versailles*, the largest of France's 30 elementary and secondary school districts, and administers the education system for all the western suburbs of Paris. In short, it's a true city with urban challenges, including traffic congestion.

Paris has three "ring roads," or beltways, but two of them are incomplete. Both incomplete roads are, perhaps not surprisingly, in the western suburbs. The A86 stops at Versailles, and picks up on the other side. Meanwhile, traffic increased, and congestion slowed traffic to a crawl.

But what was the alternative? Destroying the historical fabric of Versailles was unacceptable. Residents rejected that idea in the early 1970s. No one had figured out a way to bore underground in a cost effective manner, and the French government was not swimming in cash. So, Versailles and the residents of the region sat in traffic, willing to take the trade-off of less mobility in order to preserve the historical legacy of France.

All that changed in 1988. Cofiroute, a global engineering, construction, and design firm headquartered in France, proposed to build a tunnel under the city to preserve the historic fabric of the city while creating a new route to relieve congestion. By re-engineering its diameter and size, Cofiroute "double decked" the tunnel with two lanes going one direction on top and another two lanes going the other direction below.[2] The tunnel, scheduled to open in 2008, includes an emergency stopping lane on each deck. The $2 billion project will eventually include three interchanges, one at the beginning and end of the tunnel as well as one at the A13. The A86 West project is actually two tunnels. The east tunnel, which completes the ring road, is for light vehicles. Another tunnel on the west, linking the A12 with the A86, allows for commercial vehicles and freight as well as autos.[3]

The east tunnel boasts numerous advantages over conventional road expansion and even elevated parkways. Ninety percent of the infrastructure is hidden, preserving the picturesque landscape and historical significance of the city.[4] Noise levels and air pollution have been reduced by 15 percent through a complex series of vents and chimneys.[5] Of course, it is also self-financed, with Cofiroute using the revenues from tolls to maintain and improve the facility through a 70-year concession.

Cofiroute is also financing the tunnel using tolls, one of the few tollways in the Paris urban "agglomeration." More importantly, perhaps, free-flow traffic (at 70 kph or 43 mph) will be maintained for the entire route by using "time sensitive" pricing—tolls that change with the time of day and volume of traffic.[6] Tolls are expected to vary between $2.50 and $6.50, with steep discounts for regular users.[7]

France is not alone. Australia has effectively used tunnels to preserve neighborhoods and connect highways while greatly improving mobility in Sydney, Melbourne, and Brisbane. The Cross City Tunnel built underneath Sydney incorporates underground exits and entrances that allow travelers to reach different parts of the city without seriously disrupting the central business district. A 56 kilometer complex of tunnels is nearing completion in Madrid, Spain, that will expand and interconnect the M30 ring road with three lanes of underground traffic in each direction.[8] Table 6.1 shows some of the major urban roadway tunnel projects going on around the world.

All these examples are compelling, but we need to take urban roadway tunnels to the next level. We need to build the kind of intricate networks, such as the one underway in Shanghai, and beyond. Accomplishing this goal requires dealing with several fundamental challenges and problems.

An urban tunnel network has to be physically feasible—geologic, hydrologic, seismic and other criteria have to be met. The earthquake that recently

Table 6.1. List of Recent Large Urban Tunnels in the World

City	Tunnel	Tunneling Methods	Length (mile)	Width (ft)	Lanes	Cost (US $ Billion)	Completion
Brisbane, Australia	North-South Bypass (2 tubes)	Combination of cut-and-cover, roadheaders, and	4.2	28.5	2/tube	1.6	2010
Chongqing, China	Light Rail Daping Station (2 tubes)	Cut-and-cover	0.9	65.6	2/ tube	0.28	2007
Hong Kong, China	Kowloon Southern Link	Mixshield	1.4	28.2	2	1.8	2009
Kuala Lumpur, Malaysia	SMART- storm water	Slurry shield	6.0	43.3	-	0.52	2007
	SMART- highway (double-decker)		2.5		2/decker		
Madrid, Spain	Madrid Calle 30 Project (2 tubes)	Combination of cut-and-cover and earth pressure balanced	34.8	49.9	3/tube	5.0	2007
Paris, France	A86 West Project (double-decker)	Earth pressure balanced and slurry shield	6.2	34.1	2/decker	2.3	2009
Shanghai, China	Changjiang Under River Tunnel Project (2 tubes)	Mixshield	4.5	50.6	3/tube	1.5	2010

Source: Zongzhi Li, Jeff Budiman, and Jay Shen, *Highway Tunnels: An Overview for Planners and Policymakers*, Reason Foundation, forthcoming.

devastated the Sichuan province of China is one glaring reminder of the importance of paying attention to these issues. We have smaller scale reminders in the U.S. The Northridge Earthquake in Southern California toppled parts of the Santa Monica Freeway (the I-10), Golden State Freeway (the I-5), and the Antelope Valley Freeway (SR 41) in 1994 and caused $12.5 billion in damage. The relatively smaller "World Series Earthquake" of 1989 caused $6 billion in damage in San Francisco, but caused the collapse of the double-decked Cypress Viaduct (a section of the Nimitz Freeway) and killed 40 people.

Technology and tunneling techniques are rapidly making it possible to build tunnels under a wider range of conditions. Indeed, all the highways (and bridges) in Southern California and San Francisco have been rebuilt using higher earthquake resistant standards. As with any major infrastructure construction project, the effect of construction on existing roads and traffic, as well as on homes and businesses above and near the tunnel, have to be managed and mitigated. Tunnels also have to be integrated into the surface road network, providing adequate links to the surface roads to maintain the web.

These considerations are manageable, both from an engineering and fiscal perspective. The biggest barrier to tunnels in the United States has always been cost. Why build an expensive tunnel project when there are so many other needs? We spent several chapters earlier in this book explaining why congested cities need to expand road capacity and that a complete, functional, and sustainable congestion-free road network will require a new layer of roads in tunnels. The key is to include the benefits as well as the costs—failing to build tunnels where needed will cost much more in the long run.

That is certainly how New York City has looked at its decision to embark upon a subway expansion plan with extensive tunneling. The first phase is the expansion of the Flushing Line, or 7 train, from where it ends now at 42nd Street and 7th Avenue down and over to West 34th Street and 11th Avenue, while the more ambitious second phase is a 8.1 mile Second Avenue line from 125th Street and Park Avenue in East Harlem down to Hanover Square near Wall Street.[9] The plans show the many challenges a tunnel can overcome if the benefits are worth it:

> The 7 line will have to work around various underground features, said David Donatelli, project manager for New York-based Parsons Brinckerhoff, the design consultant. Those include the 8th Avenue subway; Amtrak's West Side rail yards, access tunnels, and open tracks; infrastructure for the Lincoln Tunnel and Port Authority Bus Terminal; the viaduct supporting 11th Avenue; and a planned $6 billion commuter rail tunnel under the Hudson River from New Jersey that would end at 34th Street and 7th Avenue.[10]

In other parts of the country as well, tunneling may be the most cost-effective and environmentally friendly solution. A case in point is a proposed connector between Palmdale and Glendale, California north of the City of Los Angeles. The major routes in the area are circuitous and highly congested (and likely to become much worse given current trends in southern California). A 21-mile mostly tunneled roadway deep below the Angeles National Forest is expected to cost about 22 percent *less* than a similar surface road, given the topography.[11] The tunnel would also have shallower grades than the surface highway, allowing higher speeds.

An analysis conducted by Reason Foundation found that the tunnel could even be self-supporting if it were built in phases and tolled using value pricing where prices are adjusted as traffic gets heavier to ensure free flow at the speed limit.[12] The study envisioned a double-decked six-lane cars-only tunnel (three lanes on each level) and a separate truck and bus tunnel that would be built later and separately. If both tunnels were built at the same time, the tolled project would cover 83 percent of the entire cost.

Still, the costs of building roadway tunnel networks cannot be taken lightly. Building tunnels can cost three to five times more than a regular surface lane (see table 6.2). Costs for individual segments of highway vary significantly, depending on soil type, grades, elevations, number and severity of curves, route choice, and regional construction costs. So, understanding benefits as well as costs are crucial to making decisions to build such structures. As congestion becomes an ever greater drain on city economies, such investments make more sense. And much of new capacity can be tolled, allowing for private capital investment to build the structures while tapping into information about people's willingness to pay, to guide decisions.

The high costs should not necessarily prevent these investments from being made. Rather, higher costs suggest that higher traffic densities or crucial net-

Table 6.2.   Estimated Costs of Urban Roadway Investments

	Cost per lane-mile	1 mile of a four-lane expressway
Urban expressway	$8.3 million	$33.2 million
Bridge/elevated	$14-18 million	$56-72 million
Tunnel	$50 million	$200 million

Note: These are general estimates presented for illustrative purposes and are not intended to reflect actual project costs.
Source: Peter Samuel, *Design Innovations* and David T. Hartgen and Gregory Fields, *Incremental Capacity Additions Necessary to Eliminate Severe Congestion*, pp. 70–71. Source of double-deck costs is Figg Engineering, see Surface Transportation Innovations, Issue No 34, Sept 2006.

work connections will be necessary to ensure that revenues or benefits are high enough to justify the investment. Moreover, if tolling is used to generate revenues, a relatively simple cost-benefit calculation is possible: if the revenues are high enough to pay for the costs of adding the highway capacity, then the benefits (measured by consumers and businesses' willingness to pay) are likely high enough to justify the investments.

Boston's "Big Dig" Debacle

We can see a lot of readers rolling their eyes and saying "haven't you heard of the Big Dig!?" Even those living outside of Boston are now familiar with the $14 billion tunneling and revitalization project that was supposed to (and did) improve traffic flows in downtown Boston. More formally known as the Central Artery/Tunnel Project, the idea was to take out an elevated portion of I-93 and replace it with a tunnel. The project ballooned from a fiscally responsible $3.2 billion investment to a $14.5 billion boondoggle. Even more disturbing, the tunnel closed during the summer of 2006 when a 2.5 ton panel of concrete fell from the ceiling, killing a motorist. The incident unleashed a highly publicized investigation of contracts and project management, ultimately resulting in the resignation of the Massachusetts Turnpike Authority's chairman. The Big Dig was the nation's largest public works project in decades, and the delays, escalating costs, and concerns about quality have severely tainted public sector investments in infrastructure as a result.

Therefore it is crucial to understand that the Big Dig was an exception, not the rule. We need to learn the key lessons from this project's problems to avoid repeating them. But this lone incident should not prevent us from building the roads we need for urban residents and economies to thrive.

The Big Dig has been scrutinized heavily.[13] A good summary of the lessons learned includes:[14]

- Work as a team;
- Set goals, benchmarks, and schedules more precisely;
- Express projected costs in construction-year dollars and, where uncertain, ranges of dollars rather than single numbers;
- Carefully estimate contingencies;
- Foster cooperation between different stakeholders;
- Enlist champions to fight for these projects;
- Be honest and transparent throughout; otherwise bad news will come as a shock and erode public confidence; and

- Guard against project creep, the tendency for the project's scope to grow by adding new elements that were not anticipated from the outset. Project creep, in fact, is the major source of cost increases for megaprojects like the Big Dig.

The success of projects overseas similar in complexity (e.g., the City Link Tunnel in Australia or the A86 tunnel outside Paris), show that the Big Dig is a cautionary tale of poor project management, not an indictment of either the need or the efficacy of investing in these projects. Indeed, large scale investments in infrastructure projects, including tunnels, are common outside the United States. Major projects are underway in Spain, France, Austria, Italy, Turkey, and other nations.

More important, most such major projects in Europe and Australia use a public-private partnership in the form of a concession that creates very strong incentives for the builder to do the project well, on time, and on cost, since they help fund the project and don't really make money until the system is operating over many years. (See table 6.3.) Projects in the United States should use such build-operate-transfer (BOT) partnerships, that:[15]

- Use a design/build method where the private partner combines the team that designs and builds the project, improving coordination and adjustment, and reduces project length and costs and ensures no one is done until the project is done.
- Provide incentives for toll revenue bond buyers and perhaps equity investors in the project to exert strong pressure on the project team to manage cost overruns, and require the design/build company to take the risk for some possible errors.
- Provide incentives to meet project deadlines. When the revenue for the private partner and investors is going to come from tolls paid once the road is open, time is almost literally money. Again, a lot of pressure is put on the design/build firm to get the project done on time and up to spec so the project can get into the operational and money-making phase.
- Require the team that designs and builds the project to operate it for many years, and then turn it over to the government in good condition at the end of the concession. This gives the private partner a strong incentive to design and build the project in ways that minimize its *life-cycle* costs, not just up-front construction costs.

**Table 6.3.   Summary of Key Differences
Between the BOT Model and the Traditional Model**

	Traditional	*Build-Operate-Transfer*
Funding source	Highway trust fund	Toll revenue bonds & equity
Procurement process	Design-Bid-Build	Design-Finance-Build-Operate-Maintain
Who pays cost overruns?	Taxpayers	Investors
Who pays for schedule slips?	Drivers	Investors
Who pays for traffic risk?	Taxpayers	Investors
Maintenance funding	Annual appropriations	Toll revenues
Maintenance incentive	Public complaints	Investors' asset value

A Tunnel Network in a U.S. City

But how feasible are tunnel projects outside of very dense, highly congested places such as Los Angeles and San Francisco? More than we may think. We and our colleagues at Reason have examined the road capacity needed to reduce congestion in Atlanta, known for its sprawling low-density landscape. Severe congestion is predicted to get much worse in Atlanta over the next several decades. Only a lot of new capacity that is well managed, with much of it priced, will solve the problem.

Reason Foundation's proposal for the first round of projects includes two tunnels. One tackles the most congested part of Atlanta's road network—the point where I-75 and I-85 converge and run together through downtown along what is called the Downtown Connector (see figure 5.1, p. 72). Our analysis estimated that at least six new lanes would be needed to relieve congestion along this stretch of highway, but space is simply too tight, and property values too high, to add them. Instead, we proposed a double-decked, three-lane tunnel located about one and half miles to the east.[16] The tunnel would parallel the Downtown Connector, linking the GA-400 toll road in the north to I-675 south of downtown. The tunnel would not be continuous. Rather, the route would consist of two tunnel segments, a northern tunnel five miles long and a southern one three miles long. Unlike the A86 West, the Atlanta tunnel could accommodate buses (and subsequently boost the cost). Overall, the proposal would add 48.6 lane-miles of tunnel and 15 lane-miles of toll road, costing about $4.8 billion (in 2005 dollars).[17] Despite this hefty price tag, toll revenues could still cover 39 percent of the total cost.[18] The other tunnel is part of a new east-west link to relieve I-20, made up of the existing Lakewood freeway, extended to the east by a new toll tunnel and to the west by upgrading portions of Campbellton Road and Camp Creek Parkway to freeway level.

Our plan to relieve Atlanta's congestion also includes substantial expansion of surface capacity and gets most of the low hanging fruit there in terms of new links to the road network. For Atlanta to complete a true road web, the two tunnels above will have to be just the first in a series of tunnels to keep up with capacity needs and connect the transportation web to match evolving travel patterns. A very similar story is true of most major cities in the U.S. We have begun examining similar proposals for Denver, Chicago, and Los Angeles, and all entail beginning to build what will ultimately have to be a second layer of roads in tunnels under the already developed parts of the city.

Thus, tunnels can be an important part of adding new road capacity, and many of them will pay their way (as we'll discuss further in chapter 11). This new infrastructure is a crucial building block of the 3-D infrastructure necessary to keep citizens and businesses mobile in the twenty-first century city. Of course, it's not the only part of the solution, either. We devote the next three chapters to exploring other strategies necessary to build the network needed to meet the transportation challenges of this century.

Notes

1. Indeed, Jane Jacobs, the iconic author of *The Death and Life of Great American Cities* (New York: Random House, 1961), became famous for stopping an urban expressway through New York City.

2. Details on the A86 West tunnel can be found at http://www.cofiroute .fr/cofiroute.nsf/web/a86-ouest.htm, accessed 19 March 2007. See also (for English speakers), http://www.a86ouest.com/a86ouest/gb/t_3a.htm, accessed 19 March 2007.

3. See http://www.a86ouest.com/a86ouest/gb/t_2a.htm, accessed 19 March 2007.

4. http://www.cofiroute.fr/cofiroute.nsf/web/a86-ouest.htm, accessed 19 March 2007.

5. Ibid.

6. http://www.a86ouest.com/a86ouest/gb/t_2a.htm, accessed 19 March 2007.

7. "CS to Renew Cofiroute's toll systems and do first ORT," TollroadsNews.com, 7 September 2005, http://tollroadsnews.info/artman/publish/article_1044.shtml, accessed 19 March 2007.

8. "M30 Madrid Calle 30 Project, Madrid, Spain," *Road Traffic Technology*, http://www.roadtraffic-technology.com/projects/m30_madrid/.

9. Tom Stabile, "New York's Subway System Finally Starting Major Expansion" Construction.com, http://www.construction.com/NewsCenter/Headlines/RP/20060523 ny.asp.

10. Ibid.

11. Parsons Brinckerhoff, *State Route 14 Corridor Improvement Alternatives Study*, (Los Angeles: Southern California Association of Governments, 2000), Section 12.

12. Robert W. Poole, Jr., Peter Samuel, and Brian F. Chase, "Building for the Future: Easing California's Transportation Crisis with Tolls and Public-Private Partnerships," Policy Study No. 324 (Los Angeles: Reason Foundation, January 2005), pp. 13–16.

13. For example the 2004 special issue of *Public Roads* focused on mega projects and the Big Dig was the center of much of the discussion, http://www.tfhrc.gov/pubrds/04jul/index.htm

14. Taken from Poole, Jr., Samuel, and Chase, "Building for the Future: pp. 32–34, http://www.reason.org/ps324.pdf

15. Based on analysis in Ibid. pp. 37–38.

16. Robert W. Poole, Jr., "Reducing Congestion in Altanta: A Bold New Approach to Increasing Mobility," Policy Study No. 351 (Los Angeles: Reason Foundation, Novemeber 2006), pp. 28–29, http://www.reason.org/ps351.pdf.

17. Ibid., p. 30.

18. The entire congestion relief program proposed by Robert Poole, however, would be self-supporting. In addition to the tunnel, Poole recommended a network of HOT lanes that would generate significant revenues to pay for other transportation improvements.

7

Seven Steps to Expanding Current Road Capacity

RETROFITTING AND REDESIGNING our road network is going to take a lot more than tunnels. Even as we add a new underground layer to our road network, creating a truly connected web-like road system will require new approaches to improving and expanding the existing surface roads, too. Technology, innovation, and modern engineering techniques allow capacity to be expanded in new and different ways that simply didn't exist a decade ago. And private capital can now help pay for it (more on this in chapter 11)

Policy makers and transportation planners will have to consider new types of overpasses, underpasses and elevated roadways. They will also have to consider managing the road network more efficiently. For example, elevated roads are getting more attention as new engineering innovations permit cheaper and more effective technologies to bring costs in line with potential revenues. Single-pylon elevated lanes are now placed in the median of existing highways, cutting down on construction costs and minimizing the need to purchase land or rights-of-way.[1] Cutting-edge engineering research at the Illinois Institute of Technology may even eliminate most pylons in the next generation of elevated local roads.

At the same time, avoiding years of congestion caused by construction on each project is crucial to making an urban capacity-building program politically and economically acceptable. Innovations that minimize the space needed for construction, shorten the duration of construction, and reduce the frequency of required maintenance road work are vital. The introduction of composite material and offsite prefabrication of elements of new construction are part of the mix in helping make urban road construction feasible

To flesh out what all of this implies, we've identified seven innovations for building new capacity on the surface or getting more out of existing capacity that will be crucial to rebuilding our transportation network into the finely differentialed mesh of the spiderweb we discussed in chapter 5, bringing transportation policy into the twenty-first century.

Queue Duckers and Jumpers

Contemporary over and underpasses in most urban areas still resemble the design of freeways, using copious amounts of open space and wide rights-of-way to separate cars. In contrast, the queue duckers or jumpers used in a number of cities around the world stay within the existing rights-of-way and transform arterial roads in built-up urban areas. The term "queue ducker" is as straightforward as it sounds. At most road intersections, a queue is formed as cars wait their turn for a signal (or for a space on a roundabout to clear). During busy times, these intersections can back up to the point travelers wait through several signal cycles, or vehicles are forced into preceding intersections. The queue ducker allows through traffic (non-local traffic) to literally jump the queue by going under the intersection (or over it with a queue jumper). Properly designed, a queue ducker is like a minitunnel and can double the through capacity of an intersection by eliminating stopping altogether.[2] (See figure 7.1.)

Take the example of a four-lane road, with two lanes going in each direction, that crosses another local road (either two or four lane). On a limited-access highway, the inside lane (left lane) is usually reserved for faster cars and the outside lane (right lane) is dedicated to slower cars or vehicles exiting and entering the highway. Take this concept and overlay it onto our four-lane arterial. Since an intersection with a local road is an obstacle to continuous traffic (using traffic lights, stop signs, or roundabouts), the local road cannot function like a highway. Indeed, the arterial design is closer to a local road (allowing, for example, left turns from the left lane).

Applying the limited-access highway design is direct—reserve the inside lanes for through traffic and allow it to pass over (or under) the intersection unimpeded. The queue ducker uses elevated roadways (or tunnels) to divert through traffic over an intersection while accommodating local traffic needs. Exiting local traffic enters a standard intersection that is regulated by a traffic light.[3] These intersections minimize traffic interruptions by using ramps to merge entering local traffic on the major arterial instead of stopping vehicles at a traffic light.[4]

Figure 7.1. This queue "ducker" diverts traffic underneath Connecticut Avenue at DuPont Circle in Washington, D.C. (Source: Samuel R. Staley)

Another version is even simpler, providing a queue ducker only for cars by having the center lanes in one direction drop under the cross street with a low clearance only for cars. One study that developed this concept and simulated how it would work on specific intersections in Honolulu found that "total travel time during the morning and evening peak hour could be reduced by 11 percent, fuel use by 24 percent and network wide stoppages 24 percent."[5] The authors point out that European experience with low-clearance over-passes for cars only shows that drivers handle them safely and efficiently, calculating that the benefits would offset the costs of putting in the overpasses in just a few years.

Most of these queue jumpers could be spliced into existing lanes either as overpasses or tunnels with minimal neighborhood impact. To some this might seem impractical. For instance, in the South and Southwest, there are few natural barriers to road expansion, and road widening seems natural and less expensive. Perhaps more importantly, many of the neighborhoods in these regions have not achieved urban densities similar to older northeastern and Midwestern cities. This is likely to change as these cities grow and their neighborhoods naturally become denser and land uses become more diverse.

Importantly, these design features are not mere extensions of the local road network. They fuse the advantages of the local road network—access to many points within a neighborhood or on an urban block—with a limited access highway—free flow travel speeds without significant disruptions. This road, however, does not provide regional access (the role of limited-access highways) or local access (the role of traditional arterials). It represents a new type of roadway.

The few queue duckers that do exist set important precedents for cities looking for creative ways to keep traffic moving, particularly in urban neighborhoods. Dupont Circle in Washington, D.C., is a classic example. It is one of the busiest neighborhoods in the District and must accommodate traffic on three of the city's busiest boulevards: Connecticut Avenue, Massachusetts Avenue, and New Hampshire Avenue. Four lanes of moving traffic on Massachusetts and New Hampshire are directed into a four-lane, signalized traffic circle (roundabout), which also accommodates east-west traffic from P Street and north-south traffic on 19th Street.

Connecticut Avenue has the highest volume, running from the White House north to Adams Morgan, Maryland, and the I-495 beltway. Connecticut Avenue is eight lanes wide (six lanes of moving traffic), separated by a median. To avoid complete gridlock at the circle, four lanes of through traffic on Connecticut Avenue are directed under the circle, resurfacing one block north (Q Street) and re-integrating into surface traffic at R Street (two blocks north of the circle).

The design moves large numbers of cars and trucks, but does not require purchasing new rights-of-way and is integrated into the urban fabric of the Dupont Circle neighborhood. Indeed, by directing traffic under the circle, more options are available to preserve pedestrian-friendly designs and minimize potential safety hazards.

A queue ducker stays as much as possible within the rights-of-way of the arterial road, elevating (or tunneling) through traffic over the intersections without obvious exit and entrance ramps. This substantially reduces the cost of the facility by keeping the lanes within existing rights-of-way and minimizing the need to acquire land. Cost control, combined with the need to manage traffic to maintain free flow travel speeds, lends itself to tools such as variable rate tolling, both to finance the new facility as well as implement performance-based management techniques.

The question facing many cities is whether they can integrate these kinds of queue duckers into a more finely grained way into the transportation system. Lee County, Florida is attempting this in Fort Myers, but the projects are not up and running yet. One project is a four-lane road at the intersection of Colonial Boulevard and Metro Parkway. Lee County's experiment will be important for another reason—it will be financed in part by a toll paid by those "jumping" over the intersection.

Elevated Expressways

Elevated expressways are a second innovation that can dramatically add new capacity without disrupting neighborhoods or existing facilities. New composite materials and technologies have greatly increased the viability of these projects by requiring less land and expanding the number of lanes they can accommodate. Elevated roadways can be two, four, or even six lanes and built on single pylons in the middle of an existing median strip. A new addition to U.S. roadways is a Florida facility: Tampa's Crosstown Expressway (see figure 7.2). The nine-mile elevated highway opened in August 2006 and boasts three lanes that reverse direction based on the time of day. Tolls are financing the facility.

In Southern California, portions of the highway network are elevated, including the Harbor Transitway approaching downtown Los Angeles. San Antonio and Austin, Texas, double-decked freeways even though they don't face the same congestion problems as travelers in Los Angeles, and many bridges crossing rivers such as the Ohio and Mississippi are double or *triple* decked. Innovations in construction and design have dramatically reduced the costs of developing these facilities, and they require little or no land acquisition because they can be built within the same "footprint" of the original roads.

Congestion Free Lanes

Orange County, California is one of the most congested places in the nation, thanks in no small measure to its role as the first modern day suburb south of Los Angeles and Long Beach. Riverside County, its neighbor to the east, is one of the nation's fastest growing. It doesn't come as much of a surprise that traffic congestion is rising at breakneck speed. The question is what to do about it.

In the mid-1990s, local officials took a gamble. They speculated that if traffic was severe enough drivers would actually be willing to pay to travel on uncongested roads. If they were right, it would address a huge problem—how to find the money to build new capacity.

Fortunately, their gamble paid off, both figuratively and literally. The 91 Express Lanes pay for themselves and give tens of thousands of travelers an uncongested alternative to the gridlocked free lanes just a few feet away. Not only

Figure 7.2. Tampa's Crosstown Expressway uses reversible lanes and variable rate tolling to manage traffic flow and congestion (Source: Tampa-Hillsborough Expressway Authority)

that, it wasn't just the fat cat business man in his Lexus using the lanes. Soccer moms use them to get their kids to athletic events and make doctors' appointments. Harried working stiff parents use them to get to daycare before the late fees pile up.

How did they do this?

Pricing. The express lanes charge drivers to use them, and they set the price to ensure that the lanes would be congestion free. So, travelers using the road paid for it, and in exchange they got a guarantee that their trip would be unimpeded at free-flow speeds. The fees change based on the time of day, and are set to ensure free flow. If traffic volumes increase, the price goes up. If traffic falls off (e.g., non-rush hour times), the price goes down.

The experiment is the clearest example to date, in the U.S., of another way to build capacity—add lanes, one at a time, and use the toll revenues to pay for the incremental addition to capacity. The projects don't always have to be grand ones. They need to provide enough value added that customers will pay for them.

Using pricing to manage traffic to ensure free flow is no longer an experiment. It's a real solution that works. It's also becoming the hottest reform in transportation policy. Literally. Lanes that charge prices to maintain free-flow travel speeds are called "HOT" lanes.

HOT lanes represent the smart evolution of a failed policy into one that works. During the 1970s and 1980s, dozens of cities created thousands of miles of carpool lanes, also called high occupancy vehicle (HOV) lanes. The idea was to get more people to group together on their trip and reduce the number of cars on the highways. Few HOV lanes successfully reduced traffic volume. The widely used lanes were often "successful" because the HOV limit was so low, sometimes just two passengers, that everyone with a child, girlfriend, or spouse could use them. Alan Pisarski estimates that as much as 55 percent of the so-called carpools in Southern California are really trips with a spouse or child. He's dubbed these "fampools," and they use the HOV lanes even though the trip would have been made anyway. On the other extreme, HOV limits in some places are so high—four or more—that no one seems to use them. Converting HOV lanes to HOT allows carpools to continue to use the lanes for free while getting full use of the capacity by letting those willing to pay a toll use them as well. HOT lanes now can be found in Denver, Minneapolis-St. Paul, and Houston.

HOT Networks

Once a city commits to HOT lanes, it has to begin thinking more broadly—how will these lanes work as part of an overall transportation *system*? Areas with a robust network of carpool lanes can convert those lanes, add some connectors, and create a network of HOT Lanes, a "HOT Network."[6] A series of interconnected HOT lanes along major thoroughfares can give motorists access to free-flow traffic lanes throughout the metropolitan area. This is what Atlanta wants to do with its proposal to convert its HOV network into a HOT network.

Atlanta ranks among the most congested urban areas in the nation. Based on current trends, the Atlanta region is likely to see travel time indexes increase dramatically, driving down average highway speeds from 51 miles per hour in 2003 to 41 miles per hour by 2030. Once a "reliability buffer" is added, average speeds will fall to below arterial free flow speeds. Put another way, a typical traveler will be able to cover just 15 miles in a half hour compared to 30 miles if they were able to travel at free flow expressway speeds. Access to the labor force will be cut by more than half.[7]

A HOT Network has the potential to mitigate these negative congestion effects. The region's transportation plan, *Mobility 2030*, calls for adding only 688 lane miles of a planned 1,200 mile HOV system now. But recent research by local agencies and the Reason Foundation recommends developing the entire 1,200-lane-mile system as HOT lanes because the transportation benefits would be much more significant and would generate critical revenue for transportation improvements.[8] Private companies have proposed to the Georgia Department of Transportation to add HOT lanes to I-75N, I-575, and GA 400 (currently Atlanta's only toll road). Under an integrated network of HOT lanes, a traveler could traverse the entire north-south route of Atlanta in under 30 minutes. In contrast, current congestion trends will effectively balkanize the Atlanta urban area by segregating the northwest section of Fulton County from the southern and eastern portions of the urban area. Adopting policies that ensure free flow speeds allows the urban area to be accessible to most of the labor force.

Even more dramatic improvements are likely to be felt in an urban area like Seattle. Unlike Atlanta, which can expand in concentric rings from the urban core, development in the Seattle area is bounded by Puget Sound on the west and lakes on the east. Development and traffic are compressed into two north-south corridors. The western corridor follows I-5 from Lynwood to Tacoma and runs through downtown Seattle. The eastern corridor runs along the I-405 and links Mountlake Terrace, Kirkland/Redmond, Bellevue, Benton, and Puyallup. Congestion currently puts average freeway speeds at about 40 miles per hour, only slightly better than unimpeded arterial free flow speeds. Current trends indicate they are likely to see speeds closer to 20 miles per hour by 2030. Lynnwood to Tacoma is currently about a 35 mile per hour trip. Congestion has already cut access from Lynnwood down to the northern reaches of the Seattle Region. Current trends will effectively cut the entire northern environs of the Seattle region off from Tacoma as well as the downtown area.

HOT networks help build the kind of capacity that makes a spiderweb network workable. They provide an entire class of options for travelers and drivers that do not exist in the current wagon-wheel network. Queue jumpers allow drivers along high volume arterials to avoid intersections altogether, avoiding slowing and stopping their vehicles. HOT networks provide congestion-free access to routes for intermediate or regional trips. These features allow traffic to become segmented more efficiently and effectively, reducing delays and increasing traffic speeds.

The key to the overall regional transportation network is providing a broad range of options that fit into a finer mesh of travel choices and trip alternatives. Recall the current road network is designed for two basic types of travelers—local and regional. A transportation system rooted in a spiderweb mesh design with numerous options for routing traffic based on individual travel needs and destinations creates a more robust transportation system. This more robust system is dynamic and can accommodate a broader range of yet to be seen twenty-first century travel behavior and choices.

BOX 7.1
Dealing with Rights-of-Way

One of the biggest practical obstacles to building new capacity on the surface is securing the rights-of-way (ROW) for new roads and infrastructure. Buying ROW can be expensive, and can add significantly to the cost of building new infrastructure. ROW acquisition by state governments for road building can exceed $1 billion per year, and the federal government estimated it spent almost $40,000 per parcel in 1999.[1] Moreover, actual costs can vary widely, increasing budgetary uncertainty for projects.[2] Clearly, minimizing ROW costs is important to the success of new infrastructure projects.

Avoiding the need to buy ROW for new projects is another reason why tunneling, trenching, elevated highways, queue jumpers, and flyovers may be more viable options in urban areas. The transportation agencies already own the right to build new facilities in these cases, avoiding the potential for litigation, the costs of legally condemning private property, and the transaction costs associated with negotiating the purchase of these rights.

While purchasing ROW at current market prices may be unavoidable in some cases, economist Randall G. Holcombe has suggested cities and transportation authorities could avoid many of these costs by engaging in more thoughtful long-term planning.[3] The city or region should consider mapping out major transportation corridors as part a long-term capital plan. The agency wouldn't have to commit to building the new facilities, but by securing the ROW well in advance, they could accomplish a number of key goals, including:

- minimizing the costs of land acquisition;
- providing certainty to the real estate market about future infrastructure investments;
- minimizing the likelihood transportation infrastructure would be subject to political manipulation.

By making these purchases years and sometimes decades in advance, the transportation agency gives itself strategic flexibility. Investments can be made as land development patterns warrant them.

Notes

1. Federal Highway Administration, "Acquisition in the 90's," data on federal-aid highway ROW acquisition available at http://www.fhwa.dot.gov/realestate/acq90s.pdf, accessed 29 June 2006.

2. See Jared D. Heiner and Kara M. Kockelman, "The Costs of Right of Way Acquisition: Methods and Models for Estimation," paper presented at the 83rd Annual Meeting of the Transportation Research Board, Washington, D.C., January 2004.

3. Randall G. Holcombe, "Growth Management in Action: The Case of Florida," in *Smarter Growth: Market-Based Strategies for Land Use Planning in the 21st Century*, eds. Randall G. Holcombe and Samuel R. Staley, pp. 131–154 (Westport, CT: Greenwood Press, 2001).

Redesigning Intersections

Major improvements in traffic flows can be accomplished through redesigns and building new intersections. Rather than using the honeycomb or figure eight design of many freeway interchanges, flyovers can be used to redirect traffic seamlessly and safely over oncoming traffic and merge it into traffic on a road going in another direction (see figure 7.3). The flyover, as the name implies, diverts traffic onto elevated roadways for exiting or merging onto roads going in a different direction. Because traffic is taken out of the general flow and "flies over" oncoming or crossing traffic, travelers can merge seamlessly once they are aligned in the new direction. Flyovers allow for left and right turn exiting without the delays of traffic signals or stops.

Figure 7.3.   Example of a "flyover" in Miami (Souce: Peter Samuel)

Another important component of a plan to reconfigure the transportation network to be more dynamic and effective will be to expand the capacity of existing arterials by redesigning intersections and arterials to accommodate more traffic at higher speeds. Among the innovative design concepts that can be used to increase the flow of traffic as well as manage existing traffic more efficiently are:

- Access roads that divert local traffic off limited-access highways at key points along the freeway network;
- Redesigning key intersections to route traffic in a specific direction using multiple lane turns that allow easy merging;
- Using flyovers to redirect traffic and bypass local intersections altogether, diverting traffic from the mainstream flow and merging it gradually in a new direction;
- Using traffic circles rather than four-way red lights when traffic direction and volumes are evenly distributed. Traffic circles have been used successfully in Europe, but they are less effective if traffic flow in one direction (e.g., east-west) dominates the pattern.

Adding New Lanes

The simplest way to add connectivity to a road network is to simply add new lanes. For some urban areas, this may be the only short-term solution because of political resistance to road-based user fees, bureaucratic inertia, or traditional ideological opposition that resists any type of reform. This approach may be as simple as converting a two-lane road into a three-lane road where the middle lane is a turn lane. For smaller and less congested urban areas, this may be the most practical solution—expanding the existing wagon wheel into a network by filling in the road gaps with higher volume arterials.

Likable Roads

A real problem with most of these ideas for expanding urban highway capacity is a long tradition of building ugly roads. No one is excited about big, blocky, grey stained cement elevated roads crisscrossing the urban landscape. When urban freeways are planned and built, aesthetics have traditionally played almost no role.[9] The ugliness and disruption of new urban highways feeds local and political opposition to such projects. But as the need to add road capacity in urban areas becomes greater, and the benefits more apparent, it makes sense to build urban roads with better design and aesthetics and make them a desirable part of the urban landscape.[10]

Urban parkways are perhaps the oldest example of roads that fit well into their surroundings and are pleasing to the eye. The elevated Crosstown Expressway in Tampa, discussed above, was designed with elegant lines and lighting on a single pillar, much more attractive than a typical trestle type of elevated road with a forest of pillars under its dark and dank belly. In Phoenix city leaders have decided that one percent of the budget for major capital projects should go to include art.[11] This has created an opportunity to involve the community in improving the aesthetics of new roads and interchanges. For example, the city engaged community groups and artists to improve the looks of the Squaw Peak Parkway (since renamed the Piestewa Freeway) interchanges (see figure 7.4). They shaped the columns under the overpasses with Native American designs and added reliefs to the walls and art to sides of the road and the grounds around the interchanges. While this project added art to a conventionally engineered interchange, it made a big difference in how it looks. Imagine if they had also been able to re-engineer the interchange to be more attractive.

Figure 7.4. Art and an interchange on the Piestewa Freeway (SR 51) in Phoenix (Source: Leonard C. Gilroy)

Nevada has learned to take into account aesthetics the hard way. They recently adopted policies and plans for aesthetics in road designs to give them "curb appeal" after a major setback in their road-building plans.

> The Carson City Bypass was originally designed to follow a rather utilitarian approach, like other projects. According to Mark Hoversten, professor of landscape architecture at the University of Nevada, Las Vegas (UNLV), when the designs for the bypass were 60 percent complete, however, several organizations and citizens in Carson City banded together to oppose the project. Part of their concern was for improved landscaping, color schemes, and aesthetic treatments for the sound walls on the project. In addition, there were other community-related issues not directly related to aesthetics, such as inclusion of a bike path required in the transportation plan and traffic calming to alleviate impacts on local neighborhoods. Therefore, NDOT abandoned the original plans and went back to square one.[12]

Some cities are even retrofitting existing roads for aesthetic reasons, pushing some urban roads closer to tunnels. Columbus, Ohio, decked over a section of I-670 just north of its downtown in order to physically connect a revitalizing historic neighborhood on North High Street with the downtown and the Arena District (the city's sports and entertainment area). Fort Washington Way in Cincinnati, Ohio, was "trenched" so that the road is sufficiently below the surface that it can be "decked" if development justifies the investment in future years.[13] Similarly, sections of the I-5 in Seattle will be covered to create grass-covered open space.

Getting from Here to There

Each urban area will require a different mix, but each can figure out how many new lanes need to be added and what it will cost. Nationally, we need to add 42,000 lane miles in 403 urban areas over the next 25 years in order to eliminate all severely congested road conditions. While this is a big job, on average it is equivalent in cost to about 28 percent of the *planned spending* over the next 25 years in those cities.

While political opposition is a constant concern, many states and local governments own enough right-of-way to permit adding lanes without costly land acquisition. Using innovative highway financing tools such as public-private partnerships can also lower costs and improve efficiency. If new pavement needs to be added, abandoned rail lines can be converted to new road routes since they often parallel high volume roads. This may be the most practical and effective solution to congestion in many urban areas, particularly smaller and mid-sized regions where urban densities have not increased to the point where tolled highway development is practical.

We too often neglect the local and feeder roads that knit our communities together. While congestion is most visible on freeways, a poorly designed system of arterials can clog roads as easily and quickly as an overburdened highway. Much of the congestion in Atlanta, for example, is a result of its poorly designed system of arterials. While Los Angeles is known as the poster child of gridlock, congestion is most debilitating on the freeways while the arterials move traffic much more efficiently. Notably, Greater Los Angeles is tied with San Francisco-Oakland and San Diego for last place among major American urban areas in freeway miles per person.[14]

Chronic congestion caused by more traffic than the road can handle constitutes about half of total congestion in a mid-size or larger urban area (the other half is cause by "incidents"—accidents, construction, weather, etc.). In certain corridors in Los Angeles and the San Francisco Bay area, for example, between 70 percent and 87 percent of congestion may be chronic.[15] While managing traffic more efficiently can improve both incident-related and chronic congestion, squeezing efficiencies out of the existing network is less likely to achieve substantial reductions in congestion.[16] Other strategies will be necessary.

Learning from Houston

We ended chapter 5 with a historical example of a city that beat gridlock by expanding its road system at the dawn of the automobile age. We spent this and the previous chapter discussing the different ways we can expand capacity. It makes sense to conclude with an example from a city that followed this strategy and achieved success.

Houston ranks among the most congested urban areas in the United States. According to the Texas Transportation Institute, Houston's travel time is ranked eighth among the 85 cities analyzed, just below Miami and Washington, D.C., in 2005.

What makes Houston different is its history. Between 1984 and 1993, Houston *reduced* congestion.[17] After 1993, congestion grew dramatically. What happened?

Houston ranks as the nation's seventh largest metropolitan area with five million people sprawling over ten counties in an area larger than Massachusetts. The region generates economic activity worth $266 billion annually.[18] If the region were its own country, its economy would rank twentieth worldwide. Outside of New York and Chicago, Houston has the highest concentration of Fortune 500 headquarters. ConocoPhillips, Marathon Oil, Halliburton, Waste Management, and Sysco are among the companies claiming Houston as their corporate home town.

Like Los Angeles, Houston's transportation network is critical to its economic success. The Port of Houston is the nation's second busiest in terms of commercial tonnage, and first among foreign tonnage. Two major railroads and eleven hundred-plus trucking companies connect Houston to the rest of North America and Mexico.

Houston was not always congested. The Texas Transportation Institute estimates that in 1975 travel times were only slightly above free flow conditions.[19] But these conditions eroded quickly. By 1985, they were faced with travel at peak travel times 25 percent longer than free flow.[20]

Recognizing the economic threat of congestion, Houston policy makers adopted a strategy that focused on congestion relief. Houston added new lanes of freeways and arterial roads. From 1982 to 1992, freeway lane miles increased 56 percent. Between 1986 and 1992, the Houston area added 100 miles each year to the network on average. Congestion began to slow and even reverse itself. Annual delay per peak traveler *fell* 21 percent.[21] The share of the total road network that was congested at peak times fell to 45 percent after peaking at 51 percent in 1984.[22] In short, as the Greater Houston Partnership observes, the Houston "region built its way out of a severe congestion problem."[23]

Houston policy makers and business leaders apparently did not learn from their success. Between 1982 and 1992, travel demand increased by 50 percent, while the road network of freeways and arterials expanded by 56 percent.[24] But then the urban road network stopped expanding in 1993. Between 1993 and 2005, travel demand increased by another 51 percent, but the road network expanded by just 15 percent.[25] By 2001, Houston had fewer lane miles per person than Fort Worth, Dallas, Austin, and San Antonio.

Not surprisingly, peak hour travel delay almost doubled between 1993 and 2003. Congestion exceeded its 1985 peak by 2000 and had almost caught up with "peer" cities that included Boston, Chicago, Detroit, New York City, Philadelphia, and Washington, D.C.

Thus, the lesson remains the same—adding capacity is critical to keeping congestion in check. Unfortunately, as we have said earlier, it's not just about adding lane miles. It's about adding the right capacity in the right place at the right time. New road capacity has to match contemporary travel patterns. We need to think through the kinds of roads that make the most sense in this new era of customized travel. Our next chapter explores this more directly by examining what we call the "missing link" in the modern transportation network.

Notes

1. Peter Samuel, *How to "Build Our Way of Congestion": Innovative Approaches to Expanding Urban Highway Capacity*, Policy Study No. 250 (Los Angeles: Reason Foundation, 1999), http://www.reason.org/ps250.html#_Toc434987288.

2. As this book is going to press, Zongzhi Li, Ph.D., and a team of engineers at the Illinois Institute of Technology are working on a prototype design of a queue jumper that would effectively eliminate stopped traffic at major intersections, doubling throughput and dramatically increasing speeds on local roads.

3. Presumably, traffic could be regulated in other ways as well, but space and right-of-way needs in urban areas probably make traffic lights the most practical way to regulate vehicles.

4. This design becomes more complicated when two high-volume arterials or boulevards intersect. Rather than having the intermediate road jump over the local road, flyovers may be needed to direct traffic onto the intersecting boulevard by using a design similar to an exit/on ramp for a limited-access highway. These ramps would

direct traffic in one direction (one lane exiting in each direction) and merging the intersecting traffic rather than have them stop at a signal that interrupts traffic flow in all directions.

5. Gregory Dehnert and Panos Prevedouros, "Urban Intersection Congestion Reduction with Low Clearance Underpasses: Investigation and Case Study," *ITE Journal*, vol. 74, March 2004, pp. 36–47

6. Robert W. Poole, Jr. and C. Kenneth Orski, *HOT Networks: A New Plan for Congestion Relief and Better Transit*, Policy Study No. 305 (Los Angeles: Reason Foundation, February 2003).

7. By cutting the circle in half, the area of the circle is cut by three quarters since the area of the circle is proportional to the radius squared.

8. Robert W. Poole, Jr., *Reducing Congestion in Atlanta: A Bold New Approach to Increasing Mobility*, Policy Study No. 351 (Los Angeles: Reason Foundation, November 2006).

9. Joseph Passonneau, "Aesthetics and Other Community Values in the Design of Roads," *Transportation Research Record*, Vol. 1549, 1996, pp. 69–74.

10. For a thorough discussion of aesthetics and urban roadways, see Peter Samuel, *Innovative Roadway Design: Making Highways More Likable*, Reason Foundation Policy Study No. 348, (Los Angeles: Reason Foundation September 2006).

11. Anthony C. Webster, "Civic Crossings: The Commissioning, Design, and Public Perception of Urban Bridges," *Journal of Urban Technology*, Vol. 2, No. 3, 1995 pp. 19–44.

12. James L. Sipes, "Curb Appeal," *Public Roads*, Vol. 69, No. 2, September/October 2005, http://www.tfhrc.gov/pubrds/05sep/04.htm

13. Samuel, *Innovative Roadway Design*, p. 17.

14. Data for urban areas with one million or more people. See U.S. Department of Transportation, Federal Highway Administration, *Highway Statistics 2004*, Table HM-72, http://www.fhwa.dot.gov/policy/ohim/hs04/re.htm.

15. Alexander Skabardoniz, Pravin P. Varaiya, and Karl F. Petty, "Measuring Recurrent and Non-Recurrent Traffic Congestion," *Transportation Research Record*, no. 1856 (2003), pp. 118–124.

16. Indeed, the two types are not independent of each other. Chronic congestion can often create higher levels of incidents such as accidents that back up traffic.

17. Shrank and Lomax, *2007 Urban Mobility Report*, Texas Transportation Institute, Texas A&M University. Complete data provided in Excel format from Texas Transportation Institute web site.

18. Estimate by The Perryman Group, a Waco-based economic consulting firm.

19. *Trip 2000: Travel Rate Improvement program for the Houston Area*, Greater Houston Partnership, p. 5.

20. Texas Transportation Institute complete data for urban areas.

21. Shrank and Lomax, *2005 Urban Mobility Report*.

22. *Trip 2000*, p. 5.

23. Houston's success was not solely due to building more roads. The region also invested in new technologies such as better coordination of traffic signals, metering on and off ramps onto highways, and reconfiguring access from feeder roads and other

arterials. But everyone now acknowledges that a big part of Houston's success was expanding the physical capacity of the highway network to accommodate its growth.

24. Travel demand as measured by vehicle miles traveled. Calculated by the authors from Texas Transportation Institute annual estimates.

25. Calculated by authors from Texas Transportation Institute annual estimates.

8

The Missing Link

The U.S. transportation network is a mess, a victim of technology, time, and changing needs. A transportation system built 50 years ago, based on commuting patterns from the industrial era, simply doesn't cut it in a global economy where a technology-driven, service-based economy is boosting telecommuting and trip chaining to new heights. Commuting and travel patterns have made large swaths of the U.S. transportation system obsolete.

We need to convert roads that no longer serve a useful purpose supporting today's transportation needs into load-bearing parts of the system, links in a mesh more closely resembling a spiderweb than a wagon wheel. We need a transportation network that functions like . . . a network. Roads need to link to other roads that serve the purposes of travelers (commercial or passenger), and these links need to be integrated into one system.

In the twentieth century, the road system functioned like pipes in a plumbing system—diverting water onto pipes of different diameters to capture flow. But, plumbing is difficult to reconfigure efficiently. "Elbows" and "Ts" can be added to the system, but the nature of a plumbing system is to use as many straight lines as possible to keep fluid flowing as consistently as possible. Curves and bends in the roads slow the flow down significantly, reducing the overall speed.

In one respect, we face the same problem engineering our road system. We're just using the wrong model. We still need those high-volume roads where large amounts of cars can be funneled through corridors. But, given the dynamic nature of commuting and trip chaining, we need more links so that travelers can exit, enter, or change direction to meet individual schedules, needs, and destinations. In short, we need a network that functions more like an electronic circuit board, where current can be diverted easily onto different paths as new needs arise (and new obstacles identified). This transportation circuit board provides the flexibility and adaptability necessary to fit the needs of the twenty-first century. It operationalizes the spiderweb.

But, what does this mean for the urban traveler/commuter?

Driving Around the Problem

As we discussed in chapter 5, our urban transportation system is caught between two worlds—a local road system designed to manage traffic at a neighborhood level and a regional system designed to channel high-speed traffic across substantial distances. Our contemporary road needs are somewhere in between. We have lots of 25 mph and 35 mph roads designed primarily for circulating people around and within neighborhoods. We have lots of 65 mph highways, designed primarily to get people from major urban centers. What we need are *more* 45 mph and 50 mph roads that take large volumes of traffic at higher speeds between neighboring parts of a metropolitan area. This is the road network's missing link.

A suburban resident today may live in a residential neighborhood one to two miles from a limited-access highway. Call her Betty and say she has an early dental appointment 14 miles from her home (but perhaps near her workplace). She will leave her home, navigate a series of local roads (usually regulated by stop signs instead of traffic lights), and then pull out onto a major arterial. This "collector" will be larger, typically four or more lanes, where traffic is regulated by traffic lights at major intersections. Finally, Betty enters a limited-access highway and joins the morning commuters in stop-and-go traffic for several miles before exiting onto another major arterial, passing through several stoplights before arriving at her dentist's office. A lot of her trip time was spent navigating local traffic, stop signs, and traffic lights. Even though she was not commuting downtown or across town, she got on the freeway rather than negotiate several more miles of stoplights.

The road system Betty drives is incomplete because it fails to account for or adapt to those travel needs that lie somewhere between local and regional. A mid-tier, intraregional road would allow traffic to skip or jump over unnecessary intersections and other trip interruptions to keep traffic unimpeded. Boulevards and parkways give us a glimpse of what this new tier of roads might look like. They are designed to move larger volumes of traffic within a large urban area, often using low volume, local roads as access points. Parkways, however, tend to resemble a subdued and tamed interstate highway system; they are limited access through ways designed to move traffic to regional destinations.

Boulevards, on the other hand, can end up being local roads on steroids. They still rely on regulating vehicles using traffic lights, ensuring most traffic stops at some (or several) points along the way. They are faster than local roads and move more vehicles, but still much slower than they need to be.

A mid-tier of roads accommodates traffic destined for points within the urban area but outside the neighborhood while minimizing stops, slow downs, and choke points that reduce travel speeds. The queue jumpers, flyovers and redesigned intersections discussed in the previous chapter are useful to show how modern engineering allows for the creation of this new type of road for the first time.

A Twenty-First Century Drive

Think of roads as part of network, providing a seamless set of options and alternatives to travelers seeking widely disparate and changing transportation goals. Designing a road strictly (or largely) for commuters no longer makes sense. The purpose of the trip is less important than the fact the trip is made. This is why road systems need to be considered in the context of an integrated, linked system rather than a functional one. This is the inevitable result of highly customized travel patterns made possible by wealth and automobility. Adding the mid-tier of roads helps complete and integrate this system.

Let's go back to Betty's trip to the dentist, but break it down in more detail and consider how different it would be on a properly designed road network. The 14-mile trip, using conventional technology and road design in place today, would take about a half hour door-to-door even though about ten miles of the trip will be spent on a limited-access highway.

For the purposes of our illustration, the journey covers the normal features of a trip from home, including travel on local roads, higher volume "collectors" and "arterials." Since we want to examine how these trips might be influenced by our intermediate tier of roads, we are also adding an urban expressway to the trip. This feature would be common for a lengthy trip like the one we envision. Overall, the trip would include three-quarters of a mile traveling on local roads, three miles (total) on arterials, and ten miles on an urban expressway tunnel. Under normal circumstances, including driving at normal speed limits (25 mph for local roads, 35 mph for arterials, and 60 mph for expressways) and stopping at intersections, this trip could easily take about a half hour. But let's trace it out in more detail to illustrate the nature of the trip and its dimensions.

When we first presented this example to one transportation expert, he was confused. We examined three different scenarios: one free flow with existing technology, one with congested travel conditions, and a third with improved travel conditions that prevent congestion from delaying traffic significantly. Our expert wasn't confused about the free flow example, or the one with rising traffic congestion. These are "normal" ways our streets and roads function. He was confused by the scenario that examined what happened to travel speeds and times when we *improved* the road network! Let's see why.

Our traveler begins her journey from her home (an apartment, townhouse, or detached home), and drives on local roads about three-quarters of a mile to a larger arterial road that will take her to the expressway. The traffic management features of local roads will likely be very similar to the current system, built out incrementally as cities and neighborhoods developed. On the front end of our journey, our hypothetical traveler would cover three-quarters of a mile on local roads (averaging 25 mph) and two miles on larger volume arterials (averaging 35 mph). She then hops on an expressway to travel ten miles, averaging 60 mph, and ends her trip with one mile on an arterial.

Normal road configurations likely place traffic signals every half mile. So, she would have to endure four traffic-light stops. If a typical traffic-light stop delays the traveler 90 seconds, her trip is extended by more than ten minutes once we factor in stops at intersections and exit/entrance ramps, and leaving the house, as well as getting to her destination.

The use of traffic engineering innovations could cut the travel time dramatically. First, traffic signal optimization, a tool explored in more depth in chapter 9, could reduce stop time by triggering signal changes using motion and weight sensors. "Smart" technology allows the traffic signal to detect waiting cars, gauge the flow of traffic on intersecting roads, and coordinate the signal with other intersections, reducing wait times and increasing average speeds.

Second, an innovative use of flyovers and queue jumpers would allow our traveler to travel faster on arterial roads. Too many of our local road systems adopt designs that fail to recognize the layered or textured approach to traveling that modern technology permits. Improvements in mobility, along with the wealth that allows us to take advantage of it, means travelers can have local destinations, long-distance destinations, and dozens of points in between. Road speeds and network design, as we've said before, should reflect this complexity. On any long-distance trip, a traveler should be able to opt onto roads designed for 25 mph, 35 mph, 45 mph, 55 mph, 65 mph, or more. Queue jumpers and flyovers allow this diversity in the road system.

Back on our hypothetical route, our traveler wouldn't have to stop at all unless she chose to or exited onto a local road. Once into the expressway tunnel, traffic can be maintained at 60 mph (or higher) using dynamic pricing. We

Table 8.1. Characteristics of One-Way,
Free-Flow Trip in a Networked Metropolitan Region

Segment	Avg. Speed	Distance (Miles)	Time (Min.)	Network traffic mgt. features encountered
Local road	25	0.75	1.8	yield signs; stop signs
Stop time			1.0	stop sign/traffic signal signal optimatization
Arterial	35	2	3.4	queue jumpers flyovers
Stop time			0	
Urban expressway	60	10	10	surface lanes elevated lanes tunneled lanes HOT lanes
Stop time			0	
Arterial (destination)	35	1	1.7	queue jumpers flyovers signal optimization
Total		13.75	17.9	

can reduce her trip time by more than one-third. By minimizing stops and maintaining free-flow traffic speeds, her 13.75 mile trip will take 17.9 minutes.

The benefits, however, go far beyond the time savings for this trip. The innovations we've added to the system—traffic signal optimization, queue jumpers, variable rate pricing—have raised the bar on expectations and performance for our road system. Most congestion "management" programs focus on increasing travel speeds to meet the engineered levels. This is the transportation equivalent to rearranging the deck chairs.

Even worse, what if the road system is allowed to deteriorate to LOS F, the standard benchmark for "severe" congestion, with stop-and-go traffic? This is, in fact, the default policy for many regional transportation agencies, as we've discussed earlier. The travel time index would go from 1.0 under free flow conditions to 1.3 or more. Traffic light delays remain the same because they are not (in this example) influenced by traffic flows which now exceed the capacity of the road network. (It's quite possible these delays would be greater since traffic would queue up to the point where a traveler would miss a light cycle.)

The delays accumulate in the slower travel speeds. At a travel time index of 1.3 Betty's trip to the dentist takes twice as long as under the network-enhanced alternative that includes flyovers and queue jumpers. More importantly, this trip probably would not have been made at all because it would just be too much. Betty would have to settle for a dentist she likes less but is closer to home. If this were a business trip, the business would not receive the patronage of our traveler, or be able to tap into the productive talents of this worker. Notably, 28 urban areas currently operate with their regional transportation networks at TTI of 1.3 or LOS F or worse. By 2030, as many as 150 million people may live in urban areas with congestion levels this severe or worse.

Transportation decisions should be focused on continuously improving performance. In practical terms, improving performance means getting people from point A to B faster and faster, as fast as is safe and cost effective. In more technical jargon, we don't just want to improve traffic flow to achieve engineered free flow speeds. Over the long run, we want to improve the system so that we improve mobility continuously, so that in the future we can improve travel speeds beyond what is currently achievable. By adding new capacity and managing traffic more efficiently, we have achieved that in our example. Eliminating arterial road time delays at intersections generated a travel time nearly 40 percent faster than using conventional technology and approaches.

Yes, that's right. These improvements actually *improve* traffic flow so that our workers and residents can move through the metropolis more quickly. Adding innovations such as flyovers and queue jumpers allows us to reset the baseline for what free flow is based on: *faster* speeds and *more* mobility.

Remember the reporter interviewing Sam at the beginning of the book? You can probably see why the reporter was initially confused by our results. The idea that technology, innovation, and facility design could create a new baseline—faster travel—is simply not within the framework of most transportation planners and engineers today. In every case, we are looking at deteriorating traffic and mobility. We are measuring progress by whether congestion increases faster than in similar cities, not whether we are improving overall speeds and increasing mobility in a measurable way. In essence, this illustration shows that we can think about improving mobility by setting a different goal. Rather than assuming free flow travel speeds under existing conditions at engineered capacity with existing technology, we should be setting our sights on ways to let people reach more of the city in less time.

So, the bottom line is this: we need to raise the bar in our transportation decisions. We need to recognize that eliminating congestion is only phase one. Long term, we need to invest in our transportation system so that mobility improves. Given changes in travel patterns and technology, that inevitably means adding capacity. That new capacity, however, will need to be the right kind, put in the right place, and at the right time. The next chapter discusses how we accomplish this by managing the road network more efficiently, before moving on to discussing strategies for financing this ambitious transportation program.

9

Taking System Management Seriously

I T'S 8:00 A.M. ON A TYPICAL WORK DAY. You look at your watch and relax. You have 30 minutes to travel 15 miles to work. Unlike when you first moved to this city of six million people, about the size of the urban area of Houston or Atlanta, you now have plenty of time.

You press the start button on your hybrid car, and pull out of the driveway. You casually drive through your neighborhood, barely stopping at the yield signs. You're the first one in line at the traffic light going out to a major road, or arterial, that will take you to a highway (or tunnel) where you will travel most of the distance of your trip. Your wait is short: sensors have triggered the traffic light to change. Within seconds, you are cruising with the rest of the early-day travelers—some commuters, and some doing other activities such as going to personal appointments, running errands, dropping children off at school.

The traffic is heavier than usual, you subconsciously note, but it doesn't impact you; your car is breezing along five miles over the speed limit. The traffic signals are synchronized, so wait times at intersections practically don't exist since you aren't stopping; cross traffic is almost nonexistent. Westwood and Main, a major intersection is coming up in a quarter mile (half a km). Ten years ago, you could count on this intersection adding five minutes to your commute. Now, you have a choice. You can stay local in the right lane and slow your trip down as you wait at the traffic signal coordinating cross traffic. Or, you can pay a quarter (invoiced electronically using video license plate recognition technology), and use the newly installed queue jumper to carry you over the local traffic at 45 mph. Your conference call is scheduled for 8:45 am, just 15 minutes after your scheduled arrival time at work, so you decide the quarter is worth saving several minutes in your trip. So you follow the signs directing you into the left lane and jump over the queue at the intersection below.

Another half mile breezes by at 45 mph, ten miles per hour faster than five years ago. Then, the periodic traffic signals created enough stop-and-go traffic that it was hard to even reach the posted speed limit. Since the queue jumper provides a longer continuous flow of traffic, average speeds have increased as well as the posted speed limit.

Yet another half mile up the road is the entrance ramp to the highway that will carry you on the longest part of your journey. You guide your hybrid car onto the ramp, hardly slowing down since the traffic has been routed in such a way that no one is forced to stop at a traffic light; cars and trucks merge from lanes that have been directed so that the entering traffic is going in the same direction before it is funneled onto the ramp.

You are now faced with another choice: Should you use the free lanes or the high performance lanes? You look at your watch. The high-performance lanes are in a tunnel and will ensure you get to the office on time, coffee in hand, files open to the topic. The high-performance lanes are tolled, and the rates change every five minutes to ensure free flow travel speeds. The "free" lanes are conventional surface expressway.

You have plenty of time to decide whether to use the toll lanes or the general purpose lanes. The signs on the entrance ramp have already told you what the price will be. The price is higher than usual, already cluing you into the heavy traffic that is already slowing the nonpriced, general purpose surface lanes down to a crawl.

You push a button on your dashboard to directly check the level of congestion leading up to the toll lane/free lane split up the road, using the GPS map on the dashboard of your car. If you have to, you can also check congestion using your cell phone. You press a button that automatically asks the GPS to calculate the time it will take to get to work; the regional traffic management center will shoot back the fastest route in seconds. (Your friends have voice recognition software in their cars, avoiding the need to press any buttons at all, but you didn't think the extra money was worth it. You're cheap, so you decided to go for the less expensive manual system.)

A multicolored route map flashes up on our dashboard screen, reflecting the five-second loop that updates traffic congestion via satellite. You decide again that the certainty of arriving on time is better than the uncertainty of bottlenecks and accordion like traffic on the "free" lanes. You merge into the free flow traffic of the high performance lanes, letting the overhead cameras scan your license plate and enter the tunnel. Your credit card bill will arrive in a couple of weeks, detailing each of the trips and their cost, just like the coffee you buy at Starbucks or the shirt you picked up at the department store.

You are now driving on lanes with cars moving at 70 mph. The regulated entry creates traffic consistency, minimizing the weaving and darting common on the general purpose lanes, and allowing the official speed limit to increase to its engineered performance level.

Your office is less than a half mile from the exit since local zoning and land use regulations allowed your office to be built nearest the high volume highways and roads that workers are most likely to use. You are just a few minutes from the parking garage as you exit the tunnel ramp and turn onto the local arterial that will take you to your office building.

By 8:35 a.m. you are sitting in your office, punching in the conference call code to start your day and your meeting.

Sound fanciful? Even Utopian? It shouldn't. While the example is hypothetical, the technology exists right now to make this trip happen.

- Traffic-signal optimization in two Los Angeles neighborhoods improved travel time by 13 percent, reduced delay by 21 percent, and eliminated 30 percent of the stops.[1]
- London, England, coordinates 3,000 traffic lights through its traffic management system, changing signal times by just a few seconds, to keep traffic moving around bottlenecks, accidents, and other incidents.
- Queue jumpers and duckers funnel traffic under busy intersections such as Dupont Circle in Washington, D.C., and the Murray Hill Tunnel in New York City that allows traffic to avoid congestion on Park Avenue.[2] Lee County, Florida, is building a tolled queue jumper slated to open in the fall of 2008.
- Beijing, China, has a traffic monitoring system that allows drivers to find the quickest route to their destination based on real-time traffic conditions that can be accessed through the worldwide web now and even cell phones in the not-so-distant future.
- Variable rate toll pricing keeps traffic moving at 65 mph speeds on the 91 Express Lanes in Orange County, California, even as the free lanes next to them crawl forward. The same approach to pricing is in place the I-15 HOT Lanes in San Diego and most recently an 11-mile section of I-394 west of Minneapolis. More are coming to Houston, Dallas, Washington, D.C., and Northern Virginia.

All these innovations are part of a general class of transportation engineering innovations called Intelligent Transportation Systems, or ITS. They are, and will continue to be, crucial components to making a speedy, free flowing traffic network a reality. In 2000, the California DOT (Caltrans) estimated the cost-benefit ratio of a package of system-operations measures and found it to have a benefit-cost ratio of 8.9 to 1. By contrast, the addition of conventional highway capacity had a benefit-cost ratio of 2.7 to 1.[3] While capacity is important, managing traffic flows on the transportation network is even more critical because it ensures existing *and* new capacity is used at maximum efficiency. For many U.S. metropolitan areas, particularly smaller and mid-size cities, this can make the difference between a severely congested regional road network and a congestion-free road network.

Changing travel patterns and current trends mean that ITS solutions will play an increasingly prominent role in transportation systems. Technology is advancing so quickly that even experts can't keep up with it. That technology, and its widespread adoption through an increasingly market-based delivery system, is also bringing down costs, allowing technology to become even more diffuse and broadly adopted. Ideally, a transportation network that expands with travel demand and is managed through pricing and other "demand management" techniques could effectively reduce bottlenecks to rare events.

In the practical work of transportation management and engineering, planners and engineers have to fully integrate supply *and* demand, recognizing the *interactive* nature of individual driving decisions and the incremental impact of new road capacity investments. The last two chapters discussed some of the physical capacity additions that will be necessary to dramatically reduce congestion and improve the flow of traffic. This chapter discusses how this system can be managed effectively.

A crucial part of the framework we develop in the following pages hinges on moving beyond the idea that traffic congestion is all about the size of the pipe. It's also about, and in many cities and regions predominantly, managing the flow in the pipe. We emphasize this because solving our urban transportation problems is not just a supply-side exercise—it requires a complete integration of travel demand—its growth, pattern, and change—into the network-planning process. It's the interactive outcome of supply and demand that maximizes the use of the network. Moreover, since we are proposing adding considerable new road capacity to urban areas, it does not make sense to build more 1950s-style capacity. We want the most mobility for the buck, or for the ton of concrete, so integrating ITS into the new capacity and managing the road like other key infrastructure networks is crucial.

Table 9.1 shows the major causes of urban congestion and their share of the problem in the first two columns, and then some possible solutions and how much they might improve things in the third and fourth columns. One way to look at this is that insufficient capacity (the first row) accounts for about one-third of congestion problems, while faulty systems operations and management (the other rows) account for about two-thirds.

Table 9.1. Estimate of the Leverage of Systems Operations and Management on Congestion and Its Causes (Urban Areas between 1 and 3 million)

Problems, challenges	% of total urban delay	Example strategy/ tools	Potential % reduction in total urban delay
• Excess of demand over capacity • Geometric discontinuities • Operational friction • Lack of options for high-value trips	20–30	Reduce variability and provide premium options Application of speed control/ramp metering/lane control Premium/priced managed lanes	5–10
Signal timing	4–13	Minimize delay and increase reliability Systematic retiming across all jurisdictions	2–5
Crashes & breakdowns	20–42	Improve safety/security Integrated Freeway service patrol with DOT/PSA combined incident management program (quick clearance, towing incentives, etc.)	10–20
Construction work	8–27	Minimize delay and improve safety MUTCD-compliant work zone traffic control automated speed control	4–13
Weather impacts (snow, ice and emergencies)	5–10	Minimize delay and improve safety Prediction/advisory Advanced treatment regimes	2–5

Source: Steve Lockwood, *The 21st Century Operations-Oriented State DOT* (Washington, D.C.: National Cooperative Highway Research Program, Transportation Research Board, April 2005), Table 5.

But, it is wrong to think of adding capacity and managing the road network as distinct and separate strategies. They are linked. Changing how existing capacity is managed can dramatically affect the amount of new capacity that is needed. And to get the most "bang for the buck" from adding new capacity, it needs to be actively managed.

To begin to see how this works, let's take a 12,000 mile trip—to Beijing, China.

Managing for Performance

A picture paints a thousand words, but an interactive picture on a computer screen can paint a revolution. That's what we thought as we listened to the top managers of Beijing's transportation department demonstrate their newly developed GPS-based traffic management system.[4]

The lines on the map bulged different colors—red for severe congestion, yellow for moderate congestion, and green for free flow—as traffic information for all city streets and highways was updated every five seconds to reflect real-time changes in conditions. More than 10,000 taxis and commercial vehicles were outfitted with GPS chips, and they sent travel speed information up to a satellite, which then sent it down to the Beijing Transportation Information Center (http://www.bjjtw.gov.cn), which then translated the data into average travel speeds on every road in the city. Hence the bulging colors.

But this wasn't particularly innovative. Sam had seen a similar process in action during a visit to London, England's traffic management system. There the information was used to coordinate traffic signal timing, dispatch emergency vehicles, and identify other bottlenecks in real time as they emerged (or dissipated). Both systems are far ahead of most traffic management systems in the U.S., which consist mainly of putting up electronic signs on the side of the road that provide information about traffic conditions further down the road. In fact, more than half of the nation's traffic monitoring systems are not fully staffed.[5]

What sets the Chinese version apart from the rest of the world, even London's system, is its interactive nature. The Chinese aren't content to provide the information—they want drivers to use it! Right now, any driver can go to the traffic management center's (Chinese language) web site (http://www.trafficview.cn), input their origin and destination, and receive instant feedback on alternative routes. The system will show the shortest route by distance and how long it takes, and suggest a faster route based on where congestion is the worst. The system works for both automobile drivers and bus routes. When we visited in the spring of 2007, the Beijing department of transportation was about to solicit formal bids from private companies to partner with them to provide the interactive technology by cell phone. Longer term plans include in-car units (akin to a GPS) and putting touch screens at key points throughout the city and in mass transit stations to allow travelers to access the system without having to directly access the Internet.

Chinese officials told us they are keen on licensing the technology outside of China, although they have been disappointed by the reception from U.S. and European transportation planners. On one level, this isn't surprising. For most transportation planners on the state and local level, congestion relief is still not a high priority. Most discussion remains focused on small, incremental and supply-side fixes; the traveling consumer is a distant priority, if she is acknowledged at all.

The Chinese don't have that luxury. In fact, the economically and environmentally debilitating effects of congestion are one of the primary motivators behind this new, consumer-based GPS technology. And this motivation was spurred, at least in part, by the need to address air quality problems before the summer Olympic Games opened in 2008.

Chinese cities are choking with congestion, and few cities exemplify the practical challenges transportation planners face more than Beijing. Eight hundred thousand new people officially move to the Chinese capital each year, and thousands others move illegally. The city's population exceeds 16 million, and will likely approach 20 million within five years. Each year more of the population can afford their first car. And rapid economic growth means more trucks moving more materials and goods in and out of the city. More people using existing transport, more cars, and more trucks have put enormous stress on the city's transportation infrastructure. Getting a grip on traffic is a political and economic imperative.

The Chinese GPS system, as well as London's signal monitoring system and other ITS technologies, brings into stark relief the significance of recognizing the importance of managing the transportation system as a *network*.

Congestion management is almost always thought of as a supply-side solution, that treats the consumer and driving behavior as if they can't be influenced. In London (as in the U.S.), ITS technologies focus on more efficiently using pavement to maximize the flow of cars, not utilizing the network properties of the transportation system to integrate real information and incentives to help the travel consumer use the alternative modes and routes more efficiently (and possibly increasing the capacity of the network).

How does Beijing's technological approach differ from the common practice in the U.S.? Every long-range transportation plan in the U.S. has a chapter (or several chapters) that outline strategies called "demand management." In practice (in the U.S. and Europe), demand management strategies assume transportation planners are puppeteers, pulling strings to induce drivers (puppets) to behave in ways that are considered, by planners and engineers, more rational and efficient.

A traveler is treated like little more than a rat in a maze. If the planners close off one route, she will use another one. But the rat doesn't think in these models. She reacts. This shouldn't be surprising since most demand-management programs adopt an engineering framework that seems to presume certain physical relationships and properties between transportation networks and the design process; if we're not rats, we're water flowing through pipes subject to the physics of flow.

Drivers are human beings, not rats, and we make rational choices. That's why ITS is critical to keeping our transportation network moving efficiently. This is recognized by Beijing's transportation policy makers. They realize that the consumer can be a proactive participant in improving the efficiency of the transportation network, whether he uses mass transit or an automobile. The web-based traffic management system in Beijing puts the consumer at the center of the decision, recognizing that drivers want to minimize the time spent traveling (an economic decision), not maximize through-put (an engineering concept).

In the U.S., the most up-to-date travel-consumer-oriented technology can be found at BeatTheTraffic.com. Triangle Software has developed a computer program that helps estimate congestion and traffic flows at peak times in 45 cities (at the time of this writing). Available by subscription, the service allows travelers to identify shortcuts and estimate delay along particular routes. Unfortunately, the recommendations are based on projected traffic flow, not real-time data, and are most useful at the time of departure. Houston's Transtar (Greater Houston Transportation and Emergency Management Center) also provides real-time information on their website (www.transtar.org) on traffic congestion on major roads. These are significant steps forward for those of us edging onto the roads for our commute, but still not where the traffic planners and engineers in Beijing are.

Beijing's traffic management system is designed interactively, providing an effective and easily accessible way for traveling consumers to choose routes (or modes) in real time using the criteria that matter the most to them—time and speed. The municipal transportation department provides information to support that decision, but does not dictate it. Transportation planners are no longer trying to anticipate the needs of drivers, or what noncongested routes would be preferred. Drivers, using their local knowledge of the road network, their individual assessments of travel priorities, and personal experience with travel modes, choose (with the help of information provided by the GPS system) the best alternative according to their priorities and needs.

How well does it work? The first week the center's website was operational in April 2006 it registered 300,000 users. And demand is going up. That's not bad for a city that would still be considered "low income" by Western standards, and where automobile ownership is less than 15 percent.

It's as if the electrons making their way through a circuit had a brain and the engineers gave them the information they needed to make their own decisions. In Beijing, 16 million people make highly individualized decisions about where they have to go, at what time, and for what purpose. Some of those decisions are generic enough that we see them in general traffic patterns. A system that allows each traveler to make customized decisions about the best (and fastest) routes to her destination is efficient, and a critical step toward achieving a high-performance transportation network that factors in supply and demand sides of facilities use.

Applying Technology and Management Solutions

Think about how other network infrastructure is operated. Water storage tanks and pipes are monitored for flow and pressure, and adjustments can be made in real time to adjust to swings in demand. This is even truer of the electricity grid where which power plants are online and how electricity is routed through the network are managed constantly. Internet Service Providers must monitor usage and bandwidth to avoid slow speeds or crashes. Only with roads do we not expect the operators of the network to actively manage it to maintain flow.

The contrast between the approach transportation managers in Beijing are taking and the approach of cities here in the U.S. is stark. Lots of our cities have transportation management systems, but they are more oriented toward gathering data than providing for active management of the road network or empowering the region's travelers with information, let alone having any interactive components. We have often heard that Houston has one of the best traffic management systems in U.S. What does it do? It provides a website for posted information and a traffic-conditions map that gives red, yellow, green status for each segment of the freeway system. The map does not include arterials and is not interactive.[6] Nor does Houston's system represent active, full-time network management akin to that of electric or water networks.

There are several reasons why we don't actively manage our road networks as we should. History is one—state and local transportation agencies were created to build and maintain infrastructure, not to manage a transportation network. Another is jurisdictions—transportation networks cut across city and county boundaries, making it hard to establish a single active manager of the network. But perhaps most of all, the dominant philosophy of local transportation agencies toward management is that we need to manage the drivers, not the network. In place of real-transportation system operations and management, we have systems of transportation demand management. For those steeped in demand management, the first reaction to table 9.1 probably was "why doesn't this talk about other modes or measures to reduce the number of cars on the road?" It is an approach to figuring out ways to have fewer people use the road network rather than manage to carry as many travelers as possible as efficiently as possible. Policies such as transit and land-use changes that are believed to reduce road use are not included in table 9.1 with good reason. Transit carries a small and declining share of travelers in metro areas outside of New York City. And while most metro areas hew to "smart growth" policies of various types, theories that altering land-use patterns can dramatically change travel behavior are incomplete and sorely lacking in empirical verification (see the appendix on land use).[7]

So what can our cities do to improve the functioning of their transportation network? Some of it is simple. Table 9.1 points out that five to ten percent of delay in a typical large city is caused by weather, and much of this delay can be eliminated by better road design, competent snow and ice clearing, and good information systems that warn travelers of weather effects on roads. We've identified some more detailed and specific uses of technology and management that we believe would dramatically improve the efficiency of our transportation system and ensure that the capacity we have (or will add) isn't wasted.

These aren't the only technologies. In fact, the California Center for Innovative Transportation at the University of California, Berkeley, (www.calccit.org) has identified more than two dozen ITS technologies that could improve transportation system efficiency. Rather, these are the six that we believe hold the most promise for making significant impacts on improving the flow of the regional transportation network.

Apply Variable Rate Tolling to Highways

Not too long ago, one of our authors was in a store with his teenage daughter on a trip. She had found a piece of pottery, and she pitched her father on providing the cash to buy it. "You have your own money," he replied. "You can decide if it's worth the price." Her face became more contemplative. "I hate it when you say that." She didn't buy the bowl.

Economists have long recognized the importance price plays in influencing behavior. Prices provide critical information about the relative cost of buying goods and services, and a metric for comparing costs to available resources.

Without prices, prioritizing decisions (and purchases) is difficult, cumbersome, and costly. Higher prices discourage consumption while lower prices encourage it.

What happens when we don't have prices? For one, we can create surpluses. Every state in the nation has a road that has been overbuilt—the barely used four-lane limited-access highway that connects two distant rural cities and nothing else. For one of our authors, it's state route 42 between the towns of Spring Valley (population 510) and Waynesville (population 2,558). We have surplus pavement because no one subjected the project to a market test— would drivers be willing to pay to have that road built?

We also create shortages. That's called congestion. Everyone, it seems, wants to get on the highway or road because no one bears the cost of slowing down everyone else on the road. Once again, the absence of a price means flow can't be regulated efficiently.

BOX 9.1
Toll Roads, Pricing and the American Way

On October 6, 2005, Texas State Representative Mike Krusee, chairman of the Texas House Transportation Committee spoke at a Public-Private Ventures conference held by the American Road and Transportation Builders Association, and ended his speech with this:

I'll conclude by telling you why tolls represent the American way.

Americans do not tolerate shortages. Breadlines are for communist countries. Breadlines in the Soviet Union were caused by the absence of a market mechanism to match supply with demand. The genius of the free-market American system is that for everything we produce, public or private, demand is anticipated, and capital is raised to build the infrastructure to meet the demand.

In the USSR, you could not raise capital. But here, we calculate how much people will pay and how many they will buy. Whether it is widgets or computer chips or water or electricity or college tuition. We borrow against that anticipated revenue and build our factories, our water treatment plants, our pipelines, our universities.

That is why America never has permanent shortages. Oh, except in one thing: transportation. And until we make the shift to a free market mechanism of finance—tolls—we will continue to have shortages—in the form of congestion.

Many Americans think congestion is inevitable; it is not. It is a breadline, it is un-American, and we should not tolerate it.

Pricing is applied to almost every part of U.S. society and economy—except for transportation. In fact, we will even threaten to vote governors and legislators out of office if they want to price transportation choices. When Indiana Governor Mitch Daniels leased the Indiana Toll Road to a private company, it became a major factor in the loss of his party's political control over the Indiana General Assembly.

This is unfortunate. The benefits of road pricing would be significant, particularly if the pricing program is designed to maximize travel speeds. Few real-world facilities have demonstrated the principle of pricing more effectively than the 91 Express Lanes in Orange County, California (www.91expresslanes.com).

The 91 Express Lanes sit in the median of a traditional highway and stretch for ten miles with two lanes in each direction. Even though the special lanes run parallel to one of the nation's most congested stretches of highway, congestion has been virtually eliminated on the express lanes. Afternoon rush hour finds thousands of cars and trucks plodding along at 15 miles per hour on the "free" lanes. Meanwhile, just a few feet away toll-paying motorists fly by at 65 mph. Pricing the roads allows the 91 Express Lanes to maintain speedy free flow traffic *and* carry half the traffic during peak hours despite providing just one third of the corridor's capacity.[8]

It's not simple keeping speeds at free flow levels, and 15 years ago it would not have been possible at all. Every three months, the Orange County Transportation Authority sets prices based on the level of traffic, or the average hourly traffic volume.[9] Prices are set for every hour of the day.

The price swings can be dramatic. During rush hour, motorists might find the price for using the lanes as high as one dollar per mile. During off peak times, the price can be as low as twelve cents per mile.[10] The price is set based on the level necessary to maintain free flow traffic. Thus, the prices change throughout the day, depending on the level of traffic and its impact on travel speeds.

Prices also change depending on traffic flow (Figure 9.1). Eastbound lanes (away from the coast) are the most heavily traveled in the afternoon when toll rates are highest. Traffic on westbound lanes (toward the coast and L.A.), on the other hand, peaks in the morning between 5:00 and 9:00 a.m. Less overall demand on the express lanes during this period also means peak rates hover at less than half the rates of the afternoon rush. The morning peak appears to be more spread out—covering four hours—while the afternoon peak is concentrated around 4:00 p.m. and 5:00 p.m., also explaining why rates are steadier on the westbound lanes compared to the eastbound lanes.

Toll rates also change depending on the day of the week. Weekends are lightly traveled, so the transportation authority sets rates lower during the

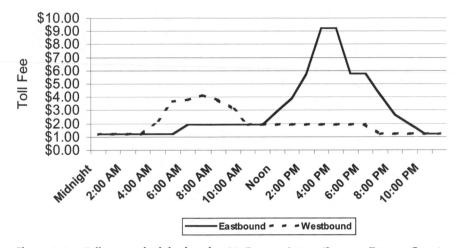

Figure 9.1. Toll rate schedule for the 91 Express Lanes (Source: Orange County Transportation Authority, www.91expresslanes.com, accessed April 15, 2008)

same period they might be high on another day. For eastbound traffic, a toll at 4:00 p.m. varies from $2.30 on Sunday to $8.50 on Thursday or Friday. For westbound traffic, tolls vary from $1.85 to $2.75 for the same time period on different days. Thus, for the 3:00 p.m. hour, on rates set October 31, 2006, tolls changed from slightly over $2.00 on Monday to $4.00 on Monday and Tuesday, to slightly more than $4.00 on Wednesday and Thursday, to $8.50 on Friday, and then dropped to $2.50 on Saturday.

Why is *variable* rate tolling so essential? Free flow speeds are the authority's benchmark, not *volume* (which would be achieved at a lower speed), because that's what users value.[11] While maximum through-put could be achieved by allowing speeds to fall below free flow levels, the service customers are willing to pay for is quick, speedy access to their jobs, homes, or appointments. Many also pay for the added certainty and reliability provided by the express lanes.

Maintaining free flow speeds may be the most important short term value maximized by the driving customer, but variable pricing provides another increasingly important benefit: it helps identify the sections of the road network in greatest need of new capacity. Variable pricing provides a *market test* for the viability of new road investments: The more tolls can cover the costs of new facilities, the more viable the projects should be. If tolls can't pay the costs, planners might consider alternatives, such as a mix of value pricing and unpriced facilities, transit, or land-use deregulation.

The 91 Express Lanes may be the most heralded example of variable pricing, but they are not the only one. They are not even the most advanced. The

I-15 express lanes outside of San Diego were created about the same time as the Orange County express lanes. The I-15 express lanes, however, use *real-time* pricing to maintain free flow speeds. Two reversible lanes were built in the median of I-15 to allow for uninterrupted traffic along an eight-mile corridor. Southbound traffic begins at 5:45 a.m. At noon, the direction of the traffic flow is reversed to accommodate northbound traffic (www.fastrak .sandag.org). Car pools and public transit buses use the lanes for free, but solo drivers pay a toll which is billed electronically.

This facility is one of the first cases where a High Occupancy Vehicle (HOV) lane was converted into High Occupancy Toll (HOT) lanes. Minneapolis converted a section of I-394 into a HOT lane, and it's using variable rate pricing to maintain free flow speeds. Denver, Salt Lake City, and Houston also have HOT lanes open and running. Eighteen other cities are actively planning or implementing HOT lane proposals.

Incident Management

Accidents, weather, and other nonrecurrent "incidents" may account for as much as half the congestion in many urban areas, particularly smaller ones.[12] Crashes alone may contribute 38 percent to delays from congestion based on national data.[13] Walter Green, a professor of emergency services management at the University of Richmond, notes that as much as 60 percent of the vehicle hours lost to delay in traffic may be due to highway incidents.[14] On the micro level, the effects can be both frustrating and dramatic. A stranded vehicle on the shoulder of an interstate can reduce capacity by as much as 26 percent.[15] An accident blocking two lanes of a highway could reduce capacity by 79 percent. Thus, managing incidents that create traffic backups or choke points more effectively can increase travel speeds and, as a result, mobility.

Fortunately, incident management has come a long way since the early days of roads. Until the 1970s, incident management really didn't exist. Emergency vehicles simply responded to emergency calls when they occurred. In the 1970s, a more systematic approach to managing road problems emerged. Local citizens used Citizens Band radio to monitor national emergency radio channels and forward reports of accidents or other incidents onto various government agencies.[16]

Now, fortunately, a subfield is emerging around the concept of incident management. Cameras and sensors detect roadway conditions and traffic flows. Combined with real-time alerts form citizens using cell phones or two-way radios, legions of emergency management units, staff, and vehicles can be dispatched depending on the severity of the incident. In some places, sophisticated incident management systems can close access to ramps and intersections, use message boards to alert drivers to delays, and dispatch vehicles quickly to clear cars, clean up accidents or treat victims.

The result of a comprehensive incident management system can be dramatic. In the mid-1980s, the state of Maryland implemented the Coordinated Highways Action Response Team (CHART) program. Originally designed to help manage traffic flows from the eastern shore to the state's interior, the system is now statewide. In 2002, CHART responded to 13,752 lane-blocking incidents and assisted 19,062 drivers of disabled vehicles that could have resulted in delays.[17] CHART cut down the average length of an incident from 39 minutes to 28 minutes. According to an evaluation commissioned by the Maryland State Highway Administration, the reduction in delays saved almost 30 million vehicle hours and 5 million gallons of fuel.[18] Cost savings to drivers topped $467 million in 2002.

Maryland's success has been repeated elsewhere. Aggressive monitoring of arterial streets and the efficient dispatch of tow trucks allowed Fairfax, Virginia, to cut average clearance times by 40 percent. Seattle paid special attention to clearing incidents involving trucks. Officials worked with towing and recovery companies with special equipment to cut clearance times from nearly six hours to less than 90 minutes.[19] San Antonio's traffic management program reduced traffic accidents by 30 percent.[20] Clearly incident management can have significant impacts on nonrecurrent congestion.

Unfortunately, many metropolitan areas and cities still do not maximize the benefits of this approach to reducing congestion. A Federal Highway Administration survey of the 75 largest urban areas found two-thirds used some form of incident-management system.[21] But, how comprehensive are these programs? While eighteen states mandate incident management, 18 percent of the agencies responding to a survey conducted by the Federal Highway Administration said incident management was not used in their jurisdiction. In many others, incident management consists mainly of directing traffic around accidents and did not represent a systematic approach to managing accidents and other incidents to keep traffic flow moving smoothly or more quickly.

Few programs think on the scale of London, England, where hundreds of video cameras monitor traffic at intersections (see the discussion below). These cameras, along with more pedestrian tools such as cell phone calls or police reports, can identify accidents or other incidents that begin to back up traffic. Engineers in the city's traffic control center, watching monitors, can assess the location and impact of these accidents and perform a variety of functions to clear them up, or manage traffic flows more efficiently. They can notify police or resynchronize traffic lights.

Incident management, while growing in importance and recognition, still remains some of the "low hanging fruit" for many transportation agencies looking for ways to maximize the efficiency of their network.

BOX 9.2
Road Maintenance and Congestion

Performing road maintenance often means closing one or more lanes of a road. This can cause long delays during rush hour, or even other times of the day. The Texas Transportation Institute uses an average value of time for each person on the road of $14.60 per hour, which means that a repaving project that causes thousands of people 15 minutes of delay each day for a week or two can be imposing millions of dollars in costs. Since, as Table 9.1 shows, "construction work," which is mostly maintenance, causes between 8 and 27 percent of delay in a typical large city, these costs are not uncommon.

There are a number of ways to avoid or minimize congestion impacts from maintenance work. The biggest is to do most of the work during low traffic times like nights and weekends. That can cost a bit more, since workers may want higher pay to work night shifts, but the benefits can be much greater. A key way to accomplish scheduling that avoids heavy delays is to make it an important part of the maintenance contract and have companies' bids include incentives to avoid traffic delays.

For example, Indiana DOT once contracted for rehabilitation on Interstate 70 and bidders had to include the cost of traffic delays caused by the road work. As a result, the winning bidder finished the work almost two months ahead of schedule, with one-third fewer lane closures than expected, saving travelers between $1 million and $1.5 million in fuel, time, and other user costs.[1]

Other strategies to reduce traffic delays caused by maintenance work include:[2]

- Providing real-time and detailed information on road work schedules, locations, and delays expected. Even better if it is integrated into an interactive information system like that in Beijing.
- Use temporary pavements to expand shoulders or otherwise created a temporary lane to replace one that is closed.
- Pay incentive bonuses or pay for longer work hours in contracts to complete work in ways that minimize traffic impacts.

Notes

1. Jim Sorenson, Ed Terry, Dan Mathis, "Maintaining the Customer-Driven Highway," *Public Roads*, Nov-Dec, 1998, http://findarticles.com/p/articles/mi_m3724/is_3_62/ai_53520288/pg_1.

2. The Ohio DOT lists a number of strategies at http://www.dot.state.oh.us/News/2005/03-08-05FS.htm.

Optimize and Integrate Traffic Signal Operations at Intersections

About 300,000 traffic signals turn red, green, and yellow every day in the U.S. According to the Institute for Traffic Engineers, three-quarters of them could be improved by updating their equipment or improving their timing. The Institute surveyed 378 traffic agencies in 49 states and discovered that only a third actively monitor traffic signals.[22] The Institute gave the nation an F on proactive management and detection systems, and a D minus on signal operation in coordinated systems. Clearly, we have a long way to go.

"Signal timing is only effective as long as the traffic patterns that were used to generate the signal timing remain reasonably similar," the Institute notes.[23] And there's the rub. Traffic patterns and volumes change all the time, and they're becoming more dynamic as the economy becomes more dynamic and people have more choices of lifestyle. Signal timing is not a onetime fix, but an ongoing management tool that has to be utilized dynamically and kept up with current data, analysis, and technology.

BOX 9.3
A Brief History of the Traffic Signal

The first traffic signal was designed based on railway signals, using semaphore arms with red and green gas lamps. Designed by railway engineer J.P. Knight, the first lights were operated manually by policemen and installed near Britain's House of Parliament in 1868. The electric light was an American invention. Salt Lake City policeman Lester Wire invented the first electric traffic light, although he didn't patent it. Nevertheless, Salt Lake remained a hotbed of traffic signal invention, and in 1917 the nation's first interconnected traffic signal system was installed. The signals controlled traffic at intersections, and were triggered manually.

The first patented electric traffic signal was installed in Cleveland in 1914 by the American Traffic Signal Company and invented by African American inventor Garrett Morgan (who applied for the patent in 1923). Automatic traffic signals were introduced in Houston in 1922. Now, more than 260,000 traffic signals turn green and red every day in the U.S.

Decades passed, however, before traffic light technology experienced another leap forward. In the 1980s, some cities began to apply computerized synchronization to their network of traffic signals. In the 1990s, the move from incandescent light bulbs to LED displays allowed for faster signal switching and the use of a broader array of colors to serve different purposes.

Traffic light optimization can improve traffic flow significantly, reducing stops by as much as 40 percent, cutting gas consumption by 10 percent, cutting emissions by 22 percent, and reducing travel times by 25 percent.[24]

In England, Transport for London, the regional transportation agency, uses 1,200 cameras to watch over the city's streets through its Traffic Control Centre. (The cameras are used solely for monitoring—nothing is actually recorded.) If there's an incident—such as a celebration for England's rugby team at Trafalgar Square, or something more minor such as a fender bender on one of the city's meandering, crowded streets—staffers can reset traffic lights remotely to improve flow, sometimes varying signal lengths by just a few seconds to smooth out traffic flows further down the network.

This strategy is also relatively cheap. One billion dollars could improve traffic signal operations *nationwide*.[25] In contrast, the Palmdale-Glendale tunnel alone would cost about $3 billion and Boston's "Big Dig" cost over $14 billion. Signal optimization benefits outweighed costs 58 to one in a California program that optimized over 3,000 signals. A study of 26 projects in Texas yielded a benefit-cost ratio of 38 to one. Although officials spent only $1.7 million on all the projects, they were able to cut fuel consumption by 13 percent, stops by 9 percent and delays by 19 percent.[26]

To fully take advantage of signal optimization, regional approaches to traffic management will have to be coordinated. Part of the success of the London program is its ability to coordinate thousands of traffic signals over a large geographic area. Moreover, successful programs need to be fully funded and staffed with professionals that can monitor traffic consistently and make the needed adjustments. Many traffic signal optimization programs fail to meet their potential because local communities do not provide the staff necessary for them to function effectively.[27]

Ramp Metering

Bottlenecks occur in a lot of different places on our roads, but the most common are often on- and off-ramps to interstate highways. Much of the so-called "accordion effect" that characterizes surging traffic is directly tied to cars and trucks merging on high-speed lanes on highways. These effects are made worse by what traffic engineers call "platooning": the tendency for traffic to bunch together in groups of four or more vehicles as they enter and exit off-ramps. Maximizing network efficiency then requires smoothing out the frequency with which vehicles enter and exit the road facilities.

Ramp metering may be the most promising technology available for smoothing out the surges in traffic flow that cluster around on- and off-ramps. In a nutshell, ramp metering regulates the flow of traffic by "holding traffic on the entrance ramp and releasing vehicles at a rate that the freeway can better absorb."[28]

Ramp metering is not new, although the technology has been improved considerably since it was first implemented in 1963 on Chicago's Eisenhower Expressway (I-290).[29] The technology was pretty basic: A police officer used hand signals to stop traffic and wave them onto the highway. Now, meters involve traffic signals that flash green for "go" and red for "stop." The typical interval is 4 to 15 seconds.[30] About 20 U.S. metropolitan areas currently use ramp metering in some form.[31] The United Kingdom and the Netherlands use ramp metering extensively as well as the cities of New York, Los Angeles, San Francisco, Chicago, Phoenix, Columbus (OH), and Minneapolis-St. Paul.

The benefits have been pretty significant. Metering can increase throughput (the number of cars that pass through a lane) by 8 percent to 22 percent, and increase speeds on the main road from 8 percent to 60 percent.[32] In the early 1990s California activated ramp meters on two highways. Average speeds went up 22 percent on the first highway and 89 percent on the second.[33] Ramp metering has also made highways safer, reducing total crashes between 15 percent and 50 percent.[34]

Ramp meters accomplish these feats by doing more than flash red and green lights at set intervals. Modern meters use an intricate system of sensors and detectors to monitor traffic. Wires buried inside the highway act as vehicle detectors. This information is then passed on to the light at the end of the on-ramp, and this is what determines when the light is green and when it's red. The duration of the red light changes depending on traffic flow, much like variable rate tolling adjusts (in principle) to the level of traffic to keep speeds flowing at free flow.

The potential impacts of ramp metering on traffic flow were dramatically illustrated during a 2000 experiment in the Minneapolis-St. Paul area. When the state Department of Transportation shut off all 433 ramp meters, highway speeds dipped by 9 percent. Motorists found their trips were lengthened by 22 percent as they dealt with more uncertainty, higher traffic volumes, and lower overall speeds because of the lower roadway capacity.[35]

After the ramp-metering program's first fourteen years, peak period speeds remained 16 percent higher than before the metering was implemented despite rapid increases in traffic volume.[36] Moreover, the peak period accident rate was 38 percent lower.[37] Ramp metering in the Twin Cities reduces annual air emissions by 1,160 tons and saves the traveling public about $40 million per year.[38] A benefit-cost study found that the benefits outweigh the costs by about five to one.[39] Other cities that have evaluated ramp metering and found that speeds have increased and accidents decreased include Portland (OR),

Seattle, Denver, and Detroit.[40] Houston, Texas, and Long Island found speeds increased, but their studies did not evaluate accident rates.[41]

Ramp metering comes with a possible downside, however. When cars are stopped at the ramp, long queues can form on the on-ramp and spill onto the surface streets and arterials. One of our colleagues has also experienced backups when ramp meters attempted to regulate traffic where two major roads merged. But the gridlock isn't necessarily a shortcoming of ramp metering; it may simply reveal a lack of attention to traffic management on the surface streets or a need for new capacity. Moreover, technology and signal coordination could eliminate some of these backups by increasing the frequency of green lights on the ramps to help clear surface streets.

Better Parking Policies

As we build better road networks that improve mobility, we will need to be able to park at our destinations. That will mean more parking spaces and better management of existing ones. Few people think about the cost of providing land to park their cars and trucks, yet these are real costs. Often, particularly in urban environments, these costs are borne by the general taxpayer, not the user. Not surprisingly, parking prices do not reflect the true cost of providing this infrastructure even though it is a crucial part of the transportation network.

Solving this problem is not as easy as it first appears. It's not clear which parking costs reflect subsidies, and which ones are benefits bundled in a particular project. It's hard to envision a shopping mall without free parking, for example. Many retailers in malls gladly pay the costs of providing "free" parking through the higher floor rents because they know the benefits come back to the store through higher revenues from high volumes of shoppers. But private land owners and shoppers consenting to pay for parking embedded in prices of goods and services is usually not the main problem. Free public parking is.

Probably no one has been more dogged in driving this and other key points about parking policy than Donald Shoup at UCLA, most recently in his book *The High Cost of Free Parking*. He starts off by pointing out that up to 30 percent of congestion in central business districts is caused by vehicles cruising around looking for curb parking. One of his recommendations is that cities price parking so that about 85 percent of spaces are filled at any given time, with prices adjusting as demand changes to always keep some spaces empty. Portland, Oregon, and Anchorage, Alaska, have adopted the 85 percent target, and San Francisco and Redwood City, California, have put into place parking prices that are higher the more popular a parking spot is.[42]

BOX 9.4
Parking Innovations*

Redwood City, in the heart of California's Silicon Valley, faced a vexing problem in 2007. During the busy lunch hour, downtown was gridlocked, with cars orbiting the block in search of one of the few prime parking spots, while just a half block away, a four-level garage was never full. So the city is trying something new: installing meters that charge more for the best spots.

As anyone who has ever circled the block for a marginally better spot knows, parking is an Amc.. .~ obsession. It occasionally boils over into rage, or worse. Since the parking meter was first introduced 70 years ago, in Oklahoma City, the field has been dominated by two simple maxims: Cities can never have too much parking, and it can never be cheap enough.

Now a small but vocal band of economists, city planners and entrepreneurs is shaking that up, promoting ideas like free-market pricing at meters and letting developers, rather than the cities, dictate the supply of off-street parking. Seattle is doing away with free street parking in a neighborhood just north of downtown. London has meters that go as high as $10 an hour. San Francisco has been trying out a system that monitors usage in real time, allowing the city to price spots to match demand. (A recent tally showed that one meter near AT&T Park brings in around $4,500 a year, while another meter about a mile away takes in less than $10.) Gainesville, Florida, has capped the number of parking spots that can be added to new buildings; Cambridge, Massachusetts, works with companies to reduce off-street parking.

San Francisco, perhaps more than any other city, shows how radically some cities are rethinking their parking. The city is one of the toughest places to find a meter spot in all of America, and there has been a spate of attacks by angry drivers against parking enforcement officers. One block near the popular Fisherman's Wharf has average stays of four hours—even though there's a two-hour time limit. Recently, the city hired a company to lay hundreds of 4-inch by 4-inch sensors along the streets in some areas. The sensors, which resemble reflectors, have recorded some 250,000 "parking events" across 200 parking spots. City planners can now tell you which spots are occupied the longest and how traffic flow affects parking supplies.

A wider rollout of the sensors would allow the city to consider a number of options. The city, for example, could temporarily charge about the same as private lots near the stadium during high demand events such as a Giants baseball game at AT&T Park. The ground sensors are also connected to the Internet wirelessly, which creates the possibility that parking enforcement officers equipped with PDAs could get real-time information on parking violations beamed to them. Consumers could get information on which parking spots are open.

About a month ago, the city also installed new kiosks that take credit cards as well as quarters, and boosted prices from a flat rate of $2 per hour to a four-hour rolling rate that starts at $3 and rises to $5, for a total of $15 for four hours. That's more than the day rate at many privately owned parking garages in the area. "We're pricing to match demand," says Tod Dykstra, chief executive of Streetline Networks, which installed the sensors.

* This is an excerpt from Conor Dougherty, "The Parking Fix," *Wall Street Journal*, February 3, 2007, Page P1.

Don is also an advocate of employee parking cash-out programs.[43] A few California businesses adopted a cash-out program for their employees with impressive results. Rather than pay for employees' parking spaces, the companies gave that money to the employee to spend on parking or whatever they wanted. Faced with a clear cash cost to parking to weigh against the benefit of driving, the number of employees driving to work fell by 13 percent on average and in one case by 24 percent.

These ideas are not without their problems. Setting market prices for public parking sounds good, but elected officials control public parking policy, and many pressures are exerted on them to deviate from market-based parking prices. Reasons to keep parking free abound. Lower density and less congested cities are in no rush to raise parking prices. People are never happy to start paying for something they thought they were getting for free, and higher parking prices hit the poor the hardest. Downtown merchants object because free parking provided by the city helps draw business. On the other hand, there are also pressures to overprice or undersupply parking. The "demand management" culture in most transportation agencies sees parking as a problem in that it enables driving, and parking policies area a tool for discouraging mobility rather than as a crucial adjunct to the road network.[44]

That said, market-based parking pricing has worked in many places that have tried it. Old Pasadena's market-based parking policies reduced congestion and improved access to and total spending in the shopping and entertainment district.[45]

Another parking issue is local zoning and planning parking mandates. Virtually every zoning code has a minimum parking requirement based on national engineering standards that requires developers to provide spaces to meet peak demand. Many of these standards rely on little empirical evidence. Shoup has found cases where standards for certain types of businesses were based on just three or four data points!

The idea that every pharmacy in America needs the same amount of parking is a bit absurd anyway. Many cities have experimented successfully with more flexible parking requirements.[46] It makes more sense for the amount of parking to be determined by the property owner and city to see what makes sense. Nevertheless, some caution is called for since under-providing parking in new developments is likely to lead to overflow and other problems. The city and developers have to take a long-term perspective when deciding how much parking a new building will need.

Conclusion

These aren't the only policies that cities could, or even should, pursue. Several others can improve the efficiency of the network was well, including encouraging telecommuting and managing access to local roads and arterials more effectively. The policies we've outlined here, however, help maximize the efficiency of the transportation network, build resilience, and encourage flexibility and adaptation of travel behavior. This is the critical task of transportation planners and policymakers in the twenty-first century.

Notes

1. France T. Banerjee, "Preliminary Evaluation Study of Adaptive Control Systems (ATCS)," City of Los Angeles, Department of Transportation, July 2001.

2. Ted Balaker and Sam Staley, "For Traffic Solutions Think Over the Box," *New York Times*, 15 July 2007, http://www.reason.org/commentaries/balaker_20070715 .shtml, accessed 28 August 2007.

3. Steve Lockwood, *The 21st Century Operations-Oriented State DOT*, Washington, D.C.: Cooperative Highway Research Program, Transportation Research Board, April 2005, p. 25.

4. A brief summary of the GPS system and its accomplishments can be found on Sam Staley's blog postings at Planetizen.com, http://www.planetizen.com/ node/24392. The information provided in this section was gathered by both authors during a visit with officials in the Beijing Municipal Department of Communications, the agency responsible for transportation planning and policy, 8 May 2007.

5. 2007 National Traffic Signal Report Card, Technical Report, p. 16, http://www .ite.org/REPORTCARD/technical_report%20final.pdf.

6. http://www.houstontranstar.org/

7. Marlon Boarnet and Randal Crane, *Travel by Design: The Influence of Urban Form on Travel* (New York: Oxford University Press, 2001).

8. "Continuation Study to Evaluate the Impacts of one SR91 Value-Priced Express Lanes: Final Report," California Department of Transportation Traffic Operations Program HOV Systems Branch Sacramento, CA December 2000, p. 48.

9. Complete details on the toll setting policy can be found at http://www
.91expresslanes.com/generalinfo/tollpolicy.asp.

10. The most recent fare schedule can be found at the 91 Express Lanes web site
(operated by the Orange County Transportation Authority), http://www.91expresslanes
.com/tollschedules.asp.

11. CPTC realized that customer service is an ongoing process, so it does not rely
just on pricing to keep the lanes clear. The 91 Express Lanes customers don't experience such delay because employees do all sorts of things to keep cars moving briskly.
They sit in a nearby traffic control center and use dozens of cameras to monitor traffic flow. If something mucks up traffic, a special patrol squad jumps into action. The
squad is there with extra gas, a new tire, a towtruck—nearly anything that will keep
traffic flowing.

12. Incidents can cover a wide range of cases. The Federal Highway Administration's *Simplified Guide to the Incident Command System for Transportation Professionals* (February 2006) lists vehicle disablement, crashes, cargo spills, debris on the road,
and hazardous material spills as examples of traffic incidents. Nontraffic incidents include industrial accidents, bridge collapses, and emergency road work. Emergency incidents include severe weather, natural disasters, wildfires, and human-caused catas-
trophes.

13. Steve Lockwood, "The 21st Century Operations-Oriented State DOT," Washington, D.C.: National Cooperative Highway Research Program, Transportation Research Board, 2005.

14. Walter G. Green, "Managing Complex Emergencies with Tight Constraints:
The Highway Incident Management Problem," paper presented at the 2003 Transportation Safety and Security Workshop, the GWU Institute for Crisis, Disaster, and
Risk Management, Washington, D.C. 29 January 2003, http://www.richmond.edu/
~wgreen/conf2.pdf, accessed 31 August 2007.

15. U.S. Department of Transportation, Federal Highway Administration, *Freeway
Incident Management Handbook* (Washington, D.C.: US Government Printing Office,
1991), cited in Green, "Managing Complex Emergencies with Tight Constraints."

16. Green, "Managing Complex Emergencies with Tight Constraints," p. 4.

17. Gang-Len Change, et al., "Performance Evaluation of CHART (Coordinated
Highways Action Response Team) Year 2002 (Final Report), Maryland State Highway
Administration, November 2003. A summary can be found at http://www.benefit-
cost.its.dot.gov/ITS/benecost.nsf/ID/9FBABB7833F303C3852571B8004D4EF5, accessed 31 August 2007.

18. Ibid.

19. David L. Helman, "Traffic Incident Management," *Public Roads*, 68, no. 3 (No-
vember/December 2004), http://www.tfhrc.gov/pubrds/04nov/03.htm.

20. http://www.ksdot.org/kcmetro/pdf/Ch1.pdf.

21. *Simplified Guide to the Incident Command System for Highway Professionals*,
U.S. Department of Transportation, Federal Highway Administration, February 2006,
http://www.ops.fhwa.dot.gov/publications/ics_guide/index.htm#chapt1, accessed 31
August 2007.

22. National Traffic Signal Report Card, Technical Report, National Transportation
Operations Coalition, 2005.

23. Institute for Transportation Engineers, http://www.ite.org/signal/index.asp, accessed 31 August 2007.

24. National Transportation Operations Coalition, *National Traffic Signal Report Card Executive Summary*, http://www.ite.org/reportcard/, accessed 31 August 2007.

25. National Traffic Signal Report Card, Technical Report, National Transportation Operations Coalition, 2005.

26. D. Fambro et al., "Benefits of the Texas Traffic Light Synchronization Grant Program," Research Report 0280-1F, Texas Transportation Institute, Texas A&M University, College Station, TX, 1995.

27. See the critique in Samuel, *Innovative Roadway Design. Making Highway Mom Likable*, Policy Study No. 348 (Los Angeles, Reason Foundation September 2006), http:///www.reason.org/ps348.pdf, p. 60.

28. *Highway Traffic Operations and Freeway Management: State-of-the-Practice: Final Report.* U.S. Department of Transportation, Federal Highway Administration, March 2003. pp. 2–5.

29. A useful summary of ramp metering can be found on Wikipedia under the entry "Ramp Meter", http://en.wikipedia.org/wiki/Ramp_meter, accessed 11 September 2007.

30. A car takes about two seconds to queue up to the line at a ramp meter. Meters that run faster than four seconds don't give drivers enough time to adjust and evaluate the timing. Meters that run longer than 15 seconds are so long that drivers typically jump the light. See the discussion on "Ramp Metering" at the ITS Decision Web Site maintained by the California Center for Innovative Transportation, a unit of the University of California, Berkeley's Institute of Transportation Studies and the California Department of Transportation, http://www.calccit.org/itsdecision/serv_and_tech/Ramp_metering/ramp_metering_report.htm#r_key, accessed 10 September 2007.

31. Ibid.

32. *Highway Traffic Operations and Freeway Management*, pp. 2–6.

33. Adam B. Summers and Ted Balaker, *A Toolbox for Congestion Relief* (Los Angeles: Reason Foundation, 2008).

34. *Highway Traffic Operations and Freeway Management*, pp. 2–6.

35. Ramp metering also offers safety benefits. Without ramp metering in Minneapolis-St. Paul, collisions increased by 26 percent. With ramp metering, the Bay Area's accident rate fell by 33 percent on the 101 and by 14 percent on the 280.

36. California Center for Innovative Transportation, "Ramp Metering."

37. Ibid.

38. *Highway Traffic Operations and Freeway Management*, pp. 2–7.

39. Ibid.

40. California Center for Innovative Transportation, "Ramp Metering," Table 6.

41. Ibid.

42. Conor Dougherty, "The Parking Fix," *Wall Street Journal*, 3 February 2007, Page P1.

43. Donald C. Shoup, *The High Cost of Free Parking* (Chicago: Planners Press 2005).

44. On the demand management approach to parking, see Valerie Knepper et al., *Developing Parking Policies to Support Smart Growth in Local Jurisdictions: Best*

Practices, San Francisco: Metropolitan Transportation Commission, June 2007, pp. 9–23, and Todd Litman, "Evaluation Parking Management Benefits," paper presented at the annual meeting of the Transportation Research Board, January 2007, http://www.vtpi.org/park_man.pdf

45. Douglas Kolozsvari and Donald Shoup, "Turning Small Change Into Big Changes," *Access,* No. 23, Fall 2003, pp. 2–7.

46. Knepper et al., *Developing Parking Policies to Support Smart Growth,* pp. 24–28.

10

Transitioning Transit

SAM'S FAVORITE TRANSIT TRIP IS ON THE YELLOW LINE on Washington, D.C.'s Metro. Frequent visitors to the District can probably guess why. It provides exceptional access to the District from Ronald Reagan National Airport. He can be just about anywhere, between Dupont Circle and Capital Hill, within forty-five minutes of the plane touching down on the tarmac. That access, and the mobility the Washington, D.C., subway provides, is valuable.

But, he also knows Metro's limits. Even during rush hour, if he's running late for a meeting, he will take a taxi. The taxi may take slightly longer en route, but it drops him off at the doorstep of his appointment. He's also aware that taxis would likely be even more competitive if he had to pay the out-of-pocket costs for the Metro, which is steeply subsidized by taxpayers.

Still, the point is that transit serves a purpose. For some, like our authors, it provides easy access to destinations for a low out-of-pocket cost. For others, it provides an essential form of mobility because they can't afford the alternatives (most notably a car) or they face physical disabilities that prevent them from driving. This begs the question: what is mass transit's role in a world that values mobility?

A New Vision for Transit

Mass transit is clearly an important part of the urban transportation network, and we believe it could become even more important in the future. But we need to be realistic about what role it can play. A lot of people use transit—10.3 billion trips in 2007 according to the American Public Transit Association—but that accounts for just 4.6 percent of all work trips.[1] Eighty-eight percent of commuters use the automobile and 2.9 percent walk. Transit trips are about 1.6 percent of all trips, and about 5 percent of all trips for households earning less than $20,000 per year.[2] In short, transit is an important mobility option for some but its regional utility is much more limited outside of a few of America's largest urban areas (such as New York).

Moreover, as we've discussed in earlier chapters, economics is working against transit. Our dynamic, decentralized life styles and work choices have created complex and variable travel patterns that don't lend themselves to fixed-route transit systems (a focus of our discussion in chapters 4 and 5). Not surprisingly, transit is losing market share. Indeed, transit's share of work and total travel has fallen steadily and is currently less than half of where it was in 1960 despite promising signs of stabilization in the early part of this decade.[3]

Yet each year we spend more on public transit because of, as one economist observes, "the general public's widespread perception that public transit helps to relieve congestion, save energy, reduce pollution, revitalize cities, provide mobility to the disadvantaged, and ensure basic mobility opportunities for everyone."[4] A great deal has been written debating the truth of these "public perceptions," but it is safe to say that transit is a crucial means of transportation for many of the poor and a desired choice for others who prefer it to driving. It is also true that if we shut down transit systems in urban areas, the extra cars entering the congested roads would likely make congestion much worse (at least in the short and intermediate terms).[5]

Still, the stark reality is that expanding existing transit services in urban areas will not effectively reduce congestion. Most people still only use transit when they have to: Only about one-third of the people who use transit choose to do so when they have a car available.[6] This harsh reality can be seen most clearly in the results of "transit-oriented development"—high density mixed use projects built near rail stations or transit centers to make it very easy for those who live there to use the transit system. These projects are created and funded expressly to increase the use of transit by those who live in them. But as the *Los Angeles Times* reports,

> [T]here is little research to back up the rosy predictions. Among the few academic studies of the subject, one that looked at buildings in the Los Angeles area showed that transit-based development successfully weaned relatively few residents from their cars. It also found that, over time, no more people in the buildings studied were taking transit 10 years after a project opened than when it was first built.[7]

The *Los Angeles Times* report wasn't a fly-by-night, deadline-driven story. It involved two months of investigations that included interviews of residents, and counting vehicle traffic and pedestrians.

The reporting showed that only a small fraction of residents shunned their cars during morning rush hour. Most people said that even though they lived close to transit stations, the trains weren't convenient enough, taking too long to arrive at destinations and lacking stops near their workplaces. Many complained that they didn't feel comfortable riding the MTA's crowded, often slow-moving buses from transit terminals to their jobs.

Moreover, the attraction of shops and cafes that are often built into developments at transit stations can actually draw more cars to neighborhoods, putting an additional traffic burden on areas that had been promised relief.[8]

This is not an isolated case. Researchers in Portland, Oregon, examining transit-oriented development projects there found very similar results.[9] In one case, the researchers staked out a site and counted. Out of 73 trips leaving the development (including bike, autos, pedestrians), only 11 trips ended at the light rail station, with only four people actually walking to the station. Indeed, research has consistently shown that transit attracts only about 10 percent to 20 percent of the trips among residents within walking distance of a transit stop.[10] Most of the rest drive. Some in very high density neighborhoods walk. (See the discussion in chapter 4 and the appendix on land use as well.)

The problem is that we have fallen into a transportation planning culture of "transit vs. automobile." Transportation decisions get very political, very quickly. In the planning process, transit and road projects compete for resources and fight over the division of spending. Transit in the form of rail and bus service is made distinct from roads, and proponents of each engage in head-to-head competition for transportation spending, as if they are competing for travelers.

This is unfortunate because everyone loses. As we have stressed in earlier chapters, driving is a practical, highly rational and efficient transportation choice because it customizes and personalizes travel. The automobile democratizes mobility. Transit needs to be a complement, not a substitute, for automobility.

Transit, like the car, is a form of transportation, a "technology," used by travelers to get from point A to point B. The traveling public chooses their transportation mode (technology) by assessing whether it can get them where they want to go fastest, at a reasonable cost. The key is to ensure transit, like a road, is provided in the right place at the right time at a reasonable cost to meet these needs. In today's economy, our wealth and service-based economy put high values on mobility *and* access. Traditional transit simply has not provided the service levels and quality travelers want (even at very steeply subsidized out-of-pocket prices). That has to change if transit wants to be a viable and competitive alternative in this century.

When transit tries to compete with auto travel by being something completely different, it loses the competition badly, as transit's declining market share shows. For decades, transit systems have evolved away from the kind of flexibility and connectivity that autos provide, and that the traveling public clearly wants. We have spent billions of dollars trying to improve transit's connectivity and level of service in an effort to lure travelers out of their cars, and this strategy has failed miserably for everyone. In many of our largest cities, 25 percent to 70 percent of all transportation spending goes to transit systems that carry one percent to two percent of travel.[11] This approach is simply not sustainable as congestion continues to march onward and upward and more and more metropolitan areas approach gridlock.

In a globally competitive, service-based economy, workers and households tailor their transportation choices to highly individualized and ever-changing needs. They don't tether their jobs and lifestyle to rail (or bus) routes that never change. Automobility has to be the fundamental building block of the transportation system and of any attempt to revitalize transit. Rather than setting itself off as a completely separate system, transit needs to be integrated with roads in ways that maximize the ways investments in infrastructure benefit multiple modes and transportation options for travelers. Some of this is already happening as transit agencies build park-and-ride lots, but it needs to be more comprehensively and strategically integrated into the transportation planning process.

This shift will be harder than many people realize. Our current approach to transit planning has purposefully moved *away* from improved mobility, connecting fewer and fewer workers with jobs, fewer employers with workers, and fewer people to places they want to go within reasonable travel times.

The evidence is pretty sobering. Public transit trips are slower than private automobile trips in almost every major urban area. An examination of work travel times for 276 metropolitan areas by demographer and transportation consultant Wendell Cox found automobile trips were faster than public transit trips in every place except four (see table 10.1 for selected cities).[12] On average, public transit riders spent 35.9 minutes traveling to work while private automobile travelers faced a 20.8 minute commute.[13]

The discrepancy between public transit and automobile travel was likely made worse by an almost ideological commitment by transportation planners to fixed-route rail systems at the federal and local level. Most of the funding for major new projects has gone to these rail projects, not flexible bus or "rub-

Table 10.1.   Work Trip Travel Times for Top 10 U.S. Metropolitan Areas

Metro Area	Automobile	Public Transit	All
New York	26.7	52.2	33.0
Los Angeles	26.9	50.0	28.0
Chicago	27.5	49.7	30.1
Philadelphia	25.1	47.4	27.1
Dallas-Ft. Worth	26.3	48.7	26.7
Miami	27.2	50.2	28.1
Houston	27.3	50.4	28.0
Washington, D.C.	28.9	47.1	30.6
Atlanta	29.4	50.3	30.1
Detroit	25.1	46.0	25.5
Average (276 metro areas)	20.8	35.9	21.1

Source: U.S. 2000 Census data reported in "Work Trip Travel Times: USA Metropolitan Areas: 2000," demographia.com, accessed 8 February 2004.

ber-tire" alternatives. Of the 208 projects funded through the federal government's "New Starts" transit program through fiscal year 2004, just 15 were for bus rapid transit projects.[14] The federal government was sinking 30 times more money into rail projects than bus. Rail lines are a limited technology that can only connect places in a thin line running across the city. Hence many, if not most, trips on rail transit include a leg on at least one bus to get to the rail line from home, or to work from the rail line. Rail transit is also very expensive, and cities that have spent large percentages of their transportation budgets have forgone adequate road building and even diverted funds from buses, allowing congestion to worsen on the roads the buses have to travel.

Clifford Winston and Vikram Maheshri of the Brookings Institution examined the net benefits of 25 rail transit systems to determine whether they were worth our investment using broad definitions of social costs and benefits.[15] Only the Bay Area Rapid Transit System, they found, generated net benefits for society. Even the much used New York and the widely heralded Washington, D.C., subway systems couldn't generate enough benefits to offset the costs. They note, echoing the points we raised in chapters 3 and 4, that:

> Rail transit's fundamental problem is its failure to attract sufficient patronage to reduce its high (and increasing) average costs. This problem has been complicated enormously by new patterns of urban development. Rail operations, unfortunately, are best suited for yesterday's concentrated central city residential development and employment opportunities; they are decidedly not suited for today's geographically dispersed residences and jobs.[16]

Public transit can facilitate a strategic transition to contemporary urban travel patterns by embracing more competitive models for delivering public services. These approaches, which can use competitive bidding and long-term concession agreements with the private sector, can help reorganize transit agencies to become more consumer oriented and directed.

Historically, U.S. cities have chosen to provide transit services directly to ensure broad access. It's time to challenge that approach. We do not insist on government ownership and provision of farms to provide food, or public ownership of oil fields and refining to provide heating oil or gasoline, or many other things we chose to subsidize to ensure people have access. We've even backed out of providing government funded and managed housing to the poor. Instead of being in the business of supplying such services, we find ways to give the people we want to help some type of voucher or direct subsidy they can use to go get the goods or services in the private market. Food stamps and housing vouchers may be two of the most visible forms of direct subsidies.

A transformation of public transit along similar lines has the potential to unleash competition, innovation, and entrepreneurship to provide transit services more people would use. In an economy and culture where personalized and customized travel is highly valued, transit agencies must be in a position to experiment with new types of services and methods for delivering those services. This probably entails a switch to transit vouchers provided to disadvantaged individuals for whom cities want to provide mobility, and as incentives for other targeted people, combined with deregulation, competitive outsourcing, and perhaps even the privatization of transit provision.

Experimentation may also mean letting the private sector operate significant portions of the transit service. The United Kingdom deregulated and privatized its bus services in the 1980s with considerable success in terms of more bus services and reduced public subsidies. There were problems in the market when bus companies acted in a predatory fashion to capture customers and that required some regulatory intervention.[17] Such problems can be solved by creating property rights for bus stops, or "curb rights." These are legal entitlements to stop at a particular spot and pick up passengers, kind of like owning a taxi stand. That solves the problem of bus companies coordinating with passengers and solves predatory behavior by letting customers choose which bus company's bus stop they will wait at.[18] Curb rights aren't abstract. They have immediate and practical application and have been implemented in Bogota and Karachi.

Of course, some glitches are likely. Privatizing British rail in the 1990s ended up creating a regulated monopoly rather than a truly competitive market. Nevertheless, the effort still reaped significant benefits for the traveling public.[19]

Contracting and limited forms of privatization are already implemented in the U.S. Private sector involvement in transit services primarily comes through contracting with private firms to operate transit services.[20] The National Research Council surveyed transit system managers on contracting out and found that:

> Hundreds of transit systems—of all sizes and types—now contract for some transit services, and many have done so for a number of years. About one-third of all federal aid recipients contract for more than 25 percent of their services, and about one-quarter contract for a smaller share. . . . Most of the general managers of systems that are now contracting reported that their contracting programs are meeting expectations. More than half stated that their expectations for contracting have been fully met overall, and another 38 percent reported that their expectations have been partially met.[21]

As these institutional changes emerge, however, cities will be faced with difficult decisions about the future of their transit systems. What is the best transit alternative for providing mobility in urban areas? One that provides fast, reliable, and convenient services. Higher income travelers who have cars are significantly more sensitive to price, convenience, and service quality because they have alternatives.[22] In very dense places, such as some parts of New York City, Washington, D.C., proper (not necessarily suburban Virginia or Maryland), or the city of San Francisco, rail can be an efficient way to transport large numbers of people. Even in these cases, however, it's not clear that the costs are worth the investment, as Winston and Maheshri point out.

The key, as we discussed in chapters 3, 4 and 5, is to provide a service that is competitive in terms of speed and accessibility. Indeed, while mass transit continues to service a very small proportion of travel outside of New York, specific types of services continue to be successful. Any corridor that is characterized by a large volume of travel to a very specific destination is likely to also find competitive transit services. Most often, these corridors will be from dense (or highly accessible) suburban locations to a downtown central business district. Increasingly, however, these corridors might also include travel to and from major suburban subcenters. Gary Barnes, for example, found that transit's share of trips increased from five to ten times the regional average for destinations that included the downtown in places such as Los Angeles, Atlanta, Minneapolis-St. Paul, and Pittsburgh.[23] Similarly, University of California, Berkeley, professor Robert Cervero has found that transit can capture about 20 percent of commuters when employment is clustered in dense locations.[24]

The Bus Alternative

Along high volume (and often congested) corridors, Bus Rapid Transit (BRT) can fill an important travel niche that is more cost effective than rail and just as effective at meeting travel needs. BRT also has the advantage of flexibility and adaptability, two key features of meeting contemporary travel needs and consistent with building the web-based road network outlined in chapter 5. BRT, according to the Federal Transit Administration, is

> an enhanced bus system that operates on bus lanes or other transitways in order to combine the flexibility of buses with the efficiency of rail. By doing so, BRT operates at faster speeds, provides greater service reliability and increased customer convenience. It also utilizes a combination of advanced technologies, infrastructure and operational investments that provide significantly better service than traditional bus service.[25]

BRT "has the advantage of being flexible," notes the U.S. General Accountability Office (GAO). "Buses can be rerouted more easily to accommodate changing travel patterns to eliminate transfers; buses can operate on busways, high-occupancy vehicle lanes, and city arterial streets."[26] The National Bus Rapid Transit Institute (www.nbrti.org) highlights systems in 18 U.S. cities that are up and running, including Pittsburgh, Chicago, Los Angeles, Albany, Boston, Miami, and Louisville. These experiments are challenging the idea that buses are noisy, slow, and polluting, unable to compete effectively with rail transit. The GAO surveyed 20 BRT systems in 2001 and found that they "were capable of moving large numbers of passengers each day."[27] The Los Angeles rapid transit lines, in particular, operated on congested arterial roads, yet averaged 32,500 riders per day. The GAO's review of 18 light rail lines found ridership averaging 29,000 per day, ranging from 7,000 to 57,000 riders per day.[28] In short, when actual ridership was compared, bus rapid transit systems compared favorably to light rail.

Moreover, the costs for rapid bus transit systems are much lower than for alternative rail projects. The GAO found that the average cost of an exclusive busway ran about $13.5 million per mile.[29] Costs for buses that used HOV lanes were much lower, averaging $9 million per mile. Light rail lines, which almost always require exclusive rights-of-way, averaged $34.8 million per mile, ranging from just $12.4 million to $118.8 million per mile.

Transit and the Spiderweb

Buses, and BRT in particular, have the potential to become much more competitive and much more effective because they can piggyback on current land-use and demographic trends. They can adjust to changing travel patterns and expand (or contract) based on the level of demand for their services. Even more ridership could be earned if investments were made in higher quality buses and bus stops and services on the buses.

Even more important, the improvements in the road network we have been describing would allow BRT to "be all it can be." A spiderweb network including mid-level roads for more mid-distance travel, the use of queue jumpers and other improvements in road design will allow the bus system to provide better and faster service.

But road pricing will also bring benefits. A HOT network can easily guarantee bus riders a speedy trip.[30] Buses can use the priced lanes for free and avoid congestion and thus travel much more rapidly. For example, Houston decided to set aside as much as 25 percent of the space on its new Katy Freeway HOT Lanes, free of charge, for transit buses and vanpoolers when it opens in 2009. Other drivers still pay a toll that goes up and down with the flow of traffic, again ensuring that everyone on the road avoids congestion.

This is even better than exclusive busways because most of the lane capacity is unused even with the highest quality bus service available (one bus leaving every one minute). If it is a HOT lane and a virtual exclusive busway the majority of the capacity is used by drivers willing to pay a price—a toll that would be adjusted to ensure traffic remains free flowing and buses remain unimpeded.

This has the advantage of generating a dedicated revenue source for the facility, relieving traffic congestion on the general-purpose lanes, and providing a practical and viable free flow alternative to single drivers (or car pools) that place a high value on time and speed. In fact, the typical light rail system recovers just 28 percent of its operating costs through fares, advertisements and other nonsubsidies while BRT covers 70 percent of its costs from nonsubsidy sources. Financially, BRT is a more sustainable transit alternative than rail.

In the end, BRT is the core of a transit system that is more integrated with the rest of the transportation network. Sharing busways with HOT networks will free up resources that can be used to improve the quality of buses and services for all users and make transit more attractive to travelers who have a choice. Best of all, investments in new capacity and pricing that reduces congestion also benefits the transit system, harmonizing both modes and ending the fruitless competition for resources that has drained both modes for so many years.

Notes

1. Alan Pisarski, *Commuting in America III*, NCHRP Report No. 550 (Washington D.C.: Transportation Research Board, 2006), Table ES-2.

2. John Pucher, "Public Transportation," in *The Geography of Urban Transportation*, ed. Susan Hanson and Genevieve Giuliano (New York: Guilford Press, 2004), pp. 208, 212.

3. Ibid., figure 8.6.

4. Ibid., p. 208.

5. This would be true at least in the short run until households and employers could make the necessary adjustments to minimize travel times through relocation. For an extensive discussion of transit's role in congestion relief, see David Shrank and Tim Lomax, *2007 Urban Mobility Report*, Texas Transportation Institute, Texas A&M University.

6. Federal Highway Administration, *Status of the Nation's Highways, Bridges, and Transit: 2002 Conditions and Performance Report* (Washington, D.C.: U.S. Department of Transportation, 2002) exhibit 14-2.

7. Sharon Bernstein and Francisco Vara-Orta, "Near the rails but still on the road," *Los Angeles Times*, 30 June 2007, http://www.latimes.com/news/local/la-me-transit 30jun30,0,4693321.story.

8. Ibid.

9. See John A. Charles, Jr. and Michael L. Barton, *The Mythical World of Transit-Oriented Development: Light Rail and the Orenco Neighborhood, Hillsboro, Oregon*, (Portland: Cascade Policy Institute, 23 April 2003) http://www.cascadepolicy .org/pdf/env/I_124.pdf, and Michael L. Barton, *The Mythical World of Transit-Oriented Development: Steele Park in Washington County, Oregon* (Portland: Cascade Policy Institute, September 2003) http://www.cascadepolicy.org/pdf/env/I_125.pdf.

10. See the discussion (and references) in Ted Balaker and Sam Staley, *The Road More Traveled: Why the Congestion Crisis Matters More Than You Think, and What We Can Do About It* (Lanham, MD: Rowman & Littlefield, 2006), pp. 47-48, 95-96.

11. David T. Hartgen and M. Gregory Fields, *Building Roads to Reduce Traffic Congestion in America's Cities: How Much and at What Cost?* Policy Study No. 346(Los Angeles: Reason Foundation, August 2006), Table 22.

12. The metropolitan areas where public transit was faster than automobile travel were Jonesboro, Arkansas; Lawrence, Kansas; Hattiesburg, Mississippi; and Gadsden, Alabama. Data are 2000 census data and reported in "Work Trip Travel Times: USA Metropolitan Areas: 2000," Demographica.com, 8 February 2004.

13. Some planners have argued this is an apples to oranges comparison because it does not compare transit trips to "competitive" automobile trips. Those living in transit accessible neighborhoods, they claim, find automobile travel is not that much faster. But, as we've seen, even in transit competitive neighborhoods transit captures a minority of all trips. Moreover, transit use is boosted in these neighborhoods because automobile options have been significantly degraded because of congestion, not because transit is providing a clearly superior alternative.

14. "Bus Rapid Transit Offers Communities a Flexible Mass Transit Option," Statement of JayEtta Hecker, Director, Physical Infrastructure Issues, U.S. General Accountability Office, before the Committee on Banking, Housing and Urban Affairs, U.S. Senate 24 June 2003, http://www.gao.gov/new.items/d03729t.pdf, table 1, p. 8.

15. Clifford Winston and Vikram Maheshri, "On the Social Desirability of Urban Rail Transit Systems," *Journal of Urban Economics*, Vol. 61, No. 2 (2007), pp. 362–382.

16. Ibid., p. 2.

17. Daniel Klein, Adrian Moore and Binyam Reja, *Curb Rights: A Foundation for Free Enterprise in Urban Transit* (Washington, D.C.: Brookings Institution Press, 1997), pp. 73–79.

18. Ibid., pp. 107–115.

19. Michael Gerald Pollitt and Andrew Smith, "The Restructuring and Privatisation of British Rail: was it really that bad?" *Fiscal Studies*, Vol. 23, No. 4 (2002), pp. 463–502, argue that with privatization "major efficiencies have been achieved and consumers have benefited through lower prices." John Preston, "The Economics of British Rail Privatization: An Assessment," *Transport Reviews*, Vol. 16, No. 1 (January 1996), pp. 1–21, argues that "the economic evidence favours a more cautious approach to railway reform."

20. Wendell Cox, "Competitive Participation in U.S. Public Transport: Special Interests Versus the Public Interest," paper presented to the 8th International Conference on Competition and Ownership in Land Passenger Transport, September 2003, http://www.publicpurpose.com/t8-cc.pdf provide a number of case studies.

21. Committee for a Study of Contracting Out Transit Services, "Contracting for Bus and Demand-Responsive Transit Services: A Survey of U.S. Practice and Experience," Transportation Research Board, National Research Council Special Report 258, (Washington, D.C.: National Academy Press, 2001), http://books.nap.edu/openbook.php?record_id=10141&page=R1.

22. This provides potential opportunities to attract ridership. See the review and discussion in Todd Litman, "Transit Price Elasticities and Cross-Elasticities," *Journal of Public Transportation*, Vol. 7, No. 2 (2004), pp. 37–58.

23. Gary Barnes, "The Importance of Trip Destination in Determining Transit Share," Journal of Public Transportation, Vol. 8, No. 2 (2005), http://www.nctr.usf.edu/jpt/pdf/JPT%208-2%20Barnes.pdf, accessed 11 September 2007.

24. See also Robert C. Cervero, "Office Development, Rail Transit, and Commuting Choices," *Journal of Public Transportation*, Vol. 9, No. 5 (2006), pp. 41–55, http://www.nctr.usf.edu/jpt/pdf/JPT%209-5%20Cervero.pdf, accessed 11 September 2007.

25. Federal Transit Administration, "Bus Rapid Transit," http://www.fta.dot.gov/assistance/technology/research_4240.html.

26. Hecker, "Bus Rapid Transit Offers Communities a Flexible Mass Transit Option," p. 4.

27. Ibid., p. 12. Interestingly, the theoretical capacity of a BRT is between 28,800 and 86,400 people per lane per hour. This exceeds the theoretical capacity of light rail and some heavy rails systems.

28. Still, bus ridership tended to have lower daily ridership. One system using HOV lines transported just 1,000 people per day. Nevertheless, the upper end of BRT

ridership matched the upper end of light rail ridership and numerous BRT lines generated ridership volume close to light rail.

29. Hecker, "Bus Rapid Transit," p. 12. See also "Mass Transit: Status of New Starts Program and Potential for Bus Rapid Transit Projects," the testimony of John H. Anderson, Jr., Managing Director, Physical Infrastructure Issues, U.S. General Accountability Office, before the Subcommittee on Highways and Transit, Committee on Transportation and Infrastructure, House of Representatives, 20 June 2002, GAO-02-840T, http://www.gao.gov/new.items/d02840t.pdf, accessed 12 September 2007.

30. Robert W. Poole, Jr. and Ted Balaker, *Virtual Exclusive Busways: Improving Urban Transit While Relieving Congestion,* Policy Study No. 337 (Los Angeles: Reason Foundation), 2005.

IV

MAKING IT WORK

11

Where's the Beef? Funding Twenty-First Century Mobility

Few EVENTS HAVE FOCUSED NATIONAL ATTENTION on our transportation crisis more than the collapse of the I-35W bridge in Minneapolis. The rush hour tragedy sent 100 vehicles plunging onto the banks of the Mississippi, killing 13 innocent drivers and passengers, one less than two years old, and injuring more than 100. The bridge collapse carries an economic as well as human toll—$400,000 per day, or $17 million in 2007 and $43 million in 2008, according to Minnesota's Department of Transportation and Department of Employment and Economic Development.

This tragedy may be a harbinger of what is to come. Nearly 25 percent of the nation's 596,580 bridges are currently considered "deficient."[1] About eight percent of urban interstates and 30 percent of urban arterials are in poor condition.[2] More than half of the nation's urban highways are congested at some point in the day.[3] All these outcomes are a consequence of insufficient resources or misallocation of them. If we are going to implement the kind of comprehensive redesign of the transportation network we propose in this book, we have to confront our transportation funding problem head on.

A Funding System in Trouble

So far we have focused on reducing congestion and unleashing the benefits of mobility through a very ambitious series of measures to improve transportation infrastructure. That will not only take vision, will, and political capital, it will take a lot of money. How will we raise the money to prevent our bridges from falling down and our roads from falling apart, let alone expand the system in size and quality as we have proposed? It doesn't matter what we might want to achieve in terms of redesigning or rebuilding the network if the money is not there to finance it. Unfortunately, our transportation needs are growing faster—much faster—than revenues. It's not just about the engineering. It's also, and perhaps even more so, about the economics and incentives.

The needs side of this financial imbalance is easy to understand. We've spent the better part of this book explaining why the current transportation network is inadequate. Travel patterns are changing to reflect greater incomes, more mobility, and technological advancement. The U.S. nearly doubled in size between 1950 and 2000, and we're going to add another 120 million people by 2050, according to the U.S. Census Bureau. There are more people and more goods traveling every year; freight traffic is expected to nearly double by 2030.[4] A growing population and economy drive steady growth in miles traveled each year, which almost doubled between 1980 and 2005.[5]

Some areas of the nation will be hit harder than others. Nearly two-thirds of the population growth over the next 25 years is expected to concentrate in just six states: California, Arizona, Texas, Florida, Georgia, and North Carolina.[6] The ports of Los Angeles and Long Beach, already responsible for 40 percent of the nation's imported goods, expect container traffic to triple by 2035 as imports from China and Asia balloon.[7] Thus, even without a substantial redesign of the existing network, significant increases in demand on our transportation network will put severe pressure on existing funding sources. How much money we will need is a big question mark.

We are proposing the most ambitious redesign and rebuilding of a road network ever. Yet, as a nation we aren't even keeping up with current needs. Throughout the middle part of this decade, a series of reports have examined transportation needs and spending. Their results are bracing.

- The American Society of Civil Engineers estimates that we need to spend $124.6 billion each year on our roads, bridges, and transit systems, compared to the roughly $44 billion we currently spend per year, just to maintain and bring our current system up to "good" repair.[8] That's not even considering the kinds of projects we outlined in earlier chapters to make our cities function effectively and improve mobility.
- The National Cooperative Highway Research Program (NCHRP) estimated that the annual gap between revenues and the investment needed to "improve" highway and transit systems was about $105 billion. Current trends will push the gap up by another third (to $134 billion) by 2017.[9] Just maintaining the current system without deterioration, the NCHRP said, would require $50.7 billion more than available revenues in 2007.

This deficit would increase to $66 billion by 2017. This adds up to a $1.3 trillion shortfall to keep the system treading water and completely ignores the need to improve or redesign the system.

- The National Surface Transportation Policy and Revenue Study Commission released its report claiming we need to spend between $241 and $286 billion every year to maintain and improve our entire transportation system (including waterways, freight railroads, Amtrak, etc.) even if we adopt aggressive strategies to slow down travel demand and price the national highway using variable rate tolling and congestion charges.[10]

The bottom line for *all* of these reports, including the ones we haven't mentioned, is that we have been underinvesting in transportation infrastructure for decades, and the gap between needs and revenues is growing.[11] By underinvesting we have allowed congestion to build up and a huge maintenance backlog to accrue. We should assume there is a lot of padding in those estimates and that some investments could be made more efficiently; our transportation system is not performance based so needs estimates are a mix of engineering and traffic modeling and politics and special interest agendas. At the end of the day though, we probably need to spend at least a trillion dollars more on transportation over the next decade than we expect in revenues if we want to keep up with growth in travel and goods movement.

The need to find a more efficient and effective funding mechanism has never been greater. Transportation projects are funded from a variety of sources. Over half the funds flowing into our surface transportation infrastructure comes from fuel and vehicle taxes.[12] Unfortunately, fuel taxes are an increasingly unsustainable funding source. Inflation steadily erodes the purchasing power of fuel tax revenues, which are rarely increased since raising gas taxes is politically unpopular. At the same time fuel efficiency for cars has increased 54 percent since 1975.[13] Thus, more people pay less in taxes for each mile they drive, even as that mile is more expensive to maintain, and even as the demand for road travel increases. And it's going to get worse. Fuel efficiency standards passed in 2007 require new auto fleets to improve 40 percent from today to an average 35 miles a gallon by 2020. This means fuel tax revenues will continue to shrink relative to use of the system. Economists have a term for this: fiscal illusion. We have created a false perception that we are paying for a public service through taxes when, in fact, we are not.[14]

The consequences are already evident in the federal highway trust fund. According to both the Congressional Budget Office and the U.S. Department of the Treasury, if nothing changes, the federal highway account will be in the red in 2009 followed by the transit account in 2012. The system is pay as you go. When the transportation accounts go into deficit, either federal transportation spending has to shrink or revenues have to come from other sources. States are facing similar challenges. If the highway trust fund were a private business, it would be looking at bankruptcy in 2009 and its bond status would be falling to junk status or lower.

In short, it's not just the design of the transportation network that needs an update. Our funding system needs a similarly comprehensive makeover. Tweaking a funding lever here or there, or rounding the edges of the current gas tax, won't cut it. These revenue streams are simply not politically sustainable.

If we are going to deal with current shortfalls in our transportation infrastructure *and* put mobility first, we need a funding system that will get the job done. That means major changes in the way we fund transportation. Simply pumping more money into the system that got us where we are now by, for example, raising fuel taxes, will only put off the day of reckoning and the problem to get worse. First and foremost, we will need a more user fee-based system that is based on performance, connecting where and how we use the transportation system with how we pay for it. Second, we will need to redefine the roles of the private sector and government in transportation funding and service provision. Third, we have to fix the problems with the way transportation dollars are spent, including better ways of setting priorities for transportation projects, linking funding to performance, and creating more accountability. We're a long way from reaching those goals, but we are in a better position than ever before to attain them.

The Primacy of User Fees

A sustainable funding system for transportation links what people pay to what they use: A direct user-fee system. By linking revenue directly to benefits, we accomplish two critical goals. First we create a constituency for continued investment in transportation. Second, paying based on what we use sends clear signals about what parts of the system are in demand and where investments should be made.

Fuel taxes are only an indirect user fee, and some could legitimately question whether they are a user fee at all. Fuel taxes generate revenue based on the energy source for the vehicle, not the wear and tear on the road, bridge, or other facility. An electric car will still wear down the pavement as much as a gasoline-powered car, but the electric car won't pay fuel taxes. General fund tax revenues, mainly from state and local governments, make up 14 percent of our total highway funding right now. Investment income and bond issue proceeds make up another 16 percent (some of which are toll revenue bonds and so are user fees). Thus, close to 30 percent of current highway funding comes from sources that are not remotely considered user fees. Moreover, the current funding system generates far less revenue than necessary just to maintain the road network (and other transportation infrastructure), and gas taxes represent a declining share of total surface transportation expenditures.[15] On the national level, attempts to increase the gas tax have failed every time they've been proposed since 1993. Yet, general taxes dilute political support for investing in transportation because nonusers pay but don't directly benefit from the system. There's our fiscal illusion. In other words, we are a very, very far away from having a funding system that is a true user fee.

Right now motorists pay about 3 cents per mile they drive.[16] But the cost of using roads is much higher, averaging 10 to 29 cents per mile traveled depending on what peak travel time and congestion costs are factored in.[17] The fares that transit users pay are usually less than 50 percent of the operating cost of their trip (and cover none of the capital costs, in contrast with highways, where user fees cover the majority of both capital and operating costs), and much of the balance comes from fuel taxes paid by road users. Heavy trucks pay a larger share, but they only pay about 80 percent of the costs they impose on the road system.[18]

We shouldn't be surprised that our transportation infrastructure is falling apart. We've provided no effective way for transportation system users to participate in the funding process in a meaningful way. We also provide few if any incentives for our transportation providers to pay attention to users. The ballot box is a cumbersome and imprecise mechanism for providing accountability for a service as tangible as a road. Real user fees will help us get around these problems.

Direct user fees like tolls that vary by road performance and demand can fully capture the appropriate share of the costs of the system imposed by each user. They provide a meaningful way for consumers to provide direct input into the system as well as a mechanism for promoting active management of the facilities. User fees, when they are calibrated to mirror consumer-based performance criteria (e.g., speeds or traffic flow), are effective market prices, promoting efficiency and creating valuable feedback loops about demand and the need for new capacity. Our willingness to pay a premium to use a road at certain times of the day is a good indicator that the route needs to be expanded or a parallel route provided. Thus, they link demand with supply— our willingness to pay is inextricably tied to the incentives road managers have to manage their facilities efficiently.

An important caveat is that ownership and incentives matter. Government toll agencies often lack the incentives to take into account the feedback that comes from pricing when making decisions on investments and setting toll rates. Political structures respond more to public pressure than accounting and traffic flow analyses of proper prices. Take the Indiana Toll Road. Prior to the state's lease of the toll road to a consortium of private toll companies, the toll rates had not been increased in nearly 20 years. *Barrons* asked Gov. Mitch Daniels how much it cost to collect a 15-cent toll. "This being government," he responded, "nobody knew, and they finally came back to me and said it was 34 cents. My response was that we'd be better off on the honor system."[19] Government-owned toll roads are on average about half as efficient at privately-owned ones.[20]

These inefficiencies have consequences. Recall the Minnesota bridge collapse and the fact that 23 percent of bridges in the U.S. are deficient. It turns out that forty-one percent of U.S. toll authority bridges are deficient—either structurally or functionally.[21]

Breaking down the federal data a little more reveals an interesting split. Tolled bridges are in *better* shape when only their structural (engineering) adequacy is considered.[22] Tolled bridges are worse than free bridges when they are compared by functional characteristics—whether the bridge meets the needs of travelers or current design standards. In other words, the dedicated revenue from tolls keeps the bridges in better shape, but it doesn't ensure that new investments are made by government toll agencies to meet changing or rising consumer demand.

Just because bridges or roads are tolled doesn't mean they are run like real businesses with the consumer's best interest at heart. Most tolls that are in place are not actively used to manage the road system's efficiency, or apply willingness-to-pay criteria to determine when, where, and how new investments in the network should be made. Most were instituted by public-sector toll agencies as pass-through mechanisms for retiring the toll facility's construction debt in place of raising general taxes. "Their accounts are primitive," observes Peter Samuel, editor of widely read web site TollroadsNews.com "Most don't depreciate more than a bit of movable equipment, [with] no attempt to do depreciation on their major assets, their road and bridge capital. They are basically cash accounts."[23] In other words, the revenues are not tied to performance in a meaningful way. A few exceptions are the 91 Express Lanes in Southern California, the I-394 HOT lanes in Minneapolis, and the I-15 HOT lanes in San Diego.

The incentive problems government toll agencies face are an important caveat, but direct user fees still have many advantages. As tolls are more widely applied, the means for dealing with incentive and political problems will likely emerge as they have on the California and Minnesota toll roads already.

We're pretty far from making direct user fees a reality on most of the current transportation system. Tolls provide only five percent of total surface transportation funding.[24] Fortunately, direct user charges in the form of tolls are becoming a more important part of the system. About one-third of new limited-access highway lane-miles built over the last decade in the United States were tolled.[25]

Many major cities and important regional corridors include toll roads and lanes as part of their overall road network. Still, over the next 15 years or so we might be able to get to where tolling accounts for 10 percent to 20 percent of new capital investment in roads and bridges. And the investment capital private companies bring to building and reconstructing roads can only fill part of the gap between current revenue and needs.

The key is to use direct user fees as we move forward to finance the redesign, rebuilding, and expansion of the existing road network to meet the dynamic needs of the twenty-first century city in a globally competitive economy. An analysis of new road projects in several major corridors of large urban areas in the U.S. by Reason Foundation found many of these projects could be fully self-supporting, or nearly self-supporting.

An even more direct user fee would be a direct mileage charge. The technology exists now to put GPS systems in cars that can keep track of the miles a vehicle drives. Each vehicle then is charged according to how much it uses the system, not how much gas it uses. The technology allows setting variable rates based on time of day, which roads are traveled, fuel efficiency or emission characteristics of the vehicles, etc.

Technology is once again providing new ways to charge road users, eroding significant barriers to the private provision of roads. The most promising U.S. experiment is taking place in Oregon. Like nearly all states, Oregon was faced

Table 11.1. User Fees and Road Finance

Project	Est. cost	Self-support (%)
South Pasadena Tunnel (4.5 mile, 4 lanes each direction)	$1.5 billion	100%
Palmdale-Glendale Tunnel (21 miles [5 miles at grade]; double decked)	$3.1 billion	83%
Riverside-Orange County Tunnel (14 miles)	$7.1 billion	59%
LA HOT Lane network (1,009 lane-miles [385 of them new])	$13.5 billion	92%
San Bernardino-Riverside Cos. HOT Lane network (410 lane-miles [320 of them new])	$5.8 billion	72%
Atlanta Congestion Mitigation (HOT Lane network, truck toll lanes, and new tunnel)	$25 billion	78%

Source: Reason Foundation

with a substantial erosion in transportation funding, as increased fuel economy reduced gasoline tax revenues per mile driven, along with strong political resistance to increasing gasoline tax rates. Using state-of-the-art GPS technology, the state experimented with levying a charge on drivers based on the miles they traveled rather than the gas they consumed. In the pilot project, the state levied a mileage charge that differed based on whether the driver was traveling in state, out of state, or at peak periods.[26]

In Oregon, motorists had a device in their car that used the GPS system to keep track of the miles the vehicles traveled. Then, each time the vehicle was refueled, the device communicated with another at the gas station. The driver then got a receipt that showed the total price for the gas, subtracted out the gas tax, and added in the mileage charge. In Germany, a GPS system of charging heavy trucks for mileage is used and a similar system is about to be implemented in the Netherlands.

Conceptually, this is a much more efficient funding system since mileage is a much better indicator of impact on the road system than fuel consumed. More importantly, with a mileage charge that varies by time of day, drivers would be given stronger and more direct information about the economic cost of traveling on particular roads at particular times. Since GPS technology provides a means for levying fees based on the specific location and time a car is driving, revenues can be raised directly from the users and prices can be used to manage traffic flow. In short, technology is helping shift roads from the classic case of a public good to a private one.

Technology is also providing a more competitive environment on the supply side. While road networks still may need to be designed in a holistic context, specific elements and segments of the road network probably should not be managed or operated through a monopoly. By allowing multiple providers to choose different levels of service and quality, regions can more effectively tailor services to specific segments of travelers. For example, operators specializing in meeting the needs of commercial truck traffic may be better owners, operators and managers of commercial roads, with stronger incentives to create (and maintain) facilities such as truck-only toll lanes. Similarly, other operators may specialize in providing road facilities for passenger traffic. Santiago, Chile, has a network of six tolled expressways operated by different firms that coordinate on tolling transponder technology, etc., and provide smooth interoperability to users.[27]

New cars are already incorporating technology capable of being used in such a system. Over time this kind of mileage charge could replace the gas tax and be integrated with toll roads to allow a direct user fee system that can adapt as the source of financing for roads changes. New technologies will allow the driver to see in real time what he is paying for a given road and will empower drivers more than ever to know and control their travel costs.

Reshaping U.S. Transportation Funding

An equally big challenge is the restructuring of the roles and responsibilities within the transportation system. Currently the federal government provides a significant share of funding to state and local transportation agencies, and sets policy and research agendas. State and local governments provide the bulk of funding and plan, build and maintain the transportation networks. The private sector plays a small but important supporting role.

The most important new idea that must be embraced is the increasingly important role of the private sector in providing roads. The fact that private capital is now being used to build a significant number of the nation's new limited-access highway lane-miles and high profile projects in states like California, Texas, and Virginia, shows that this new idea is catching on. New roads provide a lot of value to the users. Generally, people are willing to pay tolls for new roads if they know that traditional funding is not sufficient to build the road. For private investors new toll roads are an attractive investment, offering long term returns from projects that face growing demand over time. Standard and Poor's estimates that in 2006 alone $100 billion to $150 billion was raised globally by private firms to invest in infrastructure. Much of that could be invested in America if we would let it.[28] The win-win potential of public-private partnerships for a lot of new roads is pretty obvious.

Ultimately direct user pricing and private investment meld to make widespread private road networks feasible and desirable. Table 11.2 highlights how different the financing, decisions, and outcomes are in a typical privately owned network compared to the current publicly operated highway system. In the long run, a private road system will be more responsive to changing travel and needs, and less subject to the vagaries of politics.

Table 11.2. Institutional Response in Private Telecom Networks vs. Government Highway Network

	Telecom system	*Highway system*
Structure	Interconnected network, multiple providers	Interconnected network multiple providers
Ownership	Private sector investors	Public sector
Revenues	User charges	User taxes
Investment criteria	Return on investment	Political process
Pricing	Demand-based	Virtually nonexistent
Response to congestion	Raise price, add capacity	Discourage use
Incentive for maintenance	Risk of decline in asset value	When appropriations permit
Response to new technology	Entrepreneurial	Cautious

Savvy state and local governments should be looking at this willingness to invest by the private sector as an opportunity. A strategic analysis of all the investment needs combined with private sector input to help identify projects where private capital might work would free up a lot of traditional government revenues for other purposes. Revenues from new user fee systems like mileage charges could also go to system maintenance and to projects that are needed but not easily funded by tolls. The end result should be a significant filling of the gap between revenues and needs.

For an example, our colleague Robert Poole looked at how this might work in Atlanta.[29] Typical rush-hour trips there today take 46 percent longer than at free flow, and by 2030 will take 85 percent longer under current plans (exceeding today's levels in Los Angeles). Poole examined existing plans, the road network, and traffic models and created a plan for new road capacity in Atlanta to eliminate the most severe stop-and-go congestion (Level of Service F). His plan consisted of current plans for arterial projects, plus:

- A complete network of variably priced express toll lanes on the existing freeway system, totaling 1,258 lane miles, providing reliable, uncongested travel for buses, vanpools, and paying vehicles—a HOT network.
- A north-south tunnel linking the southern end of Georgia 400 with the current terminus of I-675, with interchanges at I-20 and Freedom Parkway (to serve downtown); this new link would provide the equivalent of six additional lanes on the I-75/85 Downtown Connector.
- A new east-west link to relieve I-20, made up of the existing Lakewood freeway, extended to the east by a new toll tunnel and to the west by upgrading portions of Campbellton Road and Camp Creek Parkway to freeway level.
- A separate, voluntary toll truckway system that would bypass Atlanta's congestion in exchange for paying a toll.

The estimated cost of these projects is $25.1 billion in 2005 dollars. Toll revenue would allow private firms to finance all but $4.04 billion of those costs. (But these projects would make unnecessary $4.9 billion in planned spending to add 688 lane miles of HOV and busway lanes.)

Thanks to this new HOT network, tunnels and truckways, mobility would improve dramatically. All these recommendations were run through the transportation model of the Atlanta Regional Commission. They not only eliminated severe congestion in 2030, but:

- Led to a small decrease (0.61 percent) in overall vehicle miles traveled (VMT);

- Reduced vehicle hours of travel 27.2 percent due to faster trips;
- Sped up travel time for most trips;
- Provided an alternative for individuals willing to pay a toll to avoid congestion on the freeways when they need to;
- Gave the bus transit system access to 1,133 lane-miles of congestion-free busway by 2024 rather than waiting to 2030 for a mere 688 lane miles of busway in the current transportation plan for Atlanta; and
- Increased regional personal income by $175 billion thanks to improved access for workers and firms.

Combining bold vision, private sector financing and management, and the use of tolls on new capacity would allow Atlanta to achieve mobility improvements that would be the envy of cities nationwide.

The Changing Federal Role

The federal government's current role in transportation funding was defined by the construction of the Interstate Highway System. A decades-old vision of a national highway system became a concrete plan when President Eisenhower signed the Federal Aid Highway Act in 1956. The federal gas tax was increased and dedicated to funding the construction of the system.[30] Importantly, while the federal government funded construction, state departments of transportation were responsible for identifying the details of the routes and managing the projects. They are still responsible for maintaining them, although federal regulations impose significant constraints on how these roads are managed (including prohibitions on implementing tolls and other direct user fees). State gasoline taxes are used largely to build and maintain state highways and to provide funding to local governments for local roads and transit projects. Local governments control few of their own transportation funds, depending mainly upon distributions from federal and state gas tax revenues.

The federal government, in fact, was likely the only institution capable of embarking on such a massive program in the middle of the twentieth century. Private roads and bridges were simply too small in scale and scope to be able to undertake such a project, and private markets didn't have the capacity to coordinate the capital necessary to make it work. The technology didn't exist to make market pricing a cost effective option for most roads since tollbooths and manual toll collection quickly ate into the core benefits of roads—mobility. Moreover, interstate highways would largely be a federal function because they required crossing state borders. The political hurdles were significant for states (and local governments) so a pre-emptive role of the federal government made sense. Roads on the scale envisioned in the middle of the twentieth century were, in the true economic sense, public goods.

Those times have changed. Fifty years later, the economics and politics of providing transportation infrastructure have shifted in fundamental ways. Unless the funding system reflects these changes, the process will implode. In fact, it already is imploding.

This current system is fragile. Absent a central focus and goal, federal gas taxes have become pass-through funds. Congress allocates transportation funding in a very politicized process to fund state and local transportation needs. The number of "earmarks"—specific projects inserted into legislation by individual members of Congress—has increased from just ten in 1982, to 1,850 in 1998, to 6,371 in the 2005 federal highway bill.[31]

Federal transportation dollars should be narrowly focused on transportation projects that are clearly national in scope or impact. Rather than mainly funding state programs through a highly politicized process plagued by redistribution, pork barrel spending, and projects that would never pass a cost benefit analysis, federal transportation policy should focus on key areas of national interest:

- *Interstate highway upgrades.* There are many state highways that link up regionally in fast growing corridors where eventually an upgrade to an interstate is going to make sense. It would be sensible for the federal government to play a leadership role, in cooperation with state and local governments, in planning and funding those upgrades.
- *Multi-state coordination.* As urban areas have expanded, many transportation problems and issues have taken on multi-state dimensions. Currently, Missouri and Illinois are squabbling over how to pay for a bridge over the Mississippi at St. Louis. Kentucky and Ohio have struggled to find common ground on bridges spanning the Ohio River. Some urbanized areas such as Cincinnati span two or more states. The federal government can serve a useful role in mediating and even coordinating transportation decisions, infrastructure, and funding, given its constitutional role in facilitating interstate commerce.
- *Freight corridors.* Our producers need the roads to get materials in and products out; our services need roads to interact with customers; and our consumers need roads to connect with goods and services. Major goods-movement corridors and bottlenecks that often arise in them are regional and national assets, and the federal government should prioritize adequate capacity in them. This would include routes branching out from seaports and major border crossings, and connecting manufacturing areas with population centers.

• *Transportation research, safety and related issues.* Research into new technologies and methods of managing transportation systems, coordinating common standards, incentivizing experimentation and innovation, etc. have been at times and could remain a focus of federal transportation policy.

A shift to these priorities would mean the federal government largely backing out of the regular project grant-making process. It also means that federal funds for purely local projects would go away. This would require a few years of transition as federal programs shift focus, and state and local governments adjust to fund their own transportation systems. Part of the transition should be shifting, a bit at a time, federal transportation grants to a more performance basis where the relative costs and benefits of competing projects are considered. A good example is the program for grants for new transit projects called "New Starts" which SAFETEA-LU revised to evaluate proposed project grants on a performance basis.[32]

State and Local Leadership

The biggest gap between transportation revenue and needs is at the state and local level. States face extensive maintenance burdens and many need to add new highway and expand existing one. But the real focus of need for new infrastructure, as we spent many chapters describing, is in our urban areas. Yet, local governments depend heavily on federal and state funds for most major transportation projects.

The dynamic nature of travel patterns and the changing nature of mobility in urban economic development suggest decisions about transportation infrastructure investments need to be shifted to the state and local level and away from the federal level. That is where real leadership, making transportation one of the top priorities, and a willingness to embrace new ideas and approaches will be crucial. The key is to ensure state and local leaders have the flexibility and tools they need to make these investments happen in a way that improves mobility and, subsequently, urban economic performance. They not only have to step up to meet the current shortfalls in investments, but also to fill in as the federal government focuses more narrowly. The synergy with the growth of private investment is crucial, since major increases in state and local transportation funding will be politically challenging.

States should not see a big change in the scope of their roles and responsibilities, just the scale (particularly with funding). Transportation will have to become a bigger priority for most states, commensurate with its role in the state economy and its residents' quality of life. Local governments would face a similar transition but need to be empowered. In the current system, cities and counties depend significantly on state and federal grants to fund their transportation needs. They have little control over how much funding they will receive. Much of the grant money they get comes with strings attached that limit their ability to plan and prioritize their own projects. Providing local governments with a local user fee option to generate revenues will give them the ability to tackle transportation needs locally with dedicated revenues. After all, most severe congestion in America is a local problem in urbanized areas. State legislatures should also consider passing enabling legislation that permits regional planning and funding for transportation networks, much as Texas has done through the creation of Regional Mobility Authorities with independent powers to build and fund new roads. This is particularly important in urban areas that have regional road networks spanning multiple counties. Fortunately, as toll roads become a more important part of the transportation network, local governments will be able to build new capacity funded through local user fees. Adopting a mileage charge system would make local user fees very easy.

Transit funding would change as well. Federal funds are mostly limited to special projects and capital outlays and make up under 18 percent of transit expenditures. Since the benefits of transit are almost entirely local, federal funding would be phased out.

Making It Work

All these changes unveil the 800-pound gorilla in the transportation funding quagmire: How will state and local governments make up for declining federal grants and take the lead on increasing transportation funding? State and local governments are already underinvesting in transportation, and we are asking them to increase funding substantially. Private investment can provide some of the increase. Indiana fully funded its ten-year transportation capital investment program when it leased the Indiana Toll Road to a private consortium for nearly $4 billion. Nevertheless, private funding will remain a small but important share in the short run.

But state and local governments can learn some lessons from those cities and counties that have passed local property or sales taxes to fund transportation in recent years.[33] The success of many of these taxes at the ballot box indicates citizens are willing to tax themselves at higher levels to increase transportation spending when the benefits are identifiable and the promises made by public officials credible. As tolling and mileage charges become more common, people should be even more willing to embrace these user fees as a substitute for sales and property taxes.

State and local officials should emphasize two overarching themes when approaching the general public about the need for increased transportation funding. First, people have to believe that existing funds are being well spent and new funds will be as well—that they are getting good value for money. State and local government need to pursue policies and management practices to ensure transportation systems are maintained as efficiently as possible and new projects are built as efficiently as possible. This is currently not the case in many jurisdictions. The transportation planning and management system has built up layers of process and procedures that, while solving some problems, don't emphasize outcomes and cost containment. A study looking at highway projects nationwide over the past 30 years found that it takes on average 13.1 years from planning to completion, and more time means higher costs.[34]

Policies that do not favor efficiency abound. Despite great success at reducing costs and backlogs in places where it has been tried, few states contract out significant amounts of their highway maintenance.[35] Perhaps worse, many states do not allow "design build" approaches to new transportation projects and many also do not allow public-private partnerships. While neither design build nor PPPs are always appropriate, both often can be a more efficient way to build a project, and they should be part of the toolbox for transportation and tolling agencies. Not allowing them to be considered means the government is putting protecting special interests over best value for the transportation dollar.

If the general public is going to entrust the government with more funds for transportation, they will have to know that striving to give value for money is the top priority government policy and management decisions.

Second, transparency should be a fundamental element of any proposal to fund new infrastructure. The public has to know that the right things are being done with transportation funds. The "Bridge to Nowhere" is the current poster child for earmarks, which themselves are iconic of the politicized distribution of transportation funds that too often ignores priorities based on costs and benefits. Projects that benefit a few or an obvious vocal interest group, or the district of a powerful politician, at the expense of projects widely known to be needed, greatly undermine people's willingness to invest more in the system. Projects should be funded based on a transparent process that analyzes costs and benefits and stacks them up against alternatives so everyone can see which should be the top priorities.

Conclusion

U.S. cities (and the nation) are facing a transportation funding crisis as much as a breakdown in the core infrastructure that keeps their economies flowing smoothly and efficiently. General taxes to support infrastructure have not proven to be a sustainable source of funds. The only tax that has a proven record of generating dedicated revenues for transportation—the fuel tax—is becoming less effective as technology reduces our demand for gasoline per mile traveled and inflation erodes the value of money over time. The only way we will be able to ensure our transportation is viable over the long term is to put the direct beneficiaries of the system in charge of the funding. That means, inevitably, moving toward a direct user-fee based system for funding *all* the nation's transportation infrastructure.

Phasing out the gas tax is not practical in the short run, nor are we advocating that legislators drop it tomorrow. Over a 15 to 20 year period, we can transition to a mileage based fee that generates revenue based on real-time usage in a way that we can manage the system at peak efficiency. More importantly, we will be able to use variable rate, dynamically tolled mileage charges to figure out what infrastructure needs to be built in what place and at what time. This is technically possible now. The key is to make it economically viable. The current system has no effective way to give us the information necessary to make these decisions because taxes don't coordinate supply and demand, let alone embrace the value consumers place in improving and expanding road infrastructure in economically efficient ways.

At the same time, increasing private sector participation both brings new private investment capital to meeting the funding gap, and helps us to get the most bang for our current bucks. Combined with a shift to user fees, we enable all the changes and improvements we have suggested in earlier chapters.

Notes

1. David T. Hartgen and Ravi K. Karanam, *16th Annual Report on the on the Performance of State Highway Systems (1984–2005)* Policy Study No. 360 (Los Angeles: Reason Foundation, June 2007), http://www.reason.org/ps360/, accessed 18 February 2008.

2. Federal Highway Administration, *2006 Status of the Nation's Highways, Bridges, and Transit: Conditions and Performance,* (Washington D.C.: U.S. Department of Transportation), Exhibit 3-6, http://www.fhwa.dot.gov/policy/2006cpr/chap3.htm#highway.

3. Hartgen and Karanam, *16th Annual Report.*

4. National Surface Transportation Policy and Revenue Study Commission, *Transportation for Tomorrow,* Volume II, pp. 2–11; Bureau of Transportation Statistics, National Transportation Statistics Table 1-32, July 2007.

5. Federal Highway Administration, *Highway Statistics Series,* (Washington D.C.: U.S. Department of Transportation), Table VM-1, http://www.fhwa.dot.gov/policy/ohpi/hss/

6. National Surface Transportation Policy and Revenue Study Commission, *Transportation for Tomorrow,* Volume II, pp. 2–4.

7. Ibid, pp. 2–12.

8. See the American Society of Civil Engineers Infrastructure "2005 Report Card for America's Infrastructure," http://www.asce.org/reportcard/2005/index.cfm.

9. National Cooperative Highway Research Program, *Future Financing Options to Meet Highway and Transit Needs,* NCHRP Web-Only Document 102, December 2006, pp. 2–15.

10. National Surface Transportation Policy and Revenue Study Commission, *Transportation for Tomorrow,* Final Report, December 2007, Volume II, Chapter 4, Exhibit 4-22, pp. 4–26.

11. See also U.S. Department of Transportation, *2006 Status of the Nation's Highways, Bridges, and Transit: Conditions & Performance,* 2006; National Cooperative Highway Research Program, *Future Financing Options to Meet Highway and Transit Needs,* NCHRP Web-Only Document 102, December 2006; American Association of State Highway and Transportation Officials, *Transportation, Invest in America, The Bottom Line,* 2001; and National Chamber Foundation, *Future Highway and Public Transportation Financing,* 2005.

12. National Surface Transportation Policy and Revenue Study Commission, *Transportation for Tomorrow,* Volume II, pp. 5-2, Exhibit 5-2.

13. U.S. Environmental Protection Agency, *Light-Duty Automotive Technology and Fuel Economy Trends: 1975 Through 2007,* September 2007, http://www.epa.gov/oms/cert/mpg/fetrends/420s07001.htm.

14. Technically, this might be "reverse" fiscal illusion. Fiscal illusion occurs when government spending expands because of an "illusion" that revenues were generated to cover the expenditures. Thus, a federal grant to a local government does not result in lower taxes, but higher local spending (the "flypaper effect"), because citizens and local officials are under the illusion that the local services are paid for locally. In the case of transportation, the fiscal illusion stems from the perception that revenues pay for the level of road services we need when, in fact, they fall well short.

15. Comparing Table HF-10 in the 1995 and 2005 Federal Highway Administration, *Highway Statistics,* shows that user fees' share of total transportation spending declined over 5 percent during that decade.

16. Federal Highway Administration, *Highway Statistics,* 2005, Table VM-1 and Table HF-10. Total highway vehicle miles traveled was 2.9 trillion in 2005 and total fuel tax and toll revenues were about $90 billion.

17. HLB Decision Economics Inc., U.S. Department of Transportation, Road Pricing on a National Scale, 14 March 2005, page 30, Table 7-2.

18. Federal Highway Administration, *Addendum to the1997 Federal Highway Cost Allocation Study, Final Report*, May 2000, Table 7.

19. Andrew Bary, "Paying Up," *Barrons*, 8 May 2006.

20. Robert W. Poole, Jr. and Peter Samuel, *Pennsylvania Turnpike Alternatives: A Review and Critique of the Democratic Caucus Study*, Reason Foundation Policy Brief No. 70 (Los Angeles: Reason Foundation), April 2008, http://www.reason.org/pb70.pdf examined a set of 35 toll roads in the U.S. and overseas and found that for the government toll authorities costs averaged 42.6 percent of revenue while for private toll roads costs were only 23.4 percent of revenue. Profit rates for the private toll roads are regulated by the government.

21. Peter Samuel, "Toll Bridges in Much Worse Shape Than State Bridges—FHWA Data," *TollroadsNews*, 18 February 2008, http://www.tollroadsnews.cm/node/3403, last accessed 19 February 2008.

22. "Toll bridges lag state with old geometry, structural problems of toll not as bad (Followup)," TollroadsNews, 19 February 2008, http://tollroadsnews.com/node/3404, last accessed 20 February 2008.

23. Interview with Peter Samuel, editor, TollroadsNews.com, by Sam Staley, via personal email correspondence, 19 February 2008.

24. Federal Highway Administration, *Highway Statistics*, 2005, Table HF-10.

25. Benjamin Perez and Stephen Lockwood, *Current Toll Road Activity in the U.S.: A Survey and Analysis*, Office of Transportation Studies, Federal Highway Administration, August 2006, p. 2.

26. For an overview of the final report on the Oregon VMT program, see James M. Whitty, *Oregon's Mileage Fee Concept and Road User Fee Pilot Program: Final Report*, Oregon Department of Transportation, Salem, Oregon, November 2007.

27. Jorge Garreton, "Road Warrior: Santiago Battles Traffic and Pollution with an Interconnected System of Toll Roads," *Latin Trade*, November 2005; Peter Samuel, "Santiago Pikes Make Own Charges—Draw on Central Customer Database," *TollroadsNews*, 3 June 2005; and Peter Samuel, "Santiago Chile now has one of world's largest exclusive open road toll (ORT) systems, "*TollroadsNews*, 5 December 2006.

28. Michael Wilkins, "The Amazing Growth Of Global Infrastructure Funds: Too Good To Be True?" Standard and Poor's Rating Services, 30 November 2006.

29. All of the following on Atlanta comes from Robert W. Poole, Jr., *Reducing Congestion in Atlanta: A Bold New Approach to Increasing Mobility*, Reason Foundation Policy Study No. 351 (Los Angles: Reason Foundation), November 2006.

30. Richard F. Weingroff, "Federal-Aid Highway Act of 1956: Creating the Interstate System," *Public Roads*, (Summer 1996), Vol. 60, No. 1.

31. Ronald D. Utt, "A Primer on Lobbyists, Earmarks, and Congressional Reform," Backgrounder No. 1924 (Washington, D.C.: Heritage Foundation, 27 April 2006), table 1, http://www.heritage.org/research/budget/bg1924.cfm.

32. Government Accountability Office, *New Starts Program is in a Period of Transition*, August 2006, http://www.gao.gov/new.items/d06819.pdf.

33. Todd Goldman and Martin Wachs, "A Quiet Revolution in Transportation Finance: The Rise of Local Option Transportation Taxes," *Transportation Quarterly*, Vol. 57, No. 1, (2003), pp. 19–32.

34. Federal Highway Administration, *Evaluating the Performance of Environmental Streamlining: Development of a NEPA Baseline for Measuring Continuous Performance,* 5.1 Conclusions. http://www.environment.fhwa.dot.gov/strmlng/baseline/index.asp.

35. Geoffrey F. Segal, Adrian T. Moore, and Samuel McCarthy, *Contracting for Road and Highway Maintenance,* Reason Foundation How-to-Guide No. 21, March 2003, http://www.reason.org/htg21.pdf.

12

Charting the Uncharted

W E'VE LAID OUT THE CASE FOR WHY THE U.S. transportation system is in dire need of transformation. Performance is plummeting as our urban areas are becoming more congested. Lower performance is compromising the economic competitiveness of our cities. In order to restore the competitive efficiency of our transportation system, we will need to retrofit our regional transportation networks to fit modern travel needs. We will need to invest in 3-D infrastructure and reconfigure our networks based on the mesh of a spiderweb.

This retrofitting mandates that transportation planners and policy makers embrace cars, at least for the near term, and the new capacity to move them efficiently around the city. Cars provide the automobility people want, fusing speed, flexibility, and adaptability into one travel technology. In a service-based economy faced with global competition, cars provide the most efficient, effective, and productive transportation alternative.

This doesn't mean that mass transit is useless. On the contrary, it is an important part of the transportation network that could become even more important if it is integrated into the road system rather than set off as a separate component. To be competitive in the twenty-first century, economies must cater to the customized travel and personal needs of individuals and households and transit is not immune to this requirement.

Paradoxically, it's not the automobile that will define the character of the twenty-first century transportation network. It's the customized nature of travel choices. The specific technology is less important than the types of demand for travel it serves. Thus, we need a regional transportation system that caters to, and reflects the needs of, the millions of households that make trips each day in our cities. Currently, our regional transportation networks don't reflect this dynamism or complexity. The wagon wheel must give way to the spiderweb.

This is uncharted territory. No other economy has achieved the mobility and wealth that Americans currently experience. Yet, we are in danger of losing our competitive edge if we don't embark on a comprehensive redesign of our transportation system, including a major commitment to adding new capacity, with a new layer of roads in tunnels, along with queue jumpers, elevated roads, flyovers and upgraded arterials on the surface.

If we were writing this book 100 years ago, many people would have scoffed at such an ambitious proposal. Automobiles were still a novelty. Only forward thinking entrepreneurs like Henry Ford, Ransom Olds, or Karl Benz foresaw the revolution that the car would foist upon the U.S. and the world. Similarly, the idea of a transcontinental network of interstate highways (let alone tunnels or stacked roadways) was a pipedream, waiting for an endorsement from the federal government in the form of the Clay Committee and the commitment to making it a reality by a president acutely aware of the dangers of regional fragmentation. Like the railroads in the nineteenth century, the highways pulled together disparate parts of U.S. culture and economy, galvanizing them into a juggernaut that still defines global politics and trade. We are at risk of losing that eminence absent a wholly different way of thinking about transportation and mobility in a highly competitive, service-based global economy.

The twenty-first century transportation network will need to recognize the fluid travel patterns of commuters and noncommuters alike. These trends and patterns are already in play. Delays in taking the steps necessary to adjust to them will only degrade our transportation system's efficiency further, compromising the ability of our cities and national economy to compete effectively in the global marketplace. More specifically, our new, redesigned transportation system will have to:

- Build out new capacity, within economic regions by creating a 3-D spiderweb of interconnected routes that includes a tunnel network and some elevated roads as well as horizontally, as part of a mesh of roads of different sizes, types, and functions that serve all levels and lengths of trip whether local to regional in purpose;
- Provide sufficient physical capacity at local, arterial and regional levels while using road pricing to provide congestion free alternatives in the short run, reducing congestion to zero in the long run, *and* improving travel speeds;

- Be dynamic and responsive to the short and long-term needs of travelers on a regional basis, growing to keep up with demand, adopting new technologies and engineering ideas to provide for better mobility throughout the urban area;
- Use the newest engineering technologies to add capacity through queue jumpers, flyovers, intermediate roads, tunnels, bridges, and elevated highways;
- Manage those facilities with technologies such as variable rate tolling, traffic signal synchronization, ramp metering and other practical innovations that were merely theoretical musings a decade ago;
- Entail, by necessity, a dramatic increase in private sector involvement to fund new infrastructure, manage these facilities, design them, and build them, often through public-private partnership;
- Integrate mass transit into the network and strive for systems where multiple modes benefit from any new infrastructure and from reduced congestion and respond to consumer demand through pricing;
- Rely on a sustainable funding base routed in direct user fees, so the people that directly benefit from this new system will also pay for it, and so that changes in demand send clear signals on the need for changes in prices or adding more capacity.

These features of the twenty-first century transportation system are revolutionary. But each of them is grounded in practical, incremental changes to the overall system, and each allows us to transform the transportation network into a globally competitive one. They are the basis for the inevitably dramatic changes in the institutions that make up our transportation system.

The Fundamental Transformation of Transportation

The U.S. and other high-income nations are at a historic crossroad. In one of the few instances in modern history, we are seeing a fundamental reorientation and recasting of the nature and character of an economic service. Roads and transportation more generally, by virtue of national wealth and technology, are transitioning from what economists call a "public good" to a private one. This transition bodes well for the economy because the technologies enabling the transformation will also encourage investments far larger than ever contemplated before. Tolling, and electronic tolling in particular, was the critical ingredient necessary to allow private capital to step into Australian cities and build multibillion dollar stretches of tunnels and roadway capacity to create mobility. Sydney now has built four tunnels, and private capital is building

a fifth (the Lane Cove Tunnel), all thanks to the possibilities of tolling to induce the private sector into the daunting task of addressing the city's transportation challenges.

Why are we seeing this transformation?

The economic rationale for public goods is straightforward. Government
provides a good or service because the private sector cannot, or will not, despite important social benefits. To be successful, entrepreneurs must be able to
charge a price high enough to offset the costs of production. With public
goods, the private company sometimes cannot charge a price high enough to
generate revenue that covers its costs.

Traditionally, roads have provided a textbook case of a public good. An efficient and well functioning road system is a fundamental building block of
the economy. Yet, most observers believe the private sector has not historically
provided roads at a high enough level to meet rising demand, triggering government efforts to build roads and highways to meet the needs of a growing
and diversifying economy.

The private sector has fallen short for two primary reasons:

- Other drivers could not be practically "excluded" from the road (too many
  entrances, exits, and intersections), making it impossible for the private
  provider to charge a fee that would cover the costs of providing the service.
  Particularly with local roads, everyone has access. Even if major businesses
  benefiting significantly from the road were willing to fund it, "free riders"
  would undermine their willingness to pay for a service that benefits everyone. Thus, road networks, particularly local and regional ones, have been
  provided by government and funded by general taxes.
- The costs of negotiating, enforcing, and implementing contracts with
  suppliers and consumers—the transaction costs—have been historically
  high, preventing the private sector from building and managing this type
  of transportation service profitably. Identifying and negotiating the purchase of land and securing the rights-of-way for roads have traditionally
  created significant obstacles to private sector investment.

Roads occupy a defined amount of space. As more people use the road, the
ability of other drivers to maneuver and use it at free flow speeds becomes im-
paired. If the space available for vehicles is not increased—by building new
roads, widening existing roads, or reconfiguring existing road networks—
travel becomes congested, limiting mobility and the road's usefulness (and
discouraging additional use or demand). This means one person's use of the
road limits others' ability to use it to some degree. In economics this is called
rivalness and means it can be a private good.

So, it's the other two characteristics of public goods that have traditionally kept roads public goods. Attempts to price current roads to cover their costs would be doomed to failure because the availability of unpriced alternatives would be freely available. Few mechanisms exist to prevent drivers from avoiding payment by diverting to unpriced roads except for limited-access highways such as interstates. The transaction costs of assembling land also are thought to be prohibitive for the private sector, justifying the use of eminent domain to compel the acquisition of property for new roads.[1]

These justifications are eroding quickly. Paradoxically, rising traffic congestion and limited tax revenue for new road facilities stimulated the investment in new technologies that are laying a foundation for the effective and practical privatizing of roads. The higher levels of traffic congestion make the consequences of unregulated access to a facility that is subject to rivalness more acute. In the extreme cases, the road simply cannot perform its core function of providing mobility as traffic slows to a crawl.

Naturally, entrepreneurs see these conditions as an opportunity—consumers value roads for the mobility and access to the destinations they provide. In principle, they would be willing to pay for these services. If entrepreneurs could figure out ways to eliminate, or significantly mitigate, the problems of excludability and transactions costs that limit the private provision of roads, they could exploit a market opportunity and "monetize" the value by building new road facilities that guarantee mobility, allowing users to pay for the service.

We saw the first major step toward this new model of road construction and management in Canada. Ontario's Highway 407 ETR (electronic toll road) opened in 1997, providing the world with its first look at a twenty-first century highway. The east-west limited-access highway runs 67 miles just north of Toronto. What makes this road different is how it is paid for. It's a toll road, but toll collection is completely electronic. Overhead gantries identify cars and trucks going underneath, at every entry and exit point, and drivers are charged for the number of miles they drive on Highway 407. More than three-quarters of the daily travelers use electronic transponders that allow the 407 ETR Concession Company (owned by the Spanish company Cintra) to bill users to permanent accounts similar to debit or credit cards. The other users are identified visually and billed; video cameras photograph license plates and cross match the plate number with motor vehicle records. Thus, the toll road is boothless, allowing vehicles to travel the entire distance at free-flow speeds with minimal interruption. More importantly, the facility is self-financing because the toll acts as a true user fee.

The 407 ETR Concession Company operates on a 99-year concession (long-term lease) with the Ontario provincial government using technology developed by the former Hughes Aircraft (now Raytheon). The system has been so successful the roadway has already been widened several times. The highway started as a road with two lanes going in each direction (2 x 2). It was then expanded to 3 x 3 and in some places 4 x 4. Some sections are now even 5 x 5.[2]

While the 407 ETR's boothless system, dubbed "open road tolling" or ORT, was unique in its application to an entire roadway, the use of concession agreements with private companies to finance, build, operate, and maintain such facilities was not. As we have discussed in earlier chapters, numerous nations have used these agreements to add new road capacity to their systems.[3] These international projects have demonstrated that new road facilities, whether they are highways, tunnels, or bridges, can be privately funded, built, operated, and maintained from a sustainable, customer-based funding source. In short, they made revolutionary strides toward solving both the excludability and the transactions cost barriers to the private provision of roads.

On the demand side, ORT technology helped eliminate a significant impediment to a user-fee based system for funding new roads—the delays and safety concerns associated with traffic slowing and merging to accommodate manual revenue collection at tollbooths. Indeed, the safety risks associated with tollbooths was an important consideration in the elimination of tolls on several roadways, particularly in the northeast. Open road tolling has effectively eliminated these dangers.

Electronic tolling also has the potential to substantially lower the costs of collecting tolls on existing toll roads. While transponders and license plate recognition technology requires substantial upfront capital costs, the potential for reducing operating costs is significant since the collection costs per transaction are often 50 to 80 percent lower than collecting tolls using traditional tollbooths.[4]

Dynamic, variable rate tolling may have even greater potential for privatizing roads. Most highway tolls are flat rates: one price regardless of the time of day or traffic volume, although the toll level is commonly adjusted for the length of the trip. The flat rate structure reflects the historical roll tolls have played to finance the initial construction of roads and pay off the resulting debt, not to manage them. In addition, the technology didn't exist to allow for toll rates to change within a window sufficient to influence driver behavior. Automated coin tollbooths and metal strips for toll cards were implemented in the 1960s. Most toll collections were manual, and little thought was given to measuring the actual volume of the traffic on the roadway. ORT gives road managers more flexibility for setting toll rates based on the volume of traffic at specific times of the day, as well as the ability to change the price as traffic patterns change. That's the significance of the 91 Express Lanes in Southern California.

The 91 Express Lanes fused the need to raise revenue to pay for the new capacity with the need to manage it effectively. It's the quintessential case study of the how the system needs to operate in the twenty-first century. Like the private company that originally built them, the OCTA sets the toll rates based on the traffic volume to ensure free flow traffic 24 hours a day, seven days a week. (In fact, tolls are refunded at the end of the trip if the vehicle doesn't travel at the speed limit.)[5] Users of the 91 Express Lanes shorten the time on that stretch of road from 40 minutes to less than ten minutes.

Down the road on I-15 in San Diego, HOT Lane fees change in real time based on current traffic volume and conditions. Thus, in addition to using variable rates, tolling on the I-15 HOT Lanes is *dynamic*, allowing road managers to regulate the volume and level of traffic to maximize the value to its traveling consumers.

These are examples of new highway facilities that "pay their way." While the San Diego HOT Lanes are operated by a regional, public-sector transportation authority, the 91 Express Lanes and the 407 ETR were built and successfully operated by private companies. Combined with several other international examples, they demonstrate that the private sector is capable of providing road facilities in a competitive environment.

These facilities, of course, are limited-access highways. They restrict entry and exit through entrance and exit ramps, giving travelers or users little opportunity to avoid the toll. The primary innovation in solving the excludability problem that has plagued the private provision of roads in the past has been technological—bringing down the practicality and costs of collecting tolls—not the design of the roads. Improvements in toll collection technology have created an economic environment in which private sector investment becomes feasible and sustainable. Improvements in toll collection technology—both video and electronic tags—have substantially reduced the transaction costs of collecting tolls and improved enforcement capabilities.

Local and regional roads have traditionally provided a more difficult environment for private providers. Since they involve multiple and frequent points of entrance and egress as vehicles are provided frequent access to local destinations such as restaurants, offices, residents, shopping, and entertainment. Technology is once again providing new ways to charge road users, eroding both excludability and transaction costs as significant barriers to the private provision of road facility.

The most promising U.S. experiment is a mileage fee pilot project undertaken by the Oregon Department of Transportation and discussed in chapter 11. State-of-the-art GPS technology was used to levy a charge on drivers based on the miles they traveled rather than the gas they consumed.[6] In the pilot project, the state levied a mileage charge that differed based on whether the driver was traveling in state, out of state, or at peak periods. Oregon's experiment proved popular with users as a substitute for gas taxes.

It's hard to underestimate the importance of Oregon's success or similar programs already in place in nations such as Germany and the Netherlands. Mileage-based fees are a much more efficient funding system since mileage is a much better indicator of impact on the road system than fuel consumed. More importantly, technology allows for the mileage charge to vary by time of day and traffic flow. Drivers can be given stronger and direct information about the economic cost of traveling on particular roads at particular times. Since GPS technology provides a means for levying fees based on the specific location and time a car is driving, revenues can be raised directly from the users (eliminating the problems of excludability) and prices can be used to manage traffic flow (addressing the public-good problem of rivalness).

Technology is also providing a more competitive environment on the supply side. While road networks still may need to be designed in a holistic context, specific elements and segments of the road network should probably not be managed or operated through a monopoly. By allowing multiple providers to choose different levels of service and quality, regions can more effectively tailor services to specific segments of travelers. For example, operators specializing in meeting the needs of commercial truck traffic may be better owners, operators and managers of commercial roads, with stronger incentives to create (and maintain) facilities such as truck-only toll lanes. Similarly, other operators may specialize in providing road facilities for passenger traffic.

The possibility of differentiating road facilities based on a diversity of providers is not as farfetched as it might seem. Public transport services— whether rail, trolley, ferry, or bus—have a long tradition of relying on multiple providers with varying ownership interests and types. Recall the toll road network in Santiago, Chile, where six independent toll road companies manage different parts of a toll road network that is seamless for consumers, who may never even realize their travel has involved roads maintained and operated by different private companies. Since the toll road network is an open road system, the firms had an incentive to create a seamless and user-friendly billing system to minimize toll avoidance, and they adapted and applied software already used by utilities to their toll road systems.

Combined with GPS technology, where drivers can be charged based on their location, time of day, and traffic volume, roads can be managed and operated by small as well as large companies. Indeed, within the road infrastructure investment and management industry, companies frequently combine with other competitors to manage different facilities. The Spanish infrastructure company Cintra and the Australian firm Macquarie, for example, are global competitors but joined forces to successfully bid for the Chicago Skyway concession in 2005 and the Indiana Toll Road concession in 2006.

More important than any other factor is the potential these technologies have to unleash an unprecedented new wave of infrastructure investment. By refocusing the transportation sector on willingness to pay, and providing a mechanism for tying consumer-driven revenues to new facilities, projects on a scale unknown before can be considered. We've already seen this abroad with roadway tunnels and other major projects in other nations. Private capital can now be unleashed to build new capacity in the U.S., taking advantage of the consumer's willingness to pay for a higher quality project to dramatically reconfigure the regional transportation network.

Such investments are crucial for the vitality of our cities and our quality of life. Just as important will be the way new technologies and private industry will be transformed by new technology. It would be a disaster to build a lot more of the same old dumb infrastructure we built in past decades before new technologies and a private transportation industry arose. The heart of this transformation will be the investment in large scale underground facilities—3-D infrastructure—like the A86 West tunnels outside Paris. This $2.1 billion, privately funded project couldn't even be considered as long as it was a traditional surface road. The double-decked tunnel design pioneered by the private company now building and eventually operating the facility made it feasible, providing an opportunity to bring new money into transportation decision making. Thus, private funding of some projects eases the burden on the public sector to fund new links in the spiderweb. Entire networks of new underground and elevated facilities, like the tunnel network in Sydney and the combined tunnel and elevated expressways in Shanghai, are now within the realm of possibility thanks to these new technologies and engineering innovations.

We realize that complete privatization of roads is unlikely within the next decade or two. We also recognize that we have not addressed all the concerns or objections our proposal raises. (Two of the more important objections—land use and climate change—we have tried to address separately in appendices.)

Nevertheless, the long term trends, and the adjustments we need to make, are unmistakable. With open road tolling, the potential for privatizing the management if not ownership of limited-access highways already exists, and this will be an essential component of making the twenty-first century road network a reality. By some estimates, as much as one-third of the new limited-access highway capacity added in recent decades has used tolling to finance the expansions. As we begin to build out tunnel networks that provide new route choices for drivers, they lend themselves to pricing and private sector investment and management. The expanded use of public-private partnerships (PPPs) to harness the efficiencies of private management, as well as tap into private equity markets, clearly demonstrates that the private sector recognizes the economic value in road facilities. As national, state, and local governments fine-tune and refine their PPP agreements, the full privatization of limited-access highways is conceivable by the middle of this century. With additional modifications and innovations in GPS technology, even the privatization of local roads could be feasible by the turn of the century.

Regardless of when it happens, the fundamental nature of the transportation system and travel patterns can't be disputed. Wealth and the changing economic structure of international economies (and cities) have irrevocably transformed the nature of travel and our expectations about transportation system performance. Policy makers and elected officials must embrace these changes, rather than fight them. We ignore them at our own economic peril. Granted, this is uncharted territory, not just for the U.S., but for the international community. That doesn't lessen our responsibility to chart the course for the rest of the world.

Notes

1. Whether this is necessary has recently been disputed by economist Bruce Benson. See Bruce L. Benson, "The Mythology of Holdout as a Justification for Eminent Domain and Public Provision of Roads," *Independent Review*, vol. 10, no. 2 (Fall 2005), pp. 165–194.

2. "407ETR Celebrates 10 Years of Tolling Oct 14," TollroadsNews.com, 14 October 2007, http://www.tollroadsnews.com/node/3188.

3. For a review of the international experience, see Balaker and Staley, *The Road More Traveled*, chapter 6.

4. The costs of manual (traditional tollbooth) toll collection ranges from 20 to 30 cents per transaction. Electronic transponder toll collection ranges from 5 to 15 cents. Interview with Peter Samuel, editor, TollroadsNews.com, via email correspondence with Sam Staley, 29 November 2007.

5. "91 Express Lanes Break Dollar / Mile for An Hour on Fridays Eastbound," TollroadsNews.com, 30 December 2007, http://www.tollroadsnews.com/node/3320.

6. For an overview of the final report on the Oregon VMT program, see James M. Whitty, *Oregon's Mileage Fee Concept and Road User Fee Pilot Program: Final Report*, Oregon Department of Transportation, Salem, Oregon, November 2007.

Appendix 1

Climate Change and Transportation

(Co-written with Skaidra Smith-Heisters, Policy Analyst, Reason Foundation)

MANY PEOPLE, particularly those in the planning and environmental community, will find the framework for transportation policy we have proposed in this book objectionable. Our focus on automobility, and by implication a car-based transportation system, will strike many as wildly contrary to broader global and political concerns, particularly those related to climate change.

After all, aren't cars the number one producer of carbon dioxide (CO_2), the primary greenhouse gas? Well, no. They are important, but not the primary source of greenhouse gas emissions. That dubious honor goes to industry (broadly defined). Household vehicle use currently is responsible for approximately 16 to 18 percent of U.S. greenhouse gas emissions according to the U.S. Environmental Protection Agency (EPA).[1]

This is not our main objection to addressing climate change in the book. Rather, our main point is that *mobility* is central to economic productivity and *increased mobility* will be essential for maintaining our economic competitiveness in the twenty-first century. Improving mobility requires dramatically rethinking our approach to transportation planning and networks.

Climate change factors into this analysis as a potential "externality"—a negative by-product of the strategies we advocate where the costs are not fully accounted for in our policy framework or the choices individuals and firms make about transportation alternatives. Shouldn't these externalities be carefully weighed in our decisions about public policy?

The short answer is "yes," but we believe that tying climate change to transportation policy is a mistake. It assumes a number of key relationships that simply don't hold up under careful analysis and scrutiny. It also presumes a static relationship between technology and economic progress that is both ahistorical and imprudent as the U.S. and other nations move forward with their climate change strategies.[2]

First, linking transportation and climate change, with a specific policy of discouraging one mode, such as personal automobile use, ignores ongoing institutional and technical changes that will likely dramatically impact future greenhouse gas emissions, particularly CO_2. These emissions are largely a result of burning oil, a fossil fuel, using the internal combustion engine. This technology for powering automobiles is gradually being phased out, and higher gasoline prices are likely to accelerate this trend. Already, 65 hybrid models of passenger cars and light duty trucks are expected to be on the U.S. market by 2010.[3] While hybrid sales remain a small part of the overall market, their share is growing substantially and new technologies for powering automobiles are continually being explored. Indeed, historically, market-driven economies have been effective at shifting technologies to adapt to shortages of natural resources, whether they are renewable (e.g., trees) or nonrenewable.[4] These technological shifts are likely to have a more significant impact on reducing greenhouse gas emissions from the transportation sector than attempts to shift travel behavior, as our discussion in chapter 10 and the next appendix implies. Indeed, recent data show that, even without greenhouse gas emission reduction schemes in place, fossil fuel consumption in the U.S. has lagged average annual population growth rate (1.1 percent), electricity consumption (1.9 percent), and GDP (3.0 percent) since 1990.[5]

Second, even if we would dramatically reduce our consumption of oil and other fossil fuels that generate greenhouse gases, the likely impact on climate change trends is negligible. Even draconian attempts to reduce greenhouse gas emissions are unlikely to see meaningful changes to the climate until well into the twenty-*second* century.[6] Even if the U.S. and Europe were able to reduce greenhouse gas emissions by 80 percent by 2050—an unrealistic target by almost all accounts—the rapid growth of the economies in China and India would more than offset these gains.

Of course, these observations don't imply that the proper response to climate change concerns is to do nothing. Rather, they simply point out that attempting to address greenhouse gas emissions by focusing on one sector, or one technology, is likely to be unproductive and work against long-term goals. Moreover, if, as we suggest in this book, the consequence is to reduce our economic competitiveness, we will be in a much weaker position to address climate change through technological innovation.

A third concern is that we believe personal transportation is unduly targeted for emission reductions. In part this is an accident of the way we "count" greenhouse gas emissions. For example, the EPA inventories emissions in six main categories—electricity generation, transportation, industry, agriculture, commercial and residential. When inventoried in those broad categories without adjustment, electricity generation is the largest source of greenhouse gas emissions (34 percent in 2006), followed by transportation (28 percent), industry, agriculture, commercial, through to the smallest sector, residential (5 percent). Since electrical power, however, is an industrial product "consumed" by the other economic sectors, the next step in the EPA calculation allocates electricity generation among the five smaller sectors. After these emissions are distributed, *industry* (not electricity generation) accounts for the largest share of greenhouse gas emissions (29 percent), followed by transportation (28 percent), commercial, residential and agriculture (8 percent).[7] Thus, how emissions are categorized influences how each economic sector is perceived.

But, transportation is "consumed" by the other sectors, too, just like electricity. Passenger cars, light-duty trucks, sport utility vehicles, commercial trucks, domestic aviation, military aircraft, commercial and recreational boats and emissions from all other modes of motorized transport are lumped together in the transportation sector even though they have widely divergent impacts on the environment and production of greenhouse gases.

Moreover, these "shares" of greenhouse gas emissions are likely to change even if public policy were successful at reducing personal automobile use. While we assume public transit favors well compared to the automobile, this may be a consequence of how little public transit is used. As new, cleaner, and "greener" automobile technologies are adopted, public transit alternatives may well find themselves at an environmental disadvantage. When greenhouse gas emissions associated with the underlying infrastructure required for rail transit are included in the lifetime operating emissions, new rail systems are unlikely to compare favorably to the average passenger car.[8] Moreover, already hybrid automobiles emit fewer greenhouse gases per vehicle mile traveled than buses or commuter rail.

Fourth, targeting other sources of greenhouse gas emissions may be more effective and less costly ways of meeting targets than forsaking the personal and economic benefits of mobility. Even with commercial, personal and other kinds of modes included, transportation doesn't add up to the "largest share" of total U.S. greenhouse gas emissions. Rather, it is the largest share of CO_2 generated from fossil fuel combustion—the main source of anthropogenic CO_2. Weighted for global warming potential over a 100-year horizon, EPA reports that CO_2 from fossil fuel combustion accounted for approximately 80 percent of U.S. greenhouse gas emissions in 2006.[9] The other 20 percent, including CO_2 from industrial processes, methane from livestock and landfills, nitrous oxide from agriculture, and some chemical solvents and propellants, are also potential targets of greenhouse gas reduction strategies. In fact, these latter categories provide some of the quickest and least expensive opportunities for emission reductions.

Fifth, the focus on vehicle miles travel (VMT) is misplaced. VMT has arguably the closest relationship to the actual utility (mobility) derived from vehicle use and the most distant relationship to greenhouse gas emissions. VMT estimates derived from travel-demand models are a very poor basis for estimating greenhouse gas emissions, though they are frequently used for this purpose by regional planning agencies. Greenhouse gas emission estimates derived this way fail to capture excess fuel consumed as a result of congestion, among many other factors.

The mobility improvements we discuss in this book increase travel. That's, in fact, the point. We need to unleash the huge benefits of better mobility. More travel will increase greenhouse gas emissions from transportation (unless new technology replaces fossil fuels), but the real work is about trade-offs, not pure gains or losses. There are offsetting factors. Congestion caused vehicles stuck in traffic to waste 2.9 billion gallons of fuel in 2006. That released around 25 million tons of CO_2 into the atmosphere. At the same time, our proposals include a reinvigorated transit system in urban areas that should carry many more passengers in more heavily utilized, and thus more fuel-efficient per passenger-mile vehicles.

Finally, we believe prices will have an important impact on future fuel consumption and, as a consequence, greenhouse gases emitted from personal automobiles. Consumer behavior is not completely unaccountable as the considerable response to fuel prices and other economic signals in the past couple of years has proven. The popularity of light-duty trucks and sport utility vehicles has waned, and average new vehicle fuel economy improved in 2005 and 2006 as a result. Growth in VMT among passenger vehicles, at 2.7 percent per year for the period from 1990 to 2004, dropped to an average annual growth rate of 0.8 percent from 2004 to 2006.[10] Nationwide, hybrid vehicle registrations increased 38 percent in 2007.[11]

Policy makers should not despair if, as expected, reducing CO_2 emissions from the transportation sector is more expensive in the short term than reducing greenhouse gas emissions in other sectors of the economy. Personal transportation is responsible for a relatively small share of U.S. greenhouse gas emissions and provides a value on which consumers rightly place a high priority. In the long term, consumer preferences will undoubtedly change as efficient and cost-effective new vehicle technologies become widely available.

For these reasons, we do not believe that concerns about climate change warrant a substantial revision of our belief that improving mobility is essential to improving our wellbeing, and the best course for achieving this is by improving automobility in particular.

Notes

1. U.S. Environmental Protection Agency, *Inventory of U.S. Greenhouse Gas Emissions and Sinks: 1990–2006* (Washington D.C., 2008) pp. 3–8.

2. For more discussion of these issues in the context of sustainable development, see Samuel Staley, "Sustainable development in American Planning: A Critical Appraisal," *Town Planning Review*, Vol. 77, no. 1 (2006): pp. 99–126; Samuel R. Staley, "Institutional Considerations for Sustainable Development Policy Implementation: A US Case Study," *Property Management*, Vol. 24, No. 3 (2006), pp. 232–250; Samuel R. Staley, "Missing the Forest Through the Trees? Comment on Reid Ewing and Fan Rong's "The Impact of Urban Form on U.S. Residential Energy Use," *Housing Policy Debate*, Vol. 19, no. 1 (2008), pp. 31–43.

3. J.D. Power and Associates, "Hybrid Vehicle Sales on Pace to Reach Record Sales in 2007," press release, 2 August 2007, Westlake Village, California.

4. Staley, "Missing the Forest Through the Trees?" pp. 36–39.

5. U.S. Environmental Protection Agency, *Inventory of U.S. Greenhouse Gas Emissions and Sinks*, p. ES-17.

6. Ibid., p. 34.

7. Ibid., pp. ES-15–ES-16.

8. Randal O'Toole, *Does Rail Transit Save Energy or Reduce Greenhouse Gas Emissions?*, Policy Analysis No. 615 (Washington, D.C.: Cato Institute, 14 April 2008).

9. U.S. Environmental Protection Agency, *Inventory of U.S. Greenhouse Gas Emissions and Sinks*, p. ES-7.

10. Ibid., pp. 2–22.

11. R. L. Polk & Co., *Analysis Shows Hybrid Registrations Continue To Rise*, usa.polk.com/News/LatestNews/news_2008_0421_hybrids.htm, 21 April 2008.

Appendix 2

Land Use and Transportation Choice

Think of the transportation choices the typical large city offers today. You can travel on the congested roads, on a transit system with nice rail lines that connect few of the places you want to live, work, or play, or on a bus service that has been beggared to pay for the rail system. In either case it takes you even longer to get where you are going than on uncongested roads. If we build out a more complete road network including better arterials and a HOT network integrated with a bus rapid transit system, you can see the choice set expand. Now you can pay a toll to avoid traffic on the freeways, or if you are not in such a hurry on a given trip you still have the somewhat congested lanes on the freeways, and you have the rail transit system's limited access and a bus rapid transit system that avoids most of the traffic and gets you places nearly as fast as driving. More choices mean more mobility.

Another oft overlooked mobility choice operates on a smaller scale. A non-automobile mode of transportation we use every day might be used even more if we simply recognized its value and the latent demand for it. We're talking about our feet.

The idea that walking might be valuable fits squarely in line with the main theme of this book—that the hallmark of the modern transportation system is mobility, flexibility, and adaptability. A pedestrian-friendly neighborhood, particularly if it has densities that make other forms of commerce like a convenience store viable, can be very flexible with dozens of different routes (and even alternative transportation modes) as options. A walking-friendly environment can cut out some auto trips and make it easier for people to use a good transit system.

While the empirical results from academic research are mixed, some evidence suggests that neighborhoods with more dense and mixed-land uses have higher incidences of walking and less reported vehicle miles traveled. A detailed examination of California neighborhoods by economist Marlon Boarnet and planner Randall Crane found that land use had little impact on regional automobile trips, but could have small but significant reductions in vehicle travel for trips within neighborhoods.[1] Susan Handy, a planner at the University of California, Davis, observes that "the most important variable in predicting a change in walking is a change in attractiveness: all else equal, people walk more if they move to a neighborhood with a more attractive appearance, higher level of upkeep, more variety in housing styles, and/or more big street trees than they had in their previous neighborhood."[2] Her detailed study of neighborhoods in Austin, Texas, found that while driving was less common, walking was not a substitute for many types of driving trips. This isn't change on a large scale; it takes decades for changes in land use patterns to affect enough of a metro area to show up in travel patterns. But it is a reasonable complement to the other changes we have talked about.

How do we create such opportunities? Our experience suggests top-down approaches to reducing travel through planning don't work well. Other policies designed to increase densities have had little effect on transit use and walking but substantially increased congestion—higher density leads to higher congestion.

Instead, deregulation of land uses that allows a certain amount of low density mixed land uses can marry people's preferences for less dense living with mixed-use opportunities for less local auto travel. This is what UCLA planner Brian Taylor calls "smart sprawl."[3]

Transportation planners make a big deal about access as a key element to transportation decisions.[4] Of course, access isn't valuable in and of itself; what counts is having access to the goods and services we use at a price we can afford. We get in our car because the mobility it gives us provides access to a wider variety of services, goods, and destinations. So, access to a child care center holds little value if we don't want our children to go to that center (or we don't have children). And there's the rub.

Even if we find the daycare we want, it probably can't locate near where we live. Thank the planners for that. Modern day zoning (meaning post-World War II planning) is built on the principle that land uses should be separate—each use should have its own zone and place, and they shouldn't mix. In the early days of zoning, this wasn't particularly onerous. Zoning focused mainly on limiting nuisances in residential areas.[5] After all, who wants to live next to a factory with trucks coming in and out 24 hours a day, seven days a week? Often people could still live in a commercial or industrial section of the city; the nuisances just couldn't move in next door.

But modern zoning is a different political animal altogether. Now, zoning is used to "protect" the character of the existing neighborhood by preventing change. Of any sort. Unfortunately, for most communities, this means anything other than a single family house with a yard is considered a nuisance, relegated to the special zones for noxious land uses, even when market trends and consumers *want* mixed uses. Zoning establishes a set pattern of land use regardless of the evolving needs of the community. In order to accommodate change, the laws have to be changed. In other words, the presumption is against the natural evolution of urban communities in favor of maintaining the status quo regardless of emerging market needs or preferences.

Unfortunately, we don't have the space to go into detail about a critique and possible solutions to land-use planning problems in the U.S. That discussion must be reserved for another venue (or book).[6] We can, however, note the potential implications for transportation, mobility and congestion.

America's (and increasingly the world's) reliance on zoning has made access harder for certain modes of travel, particularly those that become viable in an urban environment or an economic context in which commuting is less important. To make walking viable, streets don't have to be torn up and high-rise residential and office towers built. On the contrary, most of what we need to do is get out of the way and let our neighborhoods and cities evolve into a higher urban form.

Nevertheless, we still have to be realistic about what these changes imply for mobility on a larger scale. Little evidence suggests that incremental changes in land use, or the mix of uses, will have a substantial influence on regional travel patterns or behavior. To the extent we see any changes, they tend to be weak relationships with relatively modest impacts.

Notes

1. Marlon G. Boarnet and Randall Crane, *Travel By Design: The Influence of Urban Form on Travel* (New York: Oxford University Press, 2001).

2. Susan Handy, "Which Comes First: The Neighborhood or the Walking," *Access* No. 26, Spring 2005, p. 20.

3. Brian D. Taylor, "Rethinking Congestion," *Access*, no. 21, (Fall 2002), p.16.

4. See Todd A. Litman, "Evaluating Accessibilty for Transportation Planning," Victoria Transportation Institute, August 2007, http://www.vtpi.org/, accessed 12 October 2007 and "How Land Use Effects Travel Behavior," http://www.vtpi.org/landtravel.pdf.

5. Even in the early days, however, zoning carried strong protectionist sentiment. In the landmark Supreme Court case *Euclid v. Ambler Realty* (1926), industries were explicitly trying to use zoning to protect their financial interests.

6. We will, however, point readers to several resources for how land use planning can be reformed to accommodate an open-ended development process. See Samuel R. Staley and Lynn Scarlett, "Market-Oriented Planning: Principles and Tools for the 21st Century," *Planning and Markets*, vol. 1, no. 1 (September 1998), on-line journal, http://www-pam.usc.edu/volume1/index.html, accessed 16 October 2007; Samuel R. Staley, "Markets, Smart Growth, and the Limits of Policy," in Randall G. Holcombe and Samuel R. Staley, eds., *Smarter Growth: Market-Based Strategies for Land-Use Planning in the 21st Century*, pp. 201–217 (Westport, Conn.: Greenwood Press, 2001); Samuel R. Staley and Eric R. Claeys, "Is the Future of Development Regulation Based in the Past? Toward a Market-Oriented, Innovation Friendly Framework," *Journal of Urban Planning and Development*, vol. 131, no. 4 (December 2005), pp. 202–213.

Index

About the Authors

Samuel R. Staley, PhD, is director of urban and land-use policy for Reason Foundation (www.reason.org) and co-author (with Ted Balaker) of *The Road More Traveled: Why the Congestion Crisis Matters More Than You Think, and What We Can Do About It* (Rowman & Littlefield, 2006). He speaks regularly on urban policy and transportation nationally and internationally, and his work has appeared in leading popular and professional publications, including the *New York Times, Washington Post, Los Angeles Times, Investor's Business Daily*, the *Journal of the American Planning Association, Housing Policy Debate, Town Planning Review, Urban Land, Planning* magazine, and *Reason* magazine. He is the author or co-author of several books and symposia, including *Smarter Growth: Market-Based Strategies for Land-Use Planning in the 21st Century* (co-edited with Randall G. Holcombe) which was called the "most thorough challenge yet to regional land-use plans" by *Planning* magazine. *Governing* and *Planning* magazines have identified him as one of the nation's foremost critics of conventional smart growth and a leader in developing practical market-oriented alternatives to growth management and development regulation. He teaches urban economics as an adjunct at the University of Dayton, serves as senior fellow at the Indiana Policy Review and the Buckeye Institute, and is a regular contributor to Planetizen Interchange, a blog hosted by the web portal Planetizen.com. He received his bachelor's degree in economics-public policy from Colby College, his master's degree in applied economics from Wright State University, and PhD in public administration from the Ohio State University.

Adrian T. Moore, PhD, is vice president for research at Reason Foundation and a member of the National Surface Transportation Infrastructure Financing Commission created by the U.S. Congress. A transportation economist by training, he is co-author of the award winning book *Curb Rights: A Foundation for Free Enterprise in Urban Transit.* Adrian's work has also been published in *Public Finance and Management, Urban Affairs Review,* the *International Journal of Sustainable Transportation,* and many other professional and popular publications. He testifies before Congress and state legislatures and regularly advises federal, state and local officials on policy issues. He was awarded a *World Outsourcing Achievement Award* by PricewaterhouseCoopers and Michael F. Corbett & Associates Ltd. in 2002 for his work showing governments how to use public-private partnerships and the private sector to save taxpayer money and improve the efficiency of their agencies. He earned a PhD in Economics from the University of California, Irvine and holds a master's degree in History from California State University, Chico.